Doing Their Bit

SECOND EDITION

Doing Their Bit

Wartime American Animated Short Films, 1939–1945

SECOND EDITION

Michael S. Shull *and*
David E. Wilt

McFarland & Company, Inc., Publishers
Jefferson, North Carolina, and London

LIBRARY OF CONGRESS CATALOGUING-IN-PUBLICATION DATA

Shull, Michael S., 1949–
    Doing their bit : wartime American animated short films,
    1939–1945 / Michael S. Shull and David E. Wilt.— 2nd ed.
        p.   cm.
    Includes filmography.
    Includes bibliographical references and index.

    ISBN 0-7864-1555-X (softcover : 50# alkaline paper)

    1. World War, 1939–1945 — Motion pictures and the war.
    2. Animated films— United States— History and criticism.
    3. Short films— United States— History and criticism.   I. Wilt,
    David E., 1955–   II. Title.
    D743.23.S54   2004
    741.5'0973'09044 — dc22   2003024614

British Library cataloguing data are available

©2004 Michael S. Shull and David E. Wilt. All rights reserved

Cover art: (top) 1942's *Blitzwolf*; (center) 1943's *Fifth Column Mouse*;
(bottom) frames from *Private Snafu*

Manufactured in the United States of America

McFarland & Company, Inc., Publishers
    Box 611, Jefferson, North Carolina 28640
    www.mcfarlandpub.com

To all the ducks, geese, cats, dogs, rabbits, mice, squirrels, pigs, woodpeckers, pandas, alien supermen, spinach-eating sailors, bears, foxes, crows, turtles, wolves, and other cartoon characters who served their country well during World War II — you truly "did your bit" toward the final "V"

Acknowledgments

As in film production, the serious historical research and analysis of motion pictures is a collaborative effort. No matter how many names appear on the title page, the cooperation of a much larger cast is essential in order to successfully complete such a project.

Access to the vast resources available at the Library of Congress, Washington, D.C., is a pleasure and a privilege. The staff of the Motion Picture, Broadcasting, and Recorded Sound Division has always been courteous, professional, and willing to share the extra bits of information which can prove to be so important. Special thanks are extended to Barbara Humphrys, David Parker, Madeline Matz, and Rosemary Hanes.

George C. Pratt, the late curator emeritus of the George Eastman House in Rochester, New York, has had our admiration and appreciation. Without his willingness to share the information in his personal indexes, Mutt and Jeff's participation in the First World War would have been inadequately covered. Craig Campbell of the Academy of Motion Picture Arts and Sciences Library in Los Angeles unselfishly came through with additional citations for the chapter on World War I. David Smith, the Disney archivist, sent us detailed information as well.

On relatively short notice, executive director Chuck Green and curator Sherman Krisher of the Museum of Cartoon Art in Port Chester, New York, made their facilities available and also shared their accumulated knowledge of animated films. Numerous other people and organizations were unselfish and helpful. They include (but are not limited to) Bonnie Willette of American University, Eric Kulberg of Universal Media, animation historian and author Mike Barrier, animation historian and author Jerry Beck, James Plumer, G. Dane Wilsonne of Kit Parker Films, Richard Shale, the interlibrary loan unit of the University of Maryland libraries, and the Society of Animation Studies. Thanks also to Norman Hatch, a former Marine combat cameraman, who rescued the "Hook" cartoons from obscurity (and possible destruction). Some of these people helped with the first edition and some with the second edition (some with *both*), but all deserve thanks for their efforts. Finally, we would also like to thank our families and friends for their support.

Michael S. Shull and David E. Wilt

Contents

Preface to the Second Edition

The authors were extremely pleased to do a second edition of *Doing Their Bit*. There aren't too many cases where — after 17 years— the opportunity arises to update a published work that we thought was essentially "set in stone," so it was a welcome task to add new material, polish the writing, and (we must admit) correct a few errors.

This new edition of *Doing Their Bit* contains updated filmography entries, revised statistics, new commentary in the text, new and better illustrations, and two major additions: a chapter on the *Private Snafu* series (produced by Warner Bros. but shown only to the armed forces), as well as an extensive filmography of the Snafu cartoons and their Navy counterpart, "Mr. Hook."

When we wrote the first edition of this book, there was no Cartoon Network, no such thing as a DVD (in fact, when working on this new edition, we were chagrined to discover half of our videotaped cartoon archive from 1986 was on *Beta* format!), and no Internet. Even personal computers were in their infancy. The literature on animated cartoons was also rather limited. In the intervening years, we've seen many things come to pass— including a number of excellent books on animation history and criticism — and now, a new edition of *Doing Their Bit* is available. We hope it will be as well-received as the original was.

D. Wilt and M. Shull
January 2004

1. Not for Kids Only

Over the past four decades, social and cultural historians have persistently sought out new sources of material for scholarly research. Motion pictures, however, have been addressed with singular timidity. Animated films, particularly short cartoons, are rarely mentioned, let alone seriously examined with regard to their historical content.

This work is an analysis and annotated filmography of the historical and political material found in cartoons released to the general public in the United States between 1 January 1939 and 30 September 1945. The purpose is to demonstrate that motion pictures—in *all* forms—provide a valuable source of evidence for scholars of 20th-century American history.

The literature dealing with the Second World War is vast and continues to grow, but the rigorous historical examination of the political aspects of motion pictures throughout the war years is still comparatively limited. Yet, during these years, the average weekly attendance in American film theaters was about 85 million people, and nearly 500 cartoons were produced in Hollywood (in the 1942–45 period). Sixty-eight percent (see Appendix A) of the cartoons released in the peak year of 1943 — and 47 percent of those released in 1942–1945 (through the end of September)—contained material relevant to the worldwide struggle to which the United States was totally committed after 7 December 1941.

An attempt has been made in this book to identify all cartoons reflecting an awareness of world events. It would be foolhardy to claim to have located every such work, but the authors feel confident that the vast majority has been identified. Because of this comprehensive approach to the material, the analyses of the individual cartoons favor plot and historical relevancy over aesthetics.

The choice of chronological parameters for a historical study is a

3

tendentious exercise. It is generally accepted that World War II began on September 1, 1939, with the invasion of Poland by Nazi Germany; the United States was an actual belligerent in the war between 7 December 1941, the date of the infamous Japanese naval air assault on Pearl Harbor, and 2 September 1945, the formal capitulation of the Imperial Japanese government aboard the U.S.S. *Missouri* in Tokyo Bay. But most would agree the events leading up to the actual outbreak of hostilities took place over an extended time. One of the most critical series of occurrences prior to the war centered on the signing of the Munich Agreement on 30 September 1938, and Hitler's unilateral abrogation of these accords when his *Wehrmacht* (army) entered Czechoslovakia, unopposed, on 16 March 1939.

Thus it was not simply an arbitrary decision on the part of the authors to begin a political analysis of American cartoons with January 1, 1939. Early that year, the Western powers began rearming to resist the growing power of the totalitarian states. From this point forward, the American people would be under increasing pressure to take sides. Hollywood's productions during this period, including cartoons, provide additional historical testimony upon which to judge the attitudes of the public toward this unprecedented global struggle.

The authors concluded our content evaluation of cartoons at the end of the month of September 1945, when the unconditional surrender of the Axis powers caused a rapid demobilization throughout American society. As will be noted in the text, well into 1946 some cartoons would reflect wartime issues and immediate postwar concerns.

Studio Overview

Of all the cartoons included in this study, the commercially released shorts *not* produced by one of seven major studios may be counted on a single hand — two "This Changing World" shorts made by Cartoon Films, Ltd. and released through Columbia; *Invasion of Norway*, also produced by Cartoon Films, Ltd.; and *Cap 'n Cub*, made by Ted Eshbaugh and released by Film Classics.[1] Otherwise, all of the theatrical cartoons came from the cartoon factories run by Leon Schlesinger (Warner Bros.), Max Fleischer (later Famous Studios/Paramount), Paul Terry (20th Century–Fox), Walter Lantz (Universal), Walt Disney (RKO), Metro-Goldwyn-Mayer, and the Screen Gems subsidiary of Columbia Pictures. There were ownership and management changes in many of the units, but by 1940 the seven major studios controlled the entire market. Looking at the principal Hollywood companies in existence during the 1940s, only Republic, PRC, United

Artists, and Monogram are absent; these distribution and production organizations did not, as a rule, concern themselves with the production of short subjects at all (with one major exception, the Republic serials). Theaters which booked features from these companies generally utilized shorts from one of the seven major organizations to fill out their programs.

Leon Schlesinger got into the cartoon business in 1930, when he agreed to bankroll Hugh Harman and Rudy Ising's efforts to break into the sound-cartoon market. Schlesinger made a deal with Warner Bros., and for the next 14 years the company he managed made "Looney Tunes" and "Merrie Melodies" animated shorts for Warners release. Schlesinger has been described as a pure businessman, not an animator-turned-producer such as Walt Disney or Walter Lantz. However, for the most part Schlesinger seemed to give his workers free rein, within budgetary and time frameworks. He was also either very canny or very lucky in hiring some of the most talented men in the business— Tex Avery, Frank Tashlin, Bob Clampett, I. Freleng, Chuck Jones, Mel Blanc, and Carl W. Stalling, to name just a few. With the security the Warner Bros. contract gave him, Schlesinger did not become complacent or, conversely, overly ambitious. Warner Bros. cartoons were distinctive and eminently successful. For years Schlesinger's unit made more shorts annually than any other producer.

In 1944 Schlesinger retired and sold his company to Warner Bros., which installed Edward Selzer in the supervisory seat. The cartoons did not suffer from this change, since some excellent shorts were released between 1944 and 1950 (and even into the 1950s most Warners' cartoons were at least amusing), but personnel changes and changing styles ultimately reduced the cartoons to shadows of what they had once been.

Max Fleischer, unlike Schlesinger, was an animation veteran, entering the business before 1920. Fleischer was, by all accounts, fascinated with the cartoon form and the mechanical apparatus used to produce cartoons. He and his brother Dave organized Out of the Inkwell Films in 1921, and created a character called Koko the Clown as their star. Throughout the 1920s the Fleischers made cartoons, and in 1927 began releasing their product through Paramount. When sound came in their new character, Betty Boop, quickly eclipsed Koko in popularity, and in 1933 Popeye the Sailor made the transition from newspaper comic strip to animated cartoon.

Max Fleischer continued to experiment with new processes, including some shorts in the 1930s that utilized models or miniature "sets" with animated figures inserted. There were also three color Popeye two-reelers produced in 1937-1938, and in 1939 Fleischer completed his first feature, *Gulliver's Travels*, followed in 1941 by *Mr. Bug Goes to Town*. Also in 1941, Fleischer added the comic book character Superman to his roster of characters, and produced some well-animated color cartoons starring this character.

In 1942 Paramount Pictures forced the Fleischers out of their company — through some complex legal maneuvers — and the Famous Studios subsidiary was formed.[2] Much of the Fleischer staff was retained, and the animation of the Famous Studios product continued to be acceptable for most of the decade. Popeye remained the breadwinner, though. Superman was dropped in mid 1943, replaced by Little Lulu and a series called Noveltoons. By the 1950s, there was a spate of new characters, including Casper the Friendly Ghost, Little Audrey, Baby Huey, and others. On television these shorts are shown under the Harveytoons name, a sure sign that it's time to go to the kitchen for a sandwich.

Also released through Paramount were George Pal's "Puppetoons," stop-motion animation shorts which used wood-and-rubber models instead of drawings. Pal, born in Hungary, was trained as an architect, but the economic situation in his homeland forced him to seek work in the motion picture industry. He later moved to Germany, and by the early 1930s was the head of the animation department at Ufa, Germany's largest movie studio. After relocating to Prague, Paris, and the Netherlands, Pal finally emigrated to the USA. Securing a contract with Paramount, he set up a studio in Hollywood and made over 40 short "Puppetoons" between 1941 and 1947, before turning his hand to feature film work. Pal's most successful "Puppetoon" series character was the little African-American boy Jasper, but he also produced various shorts with other themes and settings.

Paul Terry was, like Max Fleischer, an animator from the early days. After working for J.R. Bray, the king of early animation bosses, he went out on his own in 1919. Terry created a character called Farmer Al Falfa (who continued to appear in occasional cartoons through the 1940s), and then a series based on *Aesop's Fables.* From this point on Terry had various partners and backers. In the 1930s Terrytoons were first sold to Educational Pictures, which had a deal with 20th Century–Fox to supply shorts; later, Terrytoons were released directly through Fox, although Terry was still an independent contractor. After Farmer Al Falfa, Terry had no major stars until the creation of Gandy Goose in 1938; Mighty Mouse (originally called Supermouse) came along in 1942, and Heckle and Jeckle in 1946. In 1955, Terry sold out to CBS and retired, a rich man. Terrytoons continued under new management for a few years, until production finally ceased in 1968.

The story of Walt Disney and the various companies he was responsible for is well known. Of interest in this study are the varied wartime

The Screwball Army attacks in *Tulips Shall Grow* (1942), a George Pal Puppetoon.

productions made at the Disney studio. Disney cartoon shorts and features were released exclusively through RKO for the balance of the war years, with the exception of *Victory Through Air Power* (United Artists, 1943), and the special cartoons made under contract with the coordinator for Inter-American Affairs, the Treasury Department, and the various armed services.[3] That Disney was able to produce such a high number of special cartoons, his theatrical shorts, and still come up with features such as *Bambi* (1942), *Saludos Amigos* and *Victory Through Air Power* (both 1943), and *The Three Caballeros* (1945) is nothing short of miraculous.

Walter Lantz entered animation in 1916 at the Hearst studio, then spent a number of years with J.R. Bray. Lantz eventually wound up in Hollywood, where he was chosen to head the animation department being formed by Universal Pictures. In the mid–'30s, Lantz became an independent contractor, still releasing through Universal, a situation that lasted until the early '70s, with the exception of the 1948 season, when UA released the Lantz shorts. Lantz's earliest character was Oswald the Rabbit, originally created by Walt Disney, who had lost the rights to Charles Mintz. Mintz in turn lost the character to Universal, which had been distributing his cartoons in the years just before the changeover to sound. Lantz inherited Oswald from Universal. In the '40s, Lantz's stars were

Andy Panda and his most enduring creation, Woody Woodpecker. There were also some entertaining non-series cartoons released during the war years (most of Lantz's shorts were billed as "Cartunes," and the musical specials were called "Swing Symphonies") featuring outstanding music (*The Sliphorn King of Polaroo*, 1944, highlights the singing and playing of jazz notable Jack Teagarden).

Until 1937, the cartoons released by MGM were produced by Hugh Harman and Rudy Ising. MGM promoted a man named Fred Quimby to head their new in-house animation unit in 1937, but he made little impact on the cartoons. Though he was the titular producer on nearly every MGM cartoon until his retirement in 1955, Quimby would be overshadowed by the directors who worked for him: Harman, Ising, Tex Avery, and the team of Bill Hanna and Joe Barbera. A few other shorts were directed by other men in the war years, but Harman (through 1942), Ising (through 1943), and especially Avery and Hanna-Barbera were the mainstays of MGM cartoons. Tom and Jerry, Barney Bear, and Droopy were the lasting series stars of the '40s for MGM, one of the top cartoon studios of the decade. From between 1940 through 1949, MGM won the Academy Award for cartoons six times, Disney twice, and Warner Bros. twice.[4]

The last of the "big seven" cartoon producers was Columbia Pictures, perhaps the least distinctive of the lot. This may be attributed to the frequent changes in administration among the various units making cartoons for Columbia release. Walt Disney's cartoons were released through Columbia until 1932, at the same time the company was distributing shorts made by the staff headed by Charles Mintz. Mintz, never an animator himself, had a number of talented men working for him at various times in the '30s, but the Columbia cartoons were never very successful. Their one lasting original character was a little boy named Scrappy, although Mintz did have the rights to Krazy Kat, who had been in cartoons since the silent era. Columbia took over Mintz's operation in 1939 (he died in 1940), and the Screen Gems era began. Screen Gems, a subsidiary rather than an independent production company, was supervised at various times by Frank Tashlin, Dave Fleischer, Paul Worth, and former Warner Bros. animation executive Ray Katz. Finally, in 1949, Columbia closed down its own unit and went to UPA for its cartoon needs. During the war years, Columbia's most successful characters were the Fox and the Crow, but there were also series starring comic strip character Li'l Abner, Willoughby Wren, and other, less memorable characters, released under the "Color Rhapsody" and "Phantasy" banners.

The late 1930s and the 1940s were certainly the golden age of theatrical cartoons. The overall quality of animation was amazingly high, with even the least distinctive product miles ahead of later, limited-animation efforts. Not all cartoons from the war years are classics— some are unfunny, feeble efforts (particularly plot-wise)— but the general standard was very high, and these cartoons are enjoyable today as entertainment, in addition to their value as documents of America's wartime culture.

Cartoons as Documents

In a study such as this a note of caution should be sounded, both for the researcher and scholar and for the casual reader. Animated cartoons should not be taken either too lightly or too seriously as sources of social, cultural, or historical information. Among the general public, of course, the first attitude is likely to be more prevalent.

It is important to remember that theatrical cartoons of the 1930s and 1940s were made for the entertainment of general audiences in *movie theaters* for viewers of *all* ages, from youth to mature adult. The producers of these cartoons viewed the potential audience in different ways—certain companies' products were definitely slanted toward a more juvenile sense of humor, while other releases were certainly intended to amuse all, but contained verbal and visual references aimed at adult viewers. As a whole, the cartoon industry could not afford to make only "kiddie" cartoons, because its product would then be severely restricted in its appeal: to Saturday matinees in neighborhood movie houses. Cartoons were an integral part of virtually all motion picture theater programs for more than 30 years, until the demise of the double feature system in the 1960s.

Many made-for-television cartoons, on the other hand, are produced with a narrower audience in mind. TV cartoons of the '60s, '70s, and '80s were often made to be shown during a specific time proved to be watched almost entirely by children of a determinable age. As a consequence, the content of these cartoons was geared to the intellect of a child (and, we might sometimes think, not a very bright child either). This has changed a bit in recent years, particularly with the importation of Japanese animation (or *anime*) that has developed a cult following among adults. Television cartoons have thus fragmented into those clearly made for children, and those aimed at a "hip" adult audience (like the outrageous *South Park*). Only a relative few—*The Simpsons* and other prime-time, animated sitcoms, for example — are intended to appeal to an audience as broad as the one that watched theatrical cartoons.

Therefore, theatrical animated cartoons made during World War II are not in any sense examples of "children's literature" of their period;

rather, they are documents of mass popular culture, produced for the same audience as live-action short subjects, feature films, entertainment radio, popular magazines, and other mass-media entertainment of the day.

On the other hand, lest one think the authors are making overly extravagant claims for animated cartoons as historical documents, it must be admitted that cartoons—by the nature of the medium—cannot be treated exactly as one would examine feature films, popular novels, or other aspects of popular culture. Each has its own set of standards, rules, conventions, and limitations. Cartoons *were* largely concerned with the antics of funny animals; they *were* produced (in most cases) for the purpose of making audiences laugh, rather than educating, or arousing an audience to action. Cartoons were bound with strictures of time and budget, and even the relative variance of feature-film themes is absent in the cartoon field, where the continuing series character was paramount.

But within these boundaries, theatrical cartoons of the 1930s and 1940s can certainly provide a wealth of fascinating information about American culture of the period. Dismissing them as "kids' stuff" displays neither knowledge of the motion picture industry nor an enlightened attitude toward popular culture and the study of American history.

Music

The topical references in the cartoons examined for this study fall into several categories: visual, verbal, thematic, and musical. Many cartoons combine several or all of these types of references to make their points. One of the more interesting types is the musical reference, which is perhaps unique to the animated cartoon form.

Sound and animated cartoons seem to be totally inseparable: the examples of silent cartoons extant today, even with proper musical accompaniment, seem flat and lifeless. Sound effects, dialogue, and music combined with animation resulted in the true emergence of cartoons as an entertainment medium: "The music in cartoons usually plays at least an equal role with the animation and story in establishing the humorous success of events."[5]

Much of the background music in cartoons was stereotyped, or became stereotyped after repeated use. Warner Bros., for instance, used "The Girlfriend of the Whirling Dervish" (written for the feature *Garden of the Moon* in 1938) as its standard "Arab" or "desert" theme for many years. "Trade Winds" was another oft-heard tune, usually associated with tropical islands, sailing, or a Frank Sinatra caricature (since it was one of his hits). Bing Cosby caricatures were usually found singing "When My Dreamboat Comes Home." "As Time Goes By" (repopularized in *Casablanca*, 1942) was another familiar Warner cartoon piece. A five-note piece of music (instantly recognizable to cartoon audiences) was frequently heard to underscore a character's stupidity (in fact, it is practically Private Snafu's "theme song") — whatever the tune's *real* name, the five-note theme is generally known as "You're a Horse's Ass!"

Several of the cartoon producers were fortunate to be affiliated with studios that owned the rights to a large number of popular songs. Warner Bros. is probably the outstanding example of this. Hardly a Warners cartoon of the '30s or '40s exists without the inclusion of at least one hit song (often a tune from a current feature release of the studio). MGM and Paramount, to a lesser extent, used contemporary tunes as background music, while Walter Lantz (releasing through Universal) produced animated versions of popular "swing" hits (like 1941's *Boogie Woogie Bugle Boy of Company B* and *Cow Cow Boogie*, 1943), but relied mostly upon original compositions or classical adaptations as background music for his cartoons. At other studios, the music director often did not have the backlog of recognizable songs to draw upon, and was forced to use music in the public domain, classical music, or original compositions. Terrytoons like *All Out for "V"* (1942), *Barnyard Blackout* (1943), and *Scrap for Victory* (1943) actually had catchy little original songs with topical themes.

But it is the use of recognizable popular songs that serves as a topical reference in and of itself in many World War II-vintage cartoons. For example, "Praise the Lord and Pass the Ammunition" is heard in a number of Paramount shorts, often merely a few bars to reinforce the martial message already being imparted by the visual and verbal components of the cartoon. Movie audiences of the day knew immediately what the song was, and associated it with a patriotic theme. "We Did It Before and We Can Do It Again" (copyrighted immediately after Pearl Harbor) was a favorite Warner Bros. piece. MGM frequently used of George M. Cohan's World War I classic, "Over There." Other popular musical cues of the war era included "Columbia, the Gem of the Ocean," "The Caissons Go Rolling Along," "You're in the Army Now," "The Marines' Hymn" (aka "From the Halls of Montezuma"), "Captains of the Clouds" (for Warners), and "Don't Sit Under the Apple Tree." "The Star Spangled Banner" and even "America, the Beautiful" were not often used, perhaps because the studios feared criticism of using these songs in the context of a humorous and irreverent cartoon.

An example of a musical theme that became a ubiquitous symbol of the Allies in the war was the three-dots-and-a-dash theme from

A portrait of Hitler is a little worse for wear after a ride on a junk wagon. Frame enlargement from *Scrap for Victory* (1943).

Beethoven's Fifth Symphony. Either alone on the soundtrack or in conjunction with a visualization (•••–, or a "V"), these four notes signified the Allied will to win, and were almost universally recognized by audiences. The simplicity of this musical cue allowed for adaptation to practically any situation — Popeye's nephews snoring, Popeye's pipe, a ship's smokestack, rivets, punches, and on and on. Since it was in the public domain, Beethoven's "V" theme could be used by any cartoon producer who wished to insert a patriotic reference (see Appendix C).

Sometimes the musical cues are almost subliminal. "Praise the Lord and Pass the Ammunition," mentioned earlier, is very briefly heard at the finale of *Wood Peckin'* (1943), a Popeye short. In this case it serves to underscore the patriotic (but nonspecific) words of a woodpecker about defending one's home. In *Duck Soup to Nuts* (1944), an otherwise non-topical Porky vs. Daffy cartoon, the tune "They're Either Too Young or Too Old" (sung by Bette Davis in the feature film *Thank Your Lucky Stars* in 1943) is heard on the soundtrack. This song refers to the shortage of eligible men due to the war, and was probably inserted as a joke by Carl W. Stalling, the Warner Bros. cartoon music director.

Another example of Stalling's expertise can be heard in *Draftee Daffy* (1944). Within the first *minute and a half* of the cartoon, recognizable music (instrumental and vocal) includes "You're in the Army Now" (behind the credits), "The Marines' Hymn," "Columbia, the Gem of the Ocean,"

"Yankee Doodle," "If I Could Be With You One Hour Tonight" (Daffy sings this to a portrait of General MacArthur), "Columbia, the Gem of the Ocean" (again), "The Marines' Hymn" (again — this time, Daffy sings "Oh, the lit-tle man from the dra-aft board, is coming to see me!"), and "It Had to be You."

Unfortunately, present-day viewers unfamiliar with popular music of the 1940s may miss much of the humor and topicality inherent in these musical cues. Nonetheless, for contemporary audiences, music was not simply "background"; it often played an integral part in the overall message of the cartoon.

Propaganda and Humor

During the Second World War, animated cartoons were predominantly an American phenomenon.[6] Crass humor, with origins in burlesque, was its trademark. Although it is not within the scope of this work to delve into the enigma of what constitutes comedy, some observations will be proffered with regard to humor in American film during World War II and its propagandistic relevance.

Shorn of pejorative connotations, propaganda can be briefly defined as the methodical spreading of ideas in the promotion of some cause, group, or nation. According to a French scholar of propaganda, Jacques Ellul, the most favorable moment to seize a man and influence him is when he is "alone in the mass."[7] This is precisely the situation that exists when one is a member of a movie audience.

The Office of War Information (OWI) monitored the American film industry throughout the war, and often made detailed comments on pre-production scripts vis-à-vis their relationship to the Allied war effort as well as analyzing the final print. But the OWI rarely became directly involved in the production of commercial motion pictures. Although certain general guidelines were provided to Hollywood and its product was monitored by the government, and even though OWI had ultimate control over distribution (to foreign markets) and film stock allocations, there was never anything resembling the monolithic "ministries of propaganda" associated with totalitarian regimes. Yet American films of World War II, including cartoons, were undoubtedly propagandistic.

A significant element contributing to the success of American motion pictures as propaganda was that they were almost always designed by a non-subsidized industry to appeal to the broadest possible spectrum of the public, so economic considerations were of paramount concern. Thus, films generally reinforced current values and ideas as perceived by the film establishment.

The American motion picture industry enthusiastically embraced and promoted the war effort, both onscreen and off. The real strength of American film as propaganda, though, was not so much in content (such as exhortations to buy bonds) as in its attitude. Even in the most serious war-oriented feature works, Hollywood often injected insouciance or elements of humor. This good-natured self-confidence — or outright cockiness — even in the middle of a struggle against militaristic regimes seeking world dominance, was perhaps one of the greatest strengths of American film. And it was in cartoons that such humor was often presented in its purest, albeit crudest, form.

Thus, no matter how grim the newsreels or somber the feature presentation's subject matter may have been, cartoons allowed American movie audiences to vicariously indulge in humorous exaggerations of human foibles and shared wartime adversities (such as rationing and shortages). Aside from allowing catharsis, cartoons probably (subliminally, if not consciously) instilled a greater confidence in the ultimate triumph of the United States and its allies.

The Research and Analysis Process

Due to the nonexistence of adequate American short film subject catalogues for the World War II years, the lack of a central public motion picture repository (the Library of Congress Film Division did not come into being until the mid–1940s), and the alteration (including colorization), loss, or destruction of many works from the period, serious historical film research requires an extensive expenditure of time. Furthermore, as a result of the exaggerated sensibilities of some individuals and groups today — manifestations of so-called "political correctness" — particularly with regard to racial and ethnic stereotyping, many cartoons of this period have been censored or suppressed entirely.

For instance in 1984, Donald Duck's much-heralded 50th anniversary year, Disney was quick to release commemorative videotapes, but pointedly omitted the Academy Award-winning *Der Fuehrer's Face* (1943). Vintage cartoons broadcast on the Disney Network are routinely edited to remove scenes which are perceived to be unacceptable for contemporary audiences. An episode of The Cartoon Network's "Toon Heads" program featured a number of "complete" World War II cartoons, but at least one of these (*Blitz Wolf*) had been edited to remove footage of the destruction of Japan.

Aside from the obvious frustrations such impediments present to the film researcher, this unsophisticated and myopic response to social evolution succeeds only too well in tragically distorting perceptions of our cultural heritage. Fortunately, perhaps as a backlash against well-intentioned but (at times) destructive censorship, some cartoons have been rescued from oblivion and presented in their complete form by individuals or companies who realize the value of these works as historical artifacts. Carefully labeled and presented as such, cartoons—even those containing images that today seem racially insensitive—can be studied and appreciated as reflections of the society that created them, and not judged and condemned in the context of today's attitudes.

Over a nearly two-year period of research (and more than another year's work on this revised edition), the authors were able to identify 290 commercially-released short cartoons reflecting an awareness of the world crisis (January 1939–September 1945). Over 85 percent were actually screened. Primary information for the remainder came from the comprehensive Office of War Information motion picture analyses (April 1942–August 1943), and from copyright deposit material for the individual works, both located in the Motion Picture, Broadcast, and Recorded Sound Division of the Library of Congress in Washington, D.C.

Since the original edition of this work, the authors also collaborated on *Hollywood War Films, 1937–1945*, which uses much the same methodology to examine feature motion pictures of the war era. This methodology involves modified content analysis, assigning various "coding" terms to particular concepts, personalities, and references, both overt and covert. While feature films and animated cartoons are both artificial creations, live-action films record "reality"—even if that reality is created in a movie studio—and it is therefore possible for a number of inadvertent references to appear onscreen (for instance, gas rationing stickers on car windshields). These references are still valid, but since cartoons are *wholly* created by the director, writers, and animators, topical references in animated films were almost certainly the result of *deliberate* decisions by the filmmakers (for example, a ration sticker would not appear on a car's windshield in a cartoon unless the artist specifically *drew* it there!).

This methodology is adaptable to different topics and different eras: virtually any group or concept (images of women, African-Americans, big business, Asians, the police, etc.) could be examined over time or within a particular period. However, if there is one thing the authors have learned from our experiences, it is that such research—if it is to have validity—must be as comprehensive as possible (within stated parameters). Watching a few movies and attempting to draw broad conclusions from such a limited sample is as ridiculous as someone reading two Shakespeare plays and writing about his treatment of women, or a sociologist basing a paper about the whole immigrant experience on three interviews. Unfortunately, some film scholars follow the "usual suspects" methodology, making wide extrapolations from a handful of well-known movies. Close readings of films are another matter entirely, and have validity, but should not be used — without substantial supporting evidence — to make conjectures about broader trends.

The text chapters which follow discuss the topical content of animated cartoons of the First and Second World Wars— as well as the period between these two conflicts. The filmography contains a description of each war-oriented cartoon for the period 1939–1945. It is followed by appendices which compile the statistics for these shorts. The purpose of *Doing Their Bit* is to show how animated cartoons reflected contemporary events, both to illustrate what movie audiences of the time were viewing and to demonstrate the form and extent of topical references in one segment of motion picture production during this era.

2. Moving Lines
Behind the Lines:
Cartoons of World War I

Animated pictures have their origins in the 17th-century "magic lantern" device, but the first truly animated film cartoon seems to have been created in 1906 by J. Stuart Blackton, entitled *Humorous Phases of Funny Faces.* A few years later Winsor McCay produced and distributed his now famous *Gertie the Dinosaur,* used as part of his vaudeville act.

John Randolph Bray, a well-known newspaper cartoonist, created the first cartoon film series with his 1913 introduction of the "Colonel Heeza Liar" character.[1] The diminutive, bulbous-nosed septuagenarian was a combination of the hyperbolic Baron Munchausen and former president Teddy Roosevelt (who is mentioned in the premier work, *Col. Heeza Liar in Africa*).

Current events were often mentioned or depicted in this series (one episode caricatured President Woodrow Wilson). In August 1914, the First World War erupted on the European continent. The United States would not become embroiled in that conflict until April 1917, but the war nevertheless rapidly began to involve Americans. Germany's declaration of a war zone around Britain in February 1915 led directly to the sinking of the passenger liner *Lusitania* that May. During the same month the Colonel entered the fray with his usual panache. *Col. Heeza Liar in the Trenches* (Pathé News) portrays him as a special war correspondent for the "N.Y. Daily Bluff."[2] In an August release, *War Dog,* Heeza Liar has a comic encounter with an unidentified submarine.[3] By the following spring the Colonel had become more partisan — after reading a war article in the papers, the plucky character visits No-Man's-Land in *Col. Heeza Liar Wins the Pennant*: "Give me a chance to show my skill, or by golly the Germans will." Soon after arriving, the Colonel is blown out of his "private trench" in the battle of "Dead Man's Hill No. 23 " Using a wrecked cannon barrel like a baseball bat (a la "Ty Cobb"), he drives the enemy's cannon balls back on their heads until they are in full retreat. The Colonel is last seen pulling down the pennant over the ruins of the foe's fortress.[4] At least 11 "Col. Heeza Liar" cartoons directly or indirectly addressing World War I are listed in Appendix E.

Another cartoon by J.R. Bray, *The Long Arm of Law and Order* (April 1916), allegorically addresses the punitive expedition of General Pershing into Mexico, mounted in response to the notorious March raid by Pancho Villa on Columbus, New Mexico.[5] Uncle Sam is shown standing behind a stone barrier (the "Border") watching the Mexicans misbehaving. In disgust, he finally stretches out his right arm (labeled "Army" on the sleeve) and brings forth a squealing Villa from his mountain hideout. Uncle Sam crushes the bandit in his hand, forcing him to drop his pistol and dagger, then drops the Mexican into a garbage can in which Filipino guerrilla leader Aguinaldo also rests![6]

Soon after the United States entered the war, Bray was commissioned by the Army to make animated training films.[7] They employed the new rotoscoping process developed by Max Fleischer. Many animation studios would make military training films during World War II.

Mutt and Jeff, the popular comic strip duo, also got into the act before America became an active combatant in the war. In *The Outposts* (1916), the Germans are clearly identified as the enemy. After Jeff is rejected by a British army recruiter, he grabs Mutt and visits the French recruiting office. The two misfits exit the building wearing kepis. Soon afterwards, the new soldiers arrive at "French Trench 23," where — perhaps reflecting contemporary American attitudes — Mutt states: "This trench warfare makes me sick." An unusual aspect of this scene is the presence of a German corpse in the background. There is the inevitable encounter with an enemy outpost, and the two boys flee a sentient "high speed" bullet and several angry German soldiers at the climax.

As late as December 1915, the "Keeping Up With the Joneses" series featured a pro-peace work. In *Pa McGinnis Gets the Boys Out of the Trenches*, Pa falls asleep while smoking his Christmas cigar and reading the newspaper (headlining Henry Ford's controversial "Peace Ship" sailing to Europe). He dreams of going to the front, where he quickly kicks all the belligerents and their weapons out of the trenches. A proud Pa is presented with medals by the grateful representatives of all the warring nations, including a cigarette smoking Turk and the uniformed Kaiser. This is one of the few relatively benign characterizations of Kaiser Wilhelm to appear in an animated work during the war years.

The war in Europe so stimulated interest in topical events that many film companies added or expanded newsreel programs. Animated works quickly appeared that either parodied the newsreels or were integrated into the program. Near the end of 1915, Essanay launched an animated series called the "Canimated Nooz Pictorial." It was a split reel — the latter half was made up of so-called "scenic" live-action material. The cartoons were created by Wallace A. Carlson (the "Dreamy Dud" animator) and lampooned contemporary issues, apparently by combining photographic faces with animated bodies.[8] For instance, in the 8 March 1916 edition, a meeting of the "Women's Harmony Society at Kokomo to discuss international peace" is broken up by a "sour note."[9] The following month, in Pictorial No. 8, a "war pictures" interview with "General Frank Furter" is included.[10]

The "preparedness" controversy, a major presidential campaign issue, was discussed as early as May 1916. In Pictorial No. 10, "Kernel Willyum Jenninks Bryan" (that is, William Jennings Bryan) is unflatteringly shown demonstrating the adequacy of American defenses with a popgun and a grape juice-firing squirt gun.[11] "Luther Leatherlungs" is shown in a September issue delivering a preparedness speech.[12] Protagonists "William Jynx Bryan" and "Col. Tedious Roosevelt" are depicted at a luncheon together in Pictorial No. 23.[13] Finally, on the eve of America's entrance into the war (6 April 1917), Pictorial No. 28 features a section again maligning "William Jynx Bryan." This time he is shown "drilling his megaphone regiment in the art of talking their enemies to death."[14]

Wallace Carlson also occasionally included separate animated works in the Canimated Nooz Pictorial package. The animated portion of Pictorial No. 17 concludes with a "serious" cartoon called *Signs of Peace* and one of his Dreamy Dud episodes.[15]

Two other newsreel spoofs were "Nutty News" (Pathé-Goldberg Cartoon Comedy) and Gaumont's "Kartoon Komics," released as part of their "Mutual Weekly" program. The "Kartoon Komics" were described in a trade journal ad as "animated comicalities of current events by Harry Palmer."[16] The 5 July 1916 "Kartoon Komics" was entitled *Scrambled Events* and dealt with preparedness in a "humorous way."[17]

In a 1916 *Moving Picture World* article, cartoonist Palmer discussed his ideas concerning the part animated cartoons played in the motion picture program and their relevancy to topical issues:

> The best place on the program for an animated reel is right after the big feature [which is] usually of a tense nature ... the greater relaxation for

the greatest number is secured by showing an animated picture. Events of national importance, the coming [presidential] election, the Mexican situation, and general preparedness, afford such striking subjects for caricature that the cartoonist now makes his happiest hits depicting such events in a gently satirical vein...[18]

Before the end of April 1917, Gregory LaCava's "Jerry on the Job" character joined the Navy. In *Jerry Saves the Navy*, the new sailor encounters difficulties during target practice. As best as can be ascertained from the script, though, there were no direct references to the war.[19]

Happy Hooligan, a popular comic strip character created by F. Burr Opper, also starred in a series of animated cartoons. On 8 April 1917, only two days after war with the German Empire was confirmed by the United States Congress, in *The New Recruit*, Happy is shown telling another of his outlandish yarns to the kids. Happy relates how he joined the Army and became a hero in the trenches, dodging enemy shells to deliver a message to the general. When Happy finishes his tall tale, the children decide that he should be "shot at sunrise" for telling such a whopper.[20]

A few months later, the tin can-hatted comic hero was participating in the war effort in *The Tank*.[21] While his wife Suzanne practices Red Cross bandaging on such items as furniture legs, Happy builds a tank with a trench digger in his barn. He tells sidekick Gloomy Gus, "I'm going to present it to my country." But when Gus gets behind the controls, a swath of destruction is left in the machine's wake. After the two crash into a "Powder Works" with predictably explosive results, they fall through the ceiling into Happy's home, thus providing Suzanne with live subjects on whom to practice her newly acquired first aid knowledge.[22]

In *Doing His Bit* (1918), Happy Hooligan and three children spot a "Join the U.S. Army" poster. He proceeds to spin a yarn to the kids about his heroics when he was in the "Secret Service." Aboard a ship threatened by a U-boat, he turns away an excited sailor who offers him a life preserver, stating "women and sugar first," a comic reference to wartime shortages. Happy then upsets the German calculations by taming their torpedoes. Later, after eluding a guard behind enemy lines, he steals the German war plans from Field Marshal von Hindenburg's pocket. Hitching a ride on a shell to Allied territory, he sends the bomb back to blow up the Kaiser. As Happy concludes his tall tale, a recruiter walks up and urges him to stop talking and start fighting for America. Other Happy Hooligan cartoons which may have been war-oriented include *Double-Cross Nurse* and *The Great Offensive* (both 1917), *Tramp, Tramp, Tramp!* (1918), *Knocking the "H" Out of Heinie*, and *Der Wash on Der Line* (both 1919).

"Bobby Bumps," a character created by Earl Hurd, was a little boy—his speech sprinkled with street slang—dressed in knickers and a cap, accompanied by his pet dog. Most of his adventures involved the boy's overactive imagination. In the January 1918 cartoon segment of Paramount-Bray's Pictograph No. 100 (a one-reel "magazine-on-the-screen"), Bobby Bumps builds a "tank." While attacking an "enemy" cornfield, he suffers injuries.[23] *Bobby Bumps Becomes an Ace* (July 1918) depicts Bobby's daydream as he shoots down five German airplanes and damages a U-boat (before being brought back to reality by his irate mother).

The Happy Hooligan and Bobby Bumps cartoons may be construed as an allegory of "innocent" America becoming involved in the "European" war. Hooligan, although an adult figure, is childlike in his enthusiasms and activities, while Bobby Bumps is literally a little boy. And yet, they confront—and defeat—the enemy, a concept carried over to World War II cartoons, which demonstrate the ability of non-militaristic Americans to rise to the occasion and foil evil when necessary.

Another Paramount-Bray Pictograph released during 1918 included *Putting Fritz on the Water Wagon*. A still from this film depicts "John Bull" and "France" kicking a drunken, club-wielding "Germany" into the street, past the corpse of the violated maiden "Belgium." "Uncle Sam," in the background, has lassoed Fritz and is pulling him toward the "Permanent Peace Water Wagon."[24]

The Edison studios also joined the animated cartoon war effort. Paul Terry's *Farmer Al Falfa and His Wayward Pup*, followed by *Your Flag and My Flag*, appeared on a split-reel released through K.E.S.E. (Kline, Edison, Selig, and Essanay). The second work was described as "a patriotic poem embellished with animated illustrations."[25]

During August 1917, the "Motoy Comedies" were vigorously promoted in the trade journals. Produced by Peter Pan Film Corporation, they featured animated dolls. Though described as "clean and wholesome," ads for *The Dollies of 1917* nevertheless included militaristic images suggesting a war orientation.[26]

General Film launched a semimonthly, single-reel series called "Novelty Films" in February 1918. According to *Motion Picture News*: "The headliner for each release is the animated cartoon. In several of them Kaiser Wilhelm II of the Hohenzollern tribe and the Crown Prince are the leading characters and they are put through some stunts that are expected to strike a popular chord with patriotic American audiences."[27] The Kaiser—like Hitler during World War II, and possibly even more so—was relentlessly singled out for abuse in animated works. This may have had something to do with the lack of easily caricatured alternatives, since the other enemy nations (the Central Powers)— and their leaders— were definitely in Germany's shadow.

Perhaps reflecting the slow pace of United States mobilization, it was not until the early spring of 1918 that American cartoons containing war themes began appearing in significant numbers.[28] Released near the end of America's third Liberty Loan campaign, *Liberty Bonds* (April) was produced by the Bray Studios and directed by C.T. Anderson. A mighty American bald eagle christened "Liberty Bonds" wings his way across the Atlantic and descends upon the Kaiser's pet parrot, who is monotonously repeating his master's predictions of victory. After the eagle has completed his visit with the "Imperial Parrot," the parrot has been denuded of its plumage.[29]

The creator of "Gertie the Dinosaur," Winsor McCay, released the "blood stirring pen picture" *The Sinking of the Lusitania* in the spring of 1918.[30] The film opens with a live action sequence in which McCay introduces Augustus F. Beach, a noted war correspondent who had been the first American newspaperman to interview the survivors of the 1915 incident. The animation begins, depicting the silhouette of the *Lusitania* steaming past a mist-shrouded Statue of Liberty. Off the coast of Ireland the ship is hit by two torpedoes from the U-39. Photographs of well-known American citizens who were killed then appear on the screen (including Alfred G. Vanderbilt). As the second torpedo slams into the British vessel, the passengers are seen scurrying across the deck, launching lifeboats and jumping overboard. To further emphasize German cruelty, the action shifts to a drowning mother and her baby. As she attempts to save the infant by raising it above her head, we see them slip beneath the waves. A concluding title melodramatically declaims: "The man who fired the shot was decorated for it by the Kaiser! And yet they tell us not to hate the Hun."

Due to growing anti–German sentiments throughout the United States during World War I (fired by "100% Americanism" propaganda), the "Katzenjammer Kids" cartoon series was adversely affected. Produced by Gregory LaCava under the International Film Service banner, these cartoons featured benignly comic German immigrant caricatures. War fever resulted in the shorts being released under the title "Der Captain," but in spite of this, production was sharply curtailed during the first half of 1918 and finally discontinued in July of that year.

During the war years a cartoon version of Charlie Chaplin also began appearing, produced by Universal. The first to be released was *How Charlie Captured the Kaiser*. Charlie crosses the ocean in a tub, encountering and sinking a German submarine on the way. Charlie finally reaches France by grabbing onto the feet of a large stork. At the front he captures an

The Picture that will never have a Competitor.
–will burn in your brain forever!
"The SINKING OF THE LUSITANIA"
Winsor McCay's Blood Stirring Pen Picture
_____ the World's Only Record of
the Crime that Shocked Humanity

Advertisement for *The Sinking of the Lusitania* (1918).

enemy gun and handily defeats an army of lethargic spike-helmeted incompetents. When he punctures the posterior of a particularly rotund "Boche" with his bayonet, a blast of air gushes forth. "Reducing the German front," chortles Charlie. Wearing the uniform of one of his victims, but still carrying his cane, Charlie finds and captures a pathetic Wilhelm II, disguised in civilian clothes.[31]

Universal, under the leadership of Carl Laemmle (himself a German immigrant), seems to have worked hard to cater to its perceptions of public sentiment and to closely support the American government's policies throughout the entire World War I period (1914–1918). In late 1914, for instance, Universal released the pro–Wilson administration short *Be Neutral*, but by 1918 this same studio was responsible for one of the most virulently anti–German feature films of the war, *The Kaiser, Beast of Berlin* (1918).

In August 1917, Universal released the split-reel "Powers Comic Cartoon" *Colonel Pepper's Mobilized Farm*. The colonel runs an ammunition factory in which patriotically aroused hens are busily laying for their country. Their "hen-shells" are then set aside until they grow "ripe." All the farm animals receive military training as well, in order to be able to use properly the home grown munitions.[32]

Universal's news services were particularly extensive. In addition to the "Animated Weekly," a straightforward newsreel begun in 1912, there were "Universal Current Events" and the "Screen Magazine." The former was lauded as a "wedding of press and screen" that included selected topical political cartoons from newspapers around the country as well as animated works.[33] "Screen Magazine," launched in November 1916, was devoted largely to informational or propagandistic shorts and frequently concluded with an animated work. For instance, during 1917 and 1918 the "Screen Magazine" often closed with a clay cartoon ("animated sculp-

How Charlie Captured the Kaiser (1918): The "fool Kaiser and his harebrained idiotic outfit" are foiled by the animated version of Charlie Chaplin.

ture") by Willie Hopkins. In Issue No. 16 (27 April), his work is described as showing "us a picture of the U.S. as a united nation."[34] The following month, Issue No. 20 ends with another "Miracle in Mud" by Hopkins that contains a "patriotic subject."[35] By the fall, in Issue No. 44, he made a "timely and amusing" work on conscription, *Exemption Pleas*, and in Issue No. 78 (summer 1918), Hopkins produced a parody of the "Hate the Hun" feature *The Kaiser, the Beast of Berlin*.[36]

In the winter of 1918 the United States Government's Committee on Public Information, headed by George Creel, selected a cartoon that had originally appeared in a Universal "Current Events" as a propaganda work to be given to American allies and exhibited overseas. The cartoon was by Hy Mayer and entitled *The Eagle's Blood.*[37]

"Current Events" sometimes carried cartoons produced by or for the United States Government. One such work, made for the United States Food Administration, was described under the heading "Mobilizing the Frankfurters" in the *Motion Picture News*:

> Uncle Sam in the guise of the Pied Piper summons the Great Army of the Food Supply. As his magic notes enter the home and shop, the coals leap from their beds, lumps of sugar hop out of the bowls, the wheat bundles itself off the field and the hams hasten from the butcher's. Even the sausages, forgetting their Teutonic origin, curl up on themselves and trundle merrily to join the throng.[38]

Around December 1917, the government began promoting Thrift Stamps as a less expensive alternative to Liberty Loan Bonds and War Savings Stamps. They were issued by the Treasury Department for 25 cents and could be accumulated and exchanged for interest-bearing War Savings Stamps ($4.25).[39] An unidentified animated trailer catalogued at the Library of Congress under the heading "W. S. S. Thriftettes" promotes them under the title, "Hurry the End of the War," as a horse-drawn hearse containing the Kaiser's corpse gallops by.[40]

Mutt and Jeff, created by newspaper cartoonist Bud Fisher, made their animated debut in 1916. As indicated earlier, they had engaged the Germans on the Western Front that same year, so it should not be surprising that in 1917 they, too, actively participated in the war effort. Cartoons featuring the comical pair, dubbed "The Mirth of the Nation," were donated by their creator to the United States Navy — to entertain the servicemen — in the summer of 1917.[41] William Fox concluded a contract with Fisher the following spring for worldwide distribution of Mutt and Jeff cartoons. Fisher, by then a captain of artillery in the Canadian army, was devoting much of his artwork to life at the front.[42] About half of Mutt and Jeff's 1918 Fox releases were war-related, usually comically entangling them in some way with America's enemies, who are portrayed as undemocratic and arrogant.

In *The Tale of a Pig* (June 1918), Mutt and Jeff are "moved by the spirit of patriotism" to start a pig farm.[43] Dressed up as a tree in *The 75-Mile Gun*, the two characters capture the German super railway gun "Big Bertha" that has been shelling Paris and train it on the Crown Prince, the Kaiser, and Field Marshal von Hindenburg. At its conclusion the entire German army is "frustrated" by cheese and beer.[44] The mismatched duo joins the Navy in *Hunting for U-Boats*, and in *The Kaiser's New Dentist*, they set up practice in Berlin for the royal family. When the Kaiser visits

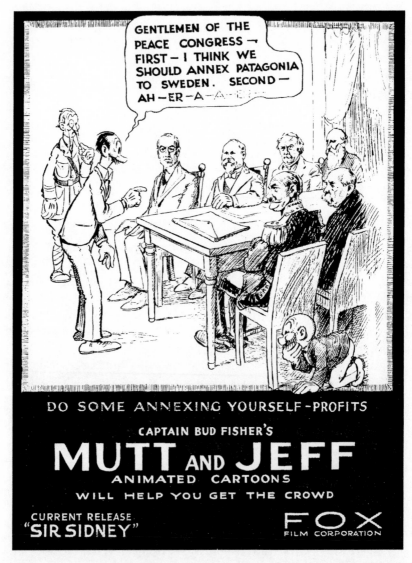

Mutt and Jeff attend the Paris Peace Conference in *Sir Sidney* (1919). Note the caricatures of world leaders Woodrow Wilson, David Lloyd George, and Georges Clemenceau.

their office, he is knocked out and bundled off to American lines.[45] Mutt and Jeff were also probably the first cartoon characters to take on the emerging Russian revolutionary leadership in *Bulling the Bolsheviki* (released 29 September 1918).[46] The following month, in *Our Four Days in Germany*, Mutt and Jeff take the place of the Kaiser's chefs, preparing a "victory dinner" attended by the Kaiser, the Crown Prince, and Admiral von Tirpitz that becomes a "banquet of defeat."[47]

Although hostilities ended with an armistice in November 1918, the Paris Peace Conference dragged on for many months afterwards. The Kaiser went into exile in the Netherlands but did not escape further animated vilification. During the spring of 1919, for instance, Mutt and Jeff took one last crack at him. In *William Hohenzollern, Sausage Maker* they tangle with the former German leader-turned-wurst-entrepreneur when they answer his suspicious ad offering to buy dogs.[48]

Thomas (Charles) Bowers, who along with Raoul Barre had produced Mutt and Jeff under contract for Bud Fisher after 1916, went out on his own in early 1919.[49] In what was probably one of his first independently animated works, *AWOL*, released through American Motion Picture Corporation (commissioned by the U.S. Army Signal Corps), the topic of demobilization of the United States Army is dealt with in a darkly humorous manner. A disgruntled doughboy addresses a group of his comrades in barracks: "We should have been discharged the minute the armistice was signed." Another soldier, his mates nodding in agreement, responds— "I'd like to get home, too. But we've got to remember that our Uncle Sam has a great big army to handle and is doing his best." A lady of pleasure ("Miss AWOL") drives up in her car, and talks the doughboy into taking a "joy" ride. He winds up penniless, ostracized and scowling behind the bars of the guard house (the bars form the letters "AWOL") as the rest of his unit is shown skipping and leapfrogging out the gate past a sign reading "Home."[50]

The Paris Peace Conference formally concluded the World War with the signing of the Versailles Treaty on 28 June 1919. Several months earlier, in *Sir Sidney*, Mutt and Jeff essentially ended pre–1930s animated participation in current international events by contributing their unique brand of advice to the peace conference delegates.[51]

3. Animated Talkies During the 1930s: A Political Overview

As discussed in the previous chapter, cartoons, like the other film forms, had been exploited for propagandistic purposes during the First World War. With the conclusion of this tragic chapter in 20th-century history, American cartoons, with the exception of a couple of anti–Bolshevik works released during the Red Scare (1918–1920), largely divorced themselves from international events and embraced the carefree, halcyon years of the 1920s.[1]

The 1930s saw a worldwide depression and the concomitant rise of authoritarian militaristic states. Among the Western democracies there arose a deep fear of extremism, along with the growth of a pacifist movement in response to these threatening developments. Cartoons, like feature films, were not immune to these sentiments.

The first animated cartoon from the l930s identified as politically topical is *Disarmament Conference* (Columbia, 1931). Several international events, such as the London Naval Disarmament Conference, had recently taken place. This Krazy Kat cartoon opens with the animal inhabitants of a jungle engaged in trench-war combat. Krazy is able to initiate a peace proclamation that brings joy to the war-weary creatures.[2]

Warner Bros.' earliest cartoon star, Bosko, appeared in several animated cartoon expressions of this trend. Parodying the feature film *The Dawn Patrol, Dumb Patrol* (WB, 1931) depicts Bosko—flying a little tublike airplane — in a World War I–style dogfight with an enemy plane (marked with a skull and crossbones). *Bosko, the Doughboy* (1932) was the cartoon counterpart to anti-war feature films like *All Quiet on the Western Front*

(1930), *The Case of Sergeant Grischa* (1930), and *Broken Lullaby* (1932). This short has a macabre scenario, with cartoon characters getting blown up in No-Man's-Land as "Am I Blue" is heard on the soundtrack.

The following year, the Great Depression was at its zenith, Hitler assumed the chancellorship in Germany, and Franklin D. Roosevelt was elected 32nd president of the United States. Paramount released a cartoon spoof a month before the presidential election, *Betty Boop for President.* At one point, while delivering her unique set of campaign promises in song, Betty's face briefly changes into the incumbent President Hoover's visage.

Benito Mussolini had been the fascist leader of Italy since late 1922. In February 1933 he made an animated appearance in *Scrappy's Party* (Columbia). In this cartoon, baby Vonsey has baked a birthday cake for Scrappy, so the birthday boy gets out of bed and suggests they have a party. The guests include caricatures of popular movie stars (Joe E. Brown, Jimmy Durante, Greta Garbo, and the Marx Brothers, for instance) as well as such disparate world figures as the Prince of Wales, a roller skating Mahatma Gandhi,[3] a money-bag-carrying John D. Rockefeller, and a dancing Mussolini.

Many of these figures (plus others like England's King George V and Maurice Chevalier) reappeared later in the year when Scrappy and little Vonsey put on a show at the Chicago World's Fair in *The World's Affair* (released in June). After sequences showing comical "inventions," the cartoon concludes with a tutu-clad chorus line consisting of Mussolini, Albert Einstein, Franklin D. Roosevelt, and Mahatma Gandhi! Although possibly making a subliminal political statement about America's new president literally embracing such ideologically diverse personalities, this scene was probably simply intended to be a humorously incongruous grouping of contemporary celebrities.

Confidence is a unique theme cartoon released in the summer of 1933 by Universal. Old Man Depression rises out of a city dump at night, envelops the earth with his toxin, and in the morning the whole world is full of gloom. On Oswald the Rabbit's chicken ranch, the hens will not even try to fill their egg baskets. Oswald runs to Dr. Pill for a cure, but the general practitioner says "There's your doctor!" and points to a picture of FDR on the wall. Oswald builds a plane and flies to Washington. When the floppy-eared rabbit enters the president's office (which has a picture of Lincoln on the wall), Roosevelt gets up dancing and cheerfully sings "Confidence."[4] Oswald returns home and injects the local citizens and farm animals with the "right serum" from a huge hypodermic needle. Imbued with the "Spirit of 1933," the barnyard band plays and the hens all lay eggs. The concept of an "economic cure" for the nation was directly inspired by Roosevelt's famous "Forgotten Man" radio address of April 1932.[5]

At about the same time, Warner Bros. produced *I Like Mountain Music* (aka *Magazine Rack*). The characters on the front pages of magazines in a drugstore come to life and interact after hours. Three crooks who step out of *Crime Stories* magazine rob the cash register. During the ensuing chase scene an angry mob — including a gun-wielding Edward G. Robinson — passes Mussolini, arms folded and chin jutting out, standing in a balcony on the title page of another magazine. *Il Duce* gives the fascist salute, then orders his blackshirts to join the pursuit. He later uses a pencil sharpener as a "machine gun" to assault the criminals. Mussolini was not unpopular in the United States at the time: this was at least his fourth appearance in a commercially released American cartoon during 1933 (in addition to the two Scrappy cartoons previously mentioned, Mussolini was also featured in *I've Got to Sing a Torch Song*, released by Warner Bros.).

Mussolini's popularity would last until Italy's invasion of Ethiopia in the fall of 1935. Since tension between the two nations had been given extensive coverage in the world press during the preceding months, it is not surprising to see fascist leader "Mausoleum" appear in the "Passé News" sequence of *Buddy's Theatre* (Warner Bros.), released in April 1935. *What Price Porky* (1938) features a fascist duck who strongly resembles the Italian leader, probably the last such caricature in cartoons prior to 1941.[6] An article in the 17 January 1939 issue of *Look* magazine suggests animation producers self-censored such references — specifically citing Mussolini and the fascist salute — for fear of losing foreign markets.

Though Adolf Hitler had just been appointed chancellor of Germany in January 1933, he made several cartoon appearances before the end of the year. *Cubby's World Flight* (Van Beuren, August 1933) depicts the aerial adventures of the little bear character. As he flies over Germany, Cubby spots Hitler and German President Paul von Hindenburg, who smile and wave their beer steins at him! In Warner Bros.' *Bosko's Picture Show* (released in September), a segment of a newsreel parody (noted as emanating from "Pretzel, Germany") depicts Hitler — wearing lederhosen and a swastika armband — chasing Jimmy Durante with an axe! The American comedian shouts "Am I mortified!"

Disney's 1933 color classic, *The Three Little Pigs*, is considered by many to be a topical allegory: the wolf is described as a symbol of the Great Depression and sometimes as a representation of the threat of fascism.[7] The theme song, "Who's Afraid of the Big Bad Wolf," seems deliberately intended to cheer up audiences — things aren't as bad as they seem, and the Depression isn't the end of the world.

At one point in *The Three Little Pigs* the wolf briefly appears as a Jewish

Frame enlargement from *I Love Mountain Music* (1933)—Italian dictator Benito Mussolini salutes his black-shirted followers.

"Shylock" caricature (deleted from the currently available Disney version of this cartoon). Released in May, this cartoon contains one of the last blatant Jewish caricatures to appear in a short commercial American cartoon. Less-than positive portrayals of Jews were not uncommon in earlier animated works. Two other examples from the early 1930s are *Laundry Blues* (Van Beuren, 1930) and *Redskin Blues* (Van Beuren, 1932). The former links Asians with Jews and the latter links American Indian stereotypes with Jews. It could be surmised that the virulent anti–Semitism of Hitler's new regime may have had some impact upon the decline of such caricatures in American animated films.

By early 1935, the peace movement was at its height in the United States. Two relevant cartoons were released before the summer. In *Sunshine Makers*, a color production from Van Beuren Studios, lugubrious black- and blue-clad gremlin-like creatures attack a community of cheerful dwarfs who bottle sunshine. Planning to black out the light, the jealous imps stealthily approach the dwarfs' sunny habitat with spray canisters filled with tar. Using a tree trunk as a cannon and their light-bottles as shells, the dwarfs fight back. Then, aboard dragonfly bombers, they go on the offensive and blow away the darkness that has enshrouded the gremlin village. At the end the dwarfs sing and dance around a flower-ringed pond: "And now the world looks bright and fair, because there's sunshine everywhere."

Released a few months later, Columbia's bizarre *Peace Conference*, starring Krazy Kat, was more explicit. Three world-power representatives (animals in top hats and tails), after being relieved of their weapons, dance together into a conference hall to discuss world peace. But they begin to quarrel as they slice off their shares of a world globe. Alerted by the doves of peace, Krazy Kat enters in a tank and shoots a shell from which Bing Crosby emerges. His crooning pacifies the delegates, but only briefly. With Uncle Sam now in attendance, the conference gets under way again, but a giant from Mars crashes to earth and disrupts the meeting. The delegates and Krazy Kat — with a Rudy Vallee–loaded shell, another Crosby shell, and a big-band shell — unite to restore world order.[8]

During 1935 a public debate developed over the alleged influence of munitions makers on America's entrance into World War I and their threat to current world peace. This issue was accented by such books as the provocatively-titled *The Merchants of Death*. Supposedly influenced by a *Fortune* magazine article devoted to the subject (probably "Arms and the Man," March 1934), Columbia released a topical cartoon entitled *Neighbors*. Its allegorical plot centers on two roosters who are happy neighbors until a crow (a vulture, according to Maltin) comes along and — disturbed by their peacefulness — tells each one lies about the other in order to create dissension. He then sells them munitions and departs. The roosters eventually annihilate each other. As they cover their own graves the two remorsefully warn others to beware of false tales.[9]

Disney entered the 1935 pacifist cartoon sweepstakes with the "Silly Symphonies" *Music Land* (released in October). A Romeo and Juliet scenario leads to war (with musical notes as shells) between a kingdom of classical strings and a rival kingdom of swinging brass instruments. *Music Land* concludes harmoniously with a double marriage.

In August 1936 Warner Bros. released *Porky's Poultry Plant*. The pig runs his chicken farm like a (benign) army camp. The buzzard-like birds that "hawknap" his hens sound like bombers and fly in military formations. When the chicken coops come under aerial attack, Porky sounds an air-raid alarm and takes off in a compact fighter plane to engage the enemy. Although the German Condor Legion that aided Franco's rebels did not go into action until November 1936, it was in July that the opposing sides in the civil war first engaged in major fighting, including the then rather controversial aerial bombing of civilian targets. Other 1936 Warner Bros. cartoons with war-like themes included *Boom Boom* (February), featuring Porky and Beans in World War I–style ground combat, and *Plane Dippy* (April), in which Porky joins the Air Corps but — after a series of mishaps — opts for the infantry instead.

A somewhat oblique pacifistic theme appears in MGM's holiday release for 1936, *The Pups' Christmas*. While romping through the family presents, a couple of puppies accidentally start up a toy tank and airplane. The two war toys (the tank is accompanied by strains of "Over There") shoot up the rest of the presents and eventually destroy each other. Three years later, MGM would portray war more explicitly in *Peace on Earth*.

The pacifist movement of the early 1930s had significantly dissipated by 1937, largely the result of the increased aggressiveness of the major authoritarian states and a growing perception of the military impotence of the democratic powers. Mussolini invaded Ethiopia in late 1935 and, unchallenged by the rest of the world, over a year later the Italians were mopping up in the bush. Hitler was unabashedly rearming Germany and unilaterally remilitarized the Rhineland in 1936. Civil war was raging in Spain, with the fascist states backing the rebels and Stalin supporting the Loyalists, while the Western powers refused to take sides officially. After years of Sino-Japanese hostilities, Japan's military leaders committed their empire to a full-scale invasion of China following the Marco Polo Bridge incident in July 1937. Britain and France, all too cognizant of their own weakness, reluctantly began belated rearmament. The only other major Western nation with the potential power to affect this world crisis, the United States, continued to rest (though uncomfortably) behind its massive oceanic shields. This policy was institutionalized through the promulgation of a series of neutrality acts.

By 1937, some Warner Bros., RKO, and 20th Century–Fox feature films reflected an awareness of the mounting crisis in world affairs. In the cartoon arena, Warner Bros. would dominate both in overall production and in social consciousness through 1941. Two Warner Bros. cartoons of 1937 made allusions to world events. The first, admittedly rather elliptical in its approach, is *Porky's Hero Agency*. Porky Pig falls asleep while reading a book on Greek mythology. In the logic-troubling dream that follows, "Porky Karkus, Hero for Sale,"[10] gets a call from "Emperor Jones" to eliminate the evil Gorgon, who is turning everyone into stone. What is significant is that the "Empy" is having a "fireside chat" with a senate made up of statues. Asking for their approval, he pulls their strings and they give him a collective fascist salute.[11]

Although the marshmallow-toasting emperor in this cartoon may or may not be a reference to *Il Duce*, a caricature of Hitler, though fleeting, is explicit in *She Was an Acrobat's Daughter*. In the local movie house, the lights are dimmed and "Dole Promise" (a reference to commentator Lowell Thomas) introduces the "Goofy Tone News" (parodying the real-life "Movietone" newsreels). Meanwhile, a patron walks to the front of the theater and takes a seat in the far corner. As he turns his head and looks up, he frowns—what he sees is a distorted shot of Hitler at an extreme angle on the screen. It lasts for only a few seconds, but shows the goosestepping *Fuehrer* in storm trooper garb (with a swastika armband) giving the fascist salute.[12] As oblique as this reference is, it comes well in advance of Warners' ground-breaking anti–Nazi feature film, *Confessions of a Nazi Spy* (1939).

Warner Bros. was almost exclusively responsible for the few cartoons referring to world events in 1938. In February they released *What Price Porky?*, an early example of a war allegory cartoon (the title spoofs *What Price Glory?*, a play and 1926 film about two American Marines fighting in France during World War I). Many more such allegories would appear, particularly in 1939 and 1940, such as *Peace on Earth* (1939, MGM) and *Ants in the Plants* (1940, Paramount). In *What Price Porky?*, the chickens on Porky Pig's farm battle a fascistic gang of ducks who steal their corn. The enemy ducks' leader is an obvious parody of Mussolini. The dispute erupts into full-scale warfare until Porky converts a clothes-wringer into a corn-firing machine gun and defeats the goose-stepping ducks, who are rounded up and put in a stockade.

In *Porky the Gob*, released later in 1938, the clumsy pig singlehandedly subdues a "pirate submarine" attacking his battleship. During the second half of 1937, so-called "pirate" submarines operating in the Mediterranean Sea had been sinking ships carrying supplies to Republican Spain. Although it was not confirmed until after the war, the culprits were vessels of the Italian Navy. Furthermore, while the skull and crossbones on the side of "Sub Zero" is the universal symbol of pirates, in 1938 it was also the well-known insignia of Mussolini's Blackshirts.

A Feud There Was was released during the final week of the Munich Crisis (September 1938). Egghead is the much-abused "peacemaker" trying to stop a feud between two families of hillbillies. Perhaps coincidentally, Egghead wears a bowler hat and stiff collar, sartorial symbols also associated with Great Britain's prime minister and appeasement advocate Neville Chamberlain.

Another Warner Bros. cartoon released in the latter part of 1938 — *You're an Education*—deserves mention. Conceptually similar to *I Like Mountain Music* (1933) and *Billboard Frolics* (1936), this short is based on brochures in a travel agency. But while almost every major country and many American states are parodied, both Germany and Japan are virtually ignored. However, the Japanese were featured in the 1938 Columbia cartoon, *Poor Little Butterfly*—a butterfly sailor assigned to a turtle battleship falls in love with a Japanese girl butterfly, with sad results.

   The discussion of this period fittingly concludes on an even more ambiguous note. Disney's *Ferdinand the Bull* was released in November 1938. Following the Christmas 1936 publication of the children's book by Munro Leaf, there had been widespread accusations that the work was a pacifist tract.[13] The allegorical implications of the bull who would rather sniff flowers than fight are debatable, but take on more weight in the context of the troubled times in which the cartoon adaptation of Leaf's book was released. The bull, for instance, could be interpreted as representing a powerful America refusing to live up to its international responsibilities, particularly the refusal to aid Republican Spain's struggle against Franco's fascist rebels.

4. Meet John Doughboy: 1939–1941

In spite of growing concern in the United States over the degree of American involvement in world events—a concern that began to appear as early as the latter half of 1938 — most Americans were undecided about "taking sides" prior to the German/Soviet invasion of Poland in September 1939. Even after the outbreak of hostilities, a majority of the public, although convinced of Nazi aggression and sympathetic to the plight of the Western Allies, was more interested in the preservation of United States neutrality than in the defeat of the totalitarian regimes.

Such complacency was shattered by the crushing defeat of France by the German *Blitzkrieg* of May-June, 1940. This event was followed in America by a congressional debate over conscription as well as the fall presidential election campaign and led to a rapid intensification of the political struggle between isolationists and "aid-short-of-war" and interventionist advocates

The implementation of America's first peacetime draft in October 1940 was a major milestone that — in the minds of many — indicated the country was on an inexorable path to direct participation in the war. In March 1941, President Franklin D. Roosevelt aided the flagging British war effort by spearheading the Lend-Lease Act; after Hitler and his allies invaded the USSR in June 1941, this program was extended (in September) to the Soviet regime.

Meanwhile, Japan was becoming more deeply entangled in its war with China and was taking advantage of the European war to put pressure on the British and French imperial systems in the Far East.

While domestic debate over American involvement in the world war continued, the United States Navy became engaged in an undeclared shooting war in the Atlantic with Germany's U-boats. The preoccupation with events in Europe, combined with an attitude of racial superiority, contributed to a tragic dismissal of the Japanese as a serious potential threat. On 7 December 1941, aircraft of the Imperial Japanese Navy taught the whole world a lasting lesson while conclusively terminating the debate in the United States with regard to its joining in the global conflict.

As discussed in the previous section, only a few cartoons of the early and mid–1930s reflected an awareness of growing world tensions. Unlike their feature film counterparts, cartoons exhibited only a very modest increase in political content until the last quarter of 1940 (up from 2.5 percent in 1939 to 6 percent in 1940 — the totals for features were 17 percent and 20 percent, respectively).[1] Warner Bros. continued to dominate in real numbers through 1941, although Universal produced a slightly higher percentage of topical releases during 1941 (30 percent to Warners' 27 percent).

The defeat of France and the subsequent passage of the Selective Service Act appear to have been most directly responsible for a dramatic increase in the political content of American animated short cartoons. Specifically, the total jumped from 11 between 1 January 1939, and 30 August 1940, to 29 between 1 September 1940, and 31 December 1941. For all of 1941, 26 commercially produced and released short cartoons (16 percent of total releases) reflected an awareness of the world crisis.

Three of the four short cartoons from 1939 have been classified as war allegories; two were released following the outbreak of World War II. All of these cartoons are pacifistic in nature. *Peace on Earth* (MGM), timed for release over the Christmas holidays, depicts a world inhabited by peace-loving animals, the humans having eliminated their own species in a cataclysmic series of wars a generation earlier.

An interesting point should be made here concerning Warner Bros.' *Old Glory*, released during the July 4th holiday, since it may reflect a growing American desire to avoid offending the British. One part of the cartoon portrays Paul Revere's famous midnight ride. Instead of shouting "The British are coming, the British are coming!" the animated Revere neutrally proclaims, "To arms! To arms!" The narrator specifically mentions America's fight for freedom from "tyranny," but who our opponent *was* during the Revolutionary War is never stated or shown.

During 1940, 10 war-related cartoons were released. Only one, *Ants in the Plants* (Paramount), is a war allegory. With its emphasis on fortifications and preparedness, this short may have been referring to France's Maginot Line. Unlike its recent predecessors, *Ants in the Plants* can in no way be construed as pacifistic. Significantly, two other 1940 cartoons refer to the draft. Universal's *Recruiting Daze*, featuring bewildered Army recruit Punchy, was released the same week the Selective Service lottery was held. The credits of *Of Fox and Hounds* (Warner Bros.), listed the draft lottery numbers of its creators instead of their names!

In 1941, for the first time since World War I, there were also a large number of comments or allusions to events and characters in Europe. Illustrating the Eurocentric attitudes of many Americans, Japan is mentioned in only one cartoon, *How War Came*, a sort of animated political lecture released through Columbia. On the other hand, the Hollywood cartoon establishment was not loath to portray the Nazis. Seven 1941 cartoons either directly or indirectly attack the Nazi regime and/or its leaders: *Broken Treaties* (Columbia), *A Coy Decoy* (WB), *How War Came* (Columbia), *Meet John Doughboy* (WB), *The Mighty NaVy* (Paramount), *One Man Navy* (20th Century–Fox), and *We the Animals Squeak* (WB).

Topical references to the Armed Forces or the draft dominate the politically conscious cartoons released in 1941. Significantly, Popeye the Sailor makes his debut as a member of the United States Navy in Paramount's *The Mighty NaVy* (he had previously been portrayed as a civilian seaman). The preoccupation of so many of the cartoons with the military mimicked a parallel emphasis in topical feature films—there were over 150 references to the U.S. military or the draft in 170 war-relevant features released in 1941 (some films had more than one reference).[2] In the majority of the animated works the characters are portrayed in comical barracks situations—*Rookie Bear* (MGM), *Rookie Revue* (WB) and *$21 a Day (Once a Month)* (Universal) are three examples. These cartoons are somewhat similar to features like *Buck Privates* (Universal, 1941) in which the peacetime conscription experience was depicted as entertaining, humorous, and even beneficial for the recruits. In *Rookie Bear*, for example, Barney Bear receives free medical care for his flat feet and bad teeth before he's stamped "government inspected." "War games" or maneuvers are spoofed in *Rookie Revue*. 1941 cartoons also contain frequent gags about Draftee #158 (the first number drawn in the conscription lottery), Draft Board #13, and the real problem of the shortage of military equipment encountered by the rapidly expanding United States Army—Jack Benny's Maxwell is depicted as substituting for a tank in *Meet John Doughboy*.

The single war allegory cartoon from 1941, Warner's *The Fighting 69½th*, is not pacifistic. Perhaps reflecting the mood of the nation, it pessimistically portrays endless fighting between ant armies over the spoils from a picnic lunch.

A unique cartoon among these works is Universal's *Boogie Woogie Bugle Boy of Company B*, which centers around the tribulations of a drafted

Harlem trumpeter (while promoting the popular title song by Hughie Prince and Don Raye). Racial stereotyping aside, it is the only American fiction film work released by a major studio between 1937 and 1945 to depict an all-black unit in the military. It was not until 1943 that the film industry would even begin producing works with positive black characters in the United States Armed Forces, and then only as individuals in supporting roles, e.g., *Bataan* (MGM) and *Crash Dive* (20th Century–Fox). In 1944, at least two government-sponsored documentaries did portray all-black units, *The Negro Soldier* and *Wings for the Man*.

As 1941 concluded, Hollywood had begun to gear up for what many felt was America's inevitable entry into the war. However, no one could have predicted how soon and in what manner war would actually arrive, and the events of 7 December 1941 changed the course of the war, America, and the world.

5. All Out for V: 1942

The attack upon Pearl Harbor may have come as a bitter shock to the American people, but the nation had already been in a state of semi-mobilization. In January 1941, the Office of Production Management had been established and had orchestrated a gradual shift from civilian to defense production. Hollywood had organized the Motion Picture Committee Cooperating for National Defense some months earlier. Immediately after war was declared, the film industry created the War Activities Committee (WAC) to coordinate and maximize the effort for victory. In addition to a myriad of training and informational films produced by Hollywood for the military and industry prior to December 7th, at least 170 feature-length motion pictures had been commercially released by the end of the year that in some way reflected an awareness of the international conflict which had erupted in 1939.[1]

In addition to the 26 commercially produced cartoons with topical references released during 1941, Warner Bros. produced — for War Activities Committee release — *Any Bonds Today?* This abbreviated cartoon features Bugs Bunny, Elmer Fudd, and Porky Pig urging Americans to buy Defense Bonds. Walt Disney had made bond-selling cartoons for the Canadian government in 1941, all of which also saw United States release.[2]

There was a tremendous surge of national unity following America's abrupt entrance into the war. This was somewhat easier in 1942 than 1917, because American society was more homogeneous (fewer recent immigrants from a major belligerent), and because of the unambiguous ideological and military threat posed by our enemies. As in any major war, there was a period of great social upheaval and anxiety — created by adjustment to living in a total-war environment as well as uncertainty over the war itself. These problems were particularly acute during the first six months of American participation in the war because of continued military setbacks in the Pacific (the loss of Wake Island and the Philippines), heavy shipping losses to the U-boat menace in the North Atlantic and in the Caribbean, and disruptions to daily life created by wartime conditions (particularly shortages).

Although the inconveniences associated with shortages and rationing would continue throughout the war, by the end of 1942 the American people appear to have willingly, if not always enthusiastically, made the necessary social modifications required to mobilize fully a nation for war. The resultant massive armaments production, linked with a series of military victories (the naval defeat of Japan at Midway in June, the British victory over Rommel at El Alamein in November, the Russian encirclement of the German Sixth Army at Stalingrad during the fall) led to a growing confidence in ultimate victory.

Due to the intensity of the military struggle through 1942, there are nearly as many topical references as in 1943, although the actual number of war-related cartoons peaked in the latter year (see Appendix A). Most frequently portrayed or referred to in 1942 cartoons was the United States military. Rationing, shortages, and home front issues were the next most popular area to receive the animated attention of Hollywood. For that matter, these categories (when combined) would be referred to almost as many times as the armed forces throughout the course of the entire war period (137 to 108).

Interestingly, the "V for victory" symbol is promoted more often in 1942 than during any of the subsequent years. One might speculate it was invoked to reassure audiences, but that after 1942 the public was so confident of final victory that the continued invocation of this symbol was deemed superfluous.

War bonds and stamps were heavily promoted, usually indirectly, in 1942 cartoons. That is, bond posters or parodies of such posters appear randomly in the works involved (as was the case in real life). However, these practically disappeared from the text of cartoons during the following two years. Perhaps the animators—who had to *draw* these posters, after all— sympathized with their fellow Americans, who now lived in a world in which such posters were omnipresent (there would be eight bond drives during the war). Besides, by the end of 1942 many feature films as well as cartoons contained a brief pitch for bonds tacked onto the end credits.[3]

A significant number of cartoons did exhort the American people, however — directly or indirectly — to participate in the war effort on the home front. These include non-commercial cartoons such as *Out of the Frying Pan, Into the Firing Line* and *The New Spirit*, both produced by Walt Disney for the government. The first short urges housewives to save their

cooking grease (which could be
used in the production of explosives), and the second suggests
that timely payment of one's
income taxes will help win the
war. Other 1942 and early 1943
cartoons promoting audience
participation in home front activities include *Sammy Salvage*
and *Scrap for Victory* (scrap metal
collection), *Doing Their Bit* (supporting the USO), *Air Raid Warden* and *Barnyard Blackout* (home
defense) and *Yankee Doodle
Swing Shift* and *Cinderella Goes
to a Party* (war production work).

Victory gardens were also
depicted as a way for civilians to
help the war effort —*Andy Panda's
Victory Garden, Barney Bear's
Victory Garden*, and *Ration fer the
Duration* are all examples of this
type of activity. Interestingly

A patriotic Donald Duck from the U.S. government-sponsored film *The New Spirit*
(1942). Courtesy of The National Archives.

enough, with the exception of a few images of women in the labor force (10
references overall in the 1942–45 period), and a handful of references to
"first aid classes," most home front activities were shown to be the bailiwick
of male characters (on the other hand, the majority of cartoon "stars" in
this era were male, which makes the imbalance somewhat understandable).

The Japanese surprise attack upon America's Pacific bastion and
reports of atrocities committed in the Philippines—combined with pre-
existing racial prejudices—resulted in the cinematic vilification of the
Japanese.[4] Animated cartoons enthusiastically participated in such
attacks—there are at least 15 pejorative references to Japanese in 1942 cartoons. The wicked, smiling, craven, buck-toothed, glasses-wearing caricatures—whether anonymous "Japs" or resembling (or merely labeled)
Emperor Hirohito or Prime Minister Tojo—were crude examples of racial
stereotyping. Sometimes, the Japanese were even portrayed as squealing
pigs, as in *Somewhere in the Pacific* (20th Century–Fox). The rare cartoons
actually portraying combat situations were virtually all directed at "inferior" Japanese servicemen, such as *Blunder Below, Scrap the Japs, You're a
Sap, Mr. Jap* (all Paramount), and *Somewhere in the Pacific* (20th Century–

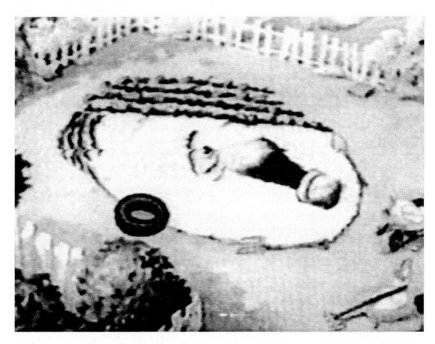

A Victory Garden becomes a Hitler caricature in *Barney Bear's Victory Garden* (1942).

Fox).[5] The Office of War Information reviewers on more than one occasion were so appalled by this misrepresentation of our Asian opponent that they felt constrained to comment that the Japanese should not be so cavalierly dismissed. Racial slurs directed at the Japanese are a little puzzling, in the light of our Chinese allies' racial similarity to the Japanese. Given the hatred and often lethal contempt for the Japanese expressed in these cartoons, it is also ironic that — unlike feature films of the same era — cartoons did not often evoke Pearl Harbor or call for revenge (Pearl Harbor was evoked in 44 features in 1942 and 36 films in 1943).

Neither the German nor the Italian people were so stigmatized in American animated cartoons, although Hitler and the Nazis were depicted as nothing less than the personification of evil. Hitler was most often caricatured as a psychopath and screeching neurotic, sometimes transmogrified into an animal, such as the vulture in *Song of Victory* (Columbia). While feature films made an effort to distinguish between so-called "good" Germans and Nazis, cartoons of the war era were not given to such subtleties, usually ignoring the existence of non–Nazi Germans (one noted exception is *Der Fuehrer's Face*, in which Donald Duck plays a tormented German worker in a shell factory).

Top: Popeye discovers why a Japanese warship is so easily destroyed ("Made in Japan" was a contemporary signifier of inferior quality): *You're a Sap, Mr. Jap* (1942). *Bottom:* Popeye has a close encounter with a Japanese naval officer in *You're a Sap, Mr. Jap* (1942) (frame enlargements).

The three animal–Axis villains of *Song of Victory* (1942).

The Italians, never considered a serious threat, were largely dismissed by the American film industry, in both features and cartoons. With the exception of a map of the tattered "boot" of Italy in *Russian Rhapsody* (WB, 1944), caricatures of Mussolini are the *only* cartoon references to fascist Italy. He is always grotesquely portrayed and frequently made to appear as a fool and the toady of Hitler. In *The Ducktators* (WB, 1942), *Song of Victory* (Columbia, 1942), *The Last Round-Up* and *Mopping Up* (both 20th Century–Fox, 1943), Mussolini is depicted as a duck, gorilla, and ape (twice).

American leaders and their counterparts in the Allied countries are far less often encountered or referred to in Hollywood cartoons. This is particularly true for 1942, when only seven references to American or Allied leaders or Allied countries were made. Again, this is quite at odds with feature films of the era, which often cited Allied leaders such as Franklin D. Roosevelt, Winston Churchill, and Joseph Stalin, as well as mentioning or depicting Allied nations like Britain, Russia, and China. Several cartoons do include Stalin and Churchill caricatures—although *Herr Meets Hare* and *Russian Rhapsody* feature Bugs Bunny disguised as Stalin and a Stalin mask, respectively, rather than depicting Stalin as a character.

However, since cartoons were fundamentally based on broad humor, it may have been felt impolitic to depict friendly leaders in such a "vulgar" context.

In sheer numbers, Warner Bros. led the way in 1942 — 22 of their 41 cartoons (54 percent) were war-relevant. However, over half of these are indirectly related to the war, and few contain blatant caricatures of the enemy. For example, *Daffy's Southern Exposure* combines quality animation, a good story, great gags, topical relevancy, catchy musical numbers, inside movie jokes and a touch of surrealism. Because he wants to see the queen of the Snow Carnival, Daffy gets stranded up north during winter. Caught in a blizzard and starving, he has a mirage in which a tree becomes a T-bone steak (something unavailable to most Americans at the time). He finds refuge, of sorts, in a cabin (which features a War Bonds poster by the door) inhabited by a fox and a weasel. After a steady diet of beans, the two mammals are anxious to host (that is, eat) the weary duck. Posing as kindly old ladies, they serenade Daffy with the song "The Latin Quarter" to the lyrics "What Is Your Order" while stuffing the duck and preparing for his oven debut. Daffy eventually finds warmth and safety in South America in the fruity hat of a Carmen Miranda–like singer. While the topical references are oblique enough to pass almost unnoticed by today's viewers— who just see a fox and a weasel trying to eat a wily duck — *Daffy's Southern Exposure* does humorously comment on food shortages, and includes references to war bonds and South America (there was a brief vogue for things Latin American in the first half of the 1940s).

The Ducktators is Warners' greatest "hard" (i.e., overt) propaganda work of 1942, tracing the barnyard career of a screeching Hitler duck. After hatching from a black egg, the "Heiling" duckling becomes a frustrated artist papering walls with swastikas, then goes into politics, haranguing his fellow fowl from a "softsoap" box, and finally seizes control of the barnyard with the aid of his Italian and Japanese cohorts. The narrator states the tardy Japanese duck has come to make a "silly Axis of himself." The yoyo-twirling, dim-witted Mussolini duck is probably the most hilarious film caricature of *Il Duce* to appear on an American screen throughout the entire war. Eventually a harassed dove of peace rises to the occasion to defeat the dictators and their motley storm troopers.

Paramount had the second most active cartoon studio during 1942. With 14 of its 23 releases containing war references, it actually had a greater portion (61 percent) of such works than Warners. Paramount's cartoon stars at the time were Popeye and Superman, and their 1942 cartoons contained

Opposite: Model sheet details of the titular characters from *The Ducktators* (1942).

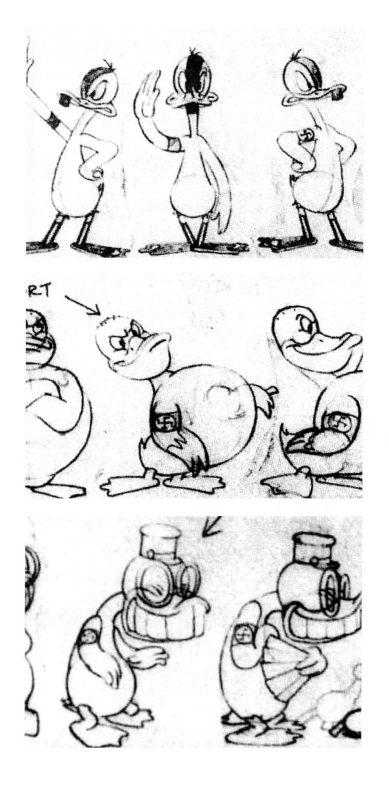

a large number of Japanese caricatures. Popeye's *Blunder Below* was the first blatantly anti–Japanese cartoon to hit American movie screens. Popeye displays no reluctance in punching the face (to the sound of shattering glass) of a bucktoothed, glasses-wearing Japanese submariner who says "So sorry!" after shooting a torpedo at the spinach-eating sailor. Because this short was released only two months after Pearl Harbor and while the siege of the Bataan peninsula was in progress, perhaps today's viewers should not be too hasty to condemn what may appear to be pure racism.

The Superman series began in 1941. Each Technicolor cartoon — drawn in a realistic style — opens with the "faster than a speeding bullet" routine (taken from the radio series) followed by a brief description of Superman's origins on the doomed planet Krypton and his arrival on earth, where he poses as mild-mannered Clark Kent of the *Daily Planet*. Three 1942 cartoons pit the laconic Man of Steel against the Axis: *Destruction, Inc.*, *The Eleventh Hour*, and *Japoteurs*. Lois Lane is one of the earliest animated characters to be portrayed as a war production worker (in *Destruction, Inc.*) while the latter two cartoons feature Japanese villains.

Paul Terry (for 20th Century–Fox) produced 11 war-related cartoons out of his annual total of 26 (42 percent). Two of these cartoons represent the total output of the short-lived Nancy series, but most of the relevant

Numerous World War II films featured references to war production work. A frame enlargement from the Superman cartoon *Destruction, Inc.* (1942).

Top: A Japanese soldier menaces Superman in *The Eleventh Hour* (1942). *Bottom:* The main title of the Superman cartoon *Japoteurs* (1942) (frame enlargement).

animated works featured Gandy Goose (an Ed Wynn sound-alike) and Sergeant Cat (formerly Sourpuss, imitating Jimmy Durante's voice). Throughout 1942, this duo's war activities were either confined to Army barracks reveries or the Pacific Theater of operations. *The Outpost,* released in July (after the American victory at Midway, but before the Marine landings on

A Japanese spy at the controls of a stolen U.S. war plane in *Japoteurs* (1942).

Model sheet details of Terrytoon star Gandy Goose, enlisted as Private Gandy for the duration.

Guadalcanal), was the first of several cartoons to portray the Japanese as squealing, pig- or rat-like creatures—some of whom are exterminated.

The best war-related Terrytoon of 1942 was the Academy Award nominee *All Out for V*, the earliest example of what would become a generic group of works featuring patriotic animals working for defense. Two more from Fox would appear during the following year: *Keep 'Em Growing* and *Shipyard Symphony*. The animation of *All Out for V* is good and the short features a song ("We're Working for Defense") written specifically for the cartoon. The "V" symbol is ubiquitous, including the use of a unique V-wipe at one point.

A Terrytoon was also responsible for the last (save one) war allegory cartoon, *Cat Meets Mouse*. Shown during the winter of 1942, this was one of the few truly allegorical cartoons of the war. Its anti-fascist message features a cat who builds a mouse "concentration camp." However, his intended victims unite and rise up to defeat their oppressor. Warner Bros. would release a somewhat similar work in 1943 entitled *Fifth Column Mouse*.

At least 10 of Columbia's 20 cartoons of 1942 make some reference to the war, although it is difficult to discuss Columbia's animated output, since many of these cartoons are unavailable for viewing today. With the exception of *Cinderella Goes to a Party*, *Old Blackout Joe*, and *Song of Victory*, Columbia cartoons in 1942 only alluded to the war.

Song of Victory portrays a vulture, a gorilla, and a hyena (Hitler, Mussolini, and Hirohito caricatures, respectively) invading a peaceful forest and enslaving its inhabitants. But the woodland creatures rebel and destroy the morale of the brutal militarists through the repetitive use of the "V for Victory" symbol. This cartoon elicited a rare note of praise from the OWI vis-à-vis its political (propagandistic) sophistication.

Universal's 1942 topical cartoons, all produced by Walter Lantz, were modest in numbers and fairly lightweight, dealing almost exclusively with home front issues. Only in *Pigeon Patrol* is the enemy (a Japanese buzzard) actually encountered. The most innovative Universal war cartoon from 1942 is *Yankee Doodle Swing Shift*, one of the best animated portrayals of the problems linked to the nation's conversion to a wartime footing. Unlike the animals in *All Out for V*, who immediately and cheerfully transform their idyllic habitat into an efficiently functioning wartime society, the "Zoot Suit Swing Cats" are despondent following Uncle Sam's scrapping of their musical instruments. Only reluctantly do they join the war effort. Once on the swing shift in a factory, miraculous feats of production do not immediately occur. Instead, it takes dormant patriotism — revived by swing music—to inspire the workers to manufacture efficiently the weapons of war needed for victory.

Only four of MGM's 15 1942 cartoons reflected an awareness of the war. For that matter, MGM's only regular character to be drafted (in 1941), Barney Bear, was mustered out and relegated to coping with victory gardens and rationing. The outstanding exception among MGM's war-related works of the year is Tex Avery's parody of the "Three Little Pigs," *Blitz Wolf*, which mercilessly lampoons Hitler and goes after the "Japs" as well.

Blitz Wolf (1942): the fortified house of the third little pig, Sgt. Pork.

"*BLITZ WOLF*"

(*The most talked about cartoon in years!*)

*Audiences will hiss, but they won't want
to miss this timely travesty from M-G-M's
new cartoon director, Fred "Tex" Avery.*

●

**An M-G-M Cartoon
In Technicolor
Available for immediate booking**

Trade magazine ad for *Blitz Wolf* (1942). "Adolf Wolf" shows his contempt for the audience.

However, the *panache* of Adolf Wolf presents something of a mixed message. He's a boastful sociopath out to conquer the pigs' domain, but he's also rather engaging, especially when compared with his primary nemesis, the humorless and stoic Sgt. Pork.

Disney studios released their commercial cartoons through RKO. Although Disney threw himself into the war effort, making many animated military training and public service works, his war-relevant commercial releases were a modest effort in 1942 (4 of 19). In three of these, Donald Duck is an incompetent Army draftee who tangles with Sergeant Pete and often peels mountains of potatoes.

Overall, the war-related output of commercial cartoons during 1942 is a very significant 71 of 158 works (45 percent). This is close to the annual percentage of war-relevant features (55 percent), and given that cartoons were essentially a single genre (comedy — except for the Superman series), feature films certainly had a greater flexibility to depict topical subjects.[6] In spite of this, almost half of all 1942 animated shorts were war-relevant: the cartoon studios were truly "Doing Their Bit."

6. Seein' Red,
White 'n' Blue: 1943

The year 1943 was the most heavily war-oriented year for animated cartoons: 68 percent of the commercially released cartoons from the seven major studios had one or more topical references. This is not surprising, since 1943 was the first full year of wartime production in the film industry as a whole. Cartoons released in 1942, especially in the first four months of the year, had been completed or were well along in production by December 7, 1941. Since the making of an animated cartoon was a lengthy, labor-intensive process, the reflection of America's actual war status (as opposed to prewar references to the war in Europe, the peacetime draft, and so on) came rather late to this segment of the movie industry. But when the cartoon producers geared up, a veritable flood of war-related shorts came forth, evidenced by the releases of the last six months of 1942 and the output for 1943.

At this point it may be instructive to examine the "racist" aspects of the anti–Japanese cartoons prevalent in 1942-43. Contrary to what some may believe, there has never been a conscious effort on the part of the American film industry to stigmatize a particular racial or ethnic group. Adverse portrayals of blacks, Asians, Mexicans, Jews, and others result more from the industry's adoption of cultural stereotypes present in many other media than from actual dislike of a particular race. No company interested in profits (which would be *all* Hollywood movie studios!) would deliberately alienate a potential segment of its audience by attacking an entire race or religion — unpleasant as some movie stereotypes may be, they seem to have been included out of ignorance or laziness, rather than as part of a master plan to malign a certain group.

One exception to this rule, however, is the anti–Japanese bias in the popular media in 1942-43, cartoons very much included. There are two reasons for this bias. First, there was undoubtedly a certain degree of racism in America during the period; just because it rarely surfaced in blatant form in the media does not mean it was not present. The Chinese were the focus of most anti–Asian caricatures prior to World War II; this is understandable, given that Chinese immigrants and second-generation Chinese-Americans greatly outnumbered other Asians in America, and thus were more familiar and accessible stereotypes. However, this anti–Asian bias was easily adapted to Japanese characters in 1942-43, and Hollywood did not have to worry about the loss of any potential audience — the United States was at war with Japan, and most Japanese-Americans (in the continental U.S.A., if not Hawaii) were interned in "relocation centers," effectively removing them from the ranks of moviegoers for the duration.

The second reason anti–Japanese feeling ran so high has been alluded to previously: the incident that brought the United States into the war, the sneak attack on Pearl Harbor. This act incensed the American sense of fair play, and subsequent tales of atrocities such as the Bataan Death March reinforced the public's attitude that the Japanese were barbarians. Interestingly enough, the Germans as a national group were considered much more "civilized" an adversary, probably because they were white, and because the complete story of Hitler's policy of genocide toward Jews, gypsies, and other select groups was not fully known at the time. Most anti–German sentiment was directed against the Nazis in general or their specific leaders (Hitler, Göring, Goebbels) rather than Germans as a nationality.

Virulent anti–Japanese caricatures in cartoons dropped off drastically after 1943 (although they never completely disappeared): realization that a racially biased attack on the Japanese also reflected negatively upon the Chinese (who were suddenly elevated to "gallant fighting ally" status after years of demeaning cook and laundryman roles) may have had something to do with this change.[1] Furthermore, portraying the enemy as animalistic incompetents in a way belittled the thousands of Allied soldiers who were dying in battle with them. Finally, as time went by, the outrage over Pearl Harbor faded somewhat, and producers of feature films and cartoons turned to other areas of the conflict.

On the whole, the tone of the 1943 cartoons was somewhat milder than that of 1942 shorts. Although still very conscious of the war, the cartoons showed a decline in ultrapatriotic themes. Racial assaults on the enemy and heavy-handed "home front" plots had peaked, although all three types of cartoons were still being made. The reason for the decline in the extreme flag-waving may have been that, after a year of war, American audiences were beginning to get used to the situation. 1942 had been a difficult year, with unfamiliar rationing, military setbacks, and the strain of massive conversion of the nation to a war footing. By 1943, audiences were taking many of these things in stride; rationing[2] could even be joked about, and there was no pressing need to educate people about blackouts, buying bonds, and so forth. These subjects were important, but they were becoming a part of everyday life, having been in existence for over a year.

Another consideration was the concern on the part of the United States government that direct attacks upon the imperial institution might actually harden Japanese resistance to surrender.[3] This sentiment may have had some bearing on the fact that only five American cartoons from 1943 made direct attacks upon Emperor Hirohito: *Seein' Red, White 'n' Blue* (with a particularly egregious caricature of the emperor, slugged by Popeye the Sailor), *Tin Pan Alley Cats, Pass the Biscuits Mirandy!, The Cocky Bantam,* and *Daffy the Commando.*

On the military side, things were also looking up. Most of the action in the first part of the year took place in Russia, where the Nazis were slowly being driven back by the Red Army, although it was to be a long and arduous process. American and British troops were engaged in North Africa, and by May had beaten Rommel, effectively ending hostilities there. In July, Sicily was invaded, and Mussolini resigned at the end of the month; by September, Italy had surrendered. The air forces of the Allies were active in Europe and in the Pacific: Berlin was heavily bombed in November, and air raids were beginning to strike at occupied France at year's end. In the Pacific, the Americans continued their advance up the Solomon Islands and had seized Tarawa atoll — but at the cost of over a thousand Marines killed on Betio Island. Japanese opposition was increasingly fanatical — few of their soldiers surrendered. It was apparent that this would not be another World War I, where America's entry had tipped the scales in a year, but things were no longer as bleak as they had seemed in early 1942.

The war-related cartoons of 1943 fall into several categories. "Hard" propaganda cartoons, taking direct aim at the enemy in various, insulting, even fatal, ways, included Disney's *Der Fuehrer's Face* and *Education for Death,* Columbia's *He Can't Make It Stick, The Last Round Up* and *Mopping Up* from 20th Century–Fox, *Seein' Red, White 'n' Blue* from Paramount, and *Tokio Jokio* (Warner Bros.).

Home front propaganda appeared in such shorts as *Barnyard Blackout* (20th Century–Fox) and *Home Defense* (RKO/Disney). *Ration fer the Duration* (Paramount), *Meatless Tuesday* (Universal) and *Ration Bored* (Universal) also looked at home front activities like rationing, but in a

Top: The "V" for Victory is graphically illustrated on this lobby card for *Fifth Column Mouse* (1943). *Left:* The evil cat briefly becomes a Japanese caricature in *Fifth Column Mouse* (1943).

funny, non-didactic way. For example, *Barnyard Blackout* tells the story of a rooster who procrastinates in the construction of a "blackout room" for his home, and illustrates the problems that ensue during a blackout. The short is humorous, but also makes its point about the importance of being prepared. On the other hand, *Ration Bored* shows Woody Woodpecker attempting to get gasoline without a ration card, then trying to *steal* enough gas to run his car. At the end he and a buffoonish cop are blown up, but

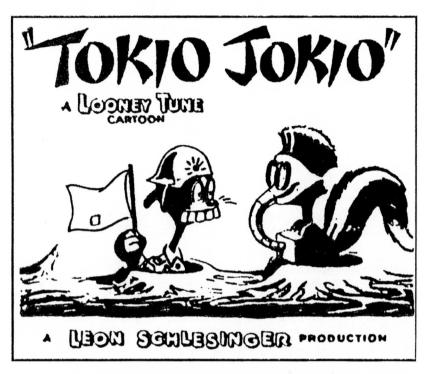

Lobby card from *Tokio Jokio* (1943), comparing a Japanese soldier with a skunk.

Woody's behavior throughout the short isn't exactly patriotic. The first cartoon treats the war as something to be concerned about, while the second uses the war's effects for comedic purposes. The latter type would begin to prevail in 1943, among all companies.

This is not to say that cartoon producers did not feel the war was a serious matter, having proved that with their spate of patriotic cartoons in 1942. But perhaps they felt that the era of "straight" war-related cartoons had passed, that they were no longer needed or wanted by audiences. Audiences wanted laughs, and the producers intended to deliver them. Still, the war was a fact of life, overshadowing practically everything else, and this is reflected in the preponderance of topical references in 1943 releases. References to the U.S. armed forces are most numerous (43), but rationing, shortages, home front, black market references (42), and Hitler caricatures (26) are close behind.

The various cartoon producers had their own styles, and the 1943 output provides some good examples. Walt Disney actually set down a plan for wartime productions. In addition to the numerous training and information films for the armed forces, Disney planned entertainment shorts

with war themes, educational cartoons like *Defense Against Invasion*—
made mostly for the Coordinator for Inter-American Affairs—and a category called "psychological" cartoons, which—although released through
commercial channels—were actually "hard" propaganda shorts like *Education for Death* and *Reason and Emotion*.[4] Of all the producers, Disney
threw his company most wholeheartedly into the war effort: in 1943, 11 of
his 13 commercially released shorts were topically related (the other two
were the "Good Neighbor" short *Pluto and the Armadillo*, originally
intended to be part of *The Three Caballeros* feature, and *Flying Jalopy*,
which has been called an anti-profiteering allegory).[5] In addition, Disney
produced the feature-length *Victory Through Air Power* on his own ini-
tiative and went outside his regular distribution company to get it shown.
There were also special shorts such as *The Spirit of '43*, made for the Treasury Department.

Disney's motives were not entirely altruistic: his company was paid
for its government work, and his theatrical shorts were made with entertainment first in mind (with the possible exception of *Education for Death*,
Reason and Emotion and *Chicken Little*, three outright propaganda pieces),
but no one was forcing him to make these films. Many producers got by
with far less, and weren't accused of hampering the war effort by their lax-
ity. Furthermore, Disney seems to have been one of the few top executives
to grasp the idea that cartoons could be used for political as well as entertainment purposes (the Columbia-released "This Changing World" series
in 1941 also showed this awareness, but it was independently produced),
and he had the power to implement his ideas (unlike the directors and
animators at other studios, who were supervised by businessmen chiefly
interested in the profit margin).

Disney's war-relevant releases in 1943 ranged from the aforemen-
tioned "hard" propaganda like *Education for Death* to a short like *Donald's
Tire Trouble*, which has one brief reference to the wartime rubber shortage. Perhaps the most famous Disney wartime cartoon was *Der Fuehrer's
Face*, officially released on January 1, 1943, but apparently released earlier
in several spots to qualify for the 1942 Academy Awards (in which it won
the Best Cartoon Oscar). This was also one of the few cartoons that focused
on Hitler's Germany, rather than Hitler himself—almost all the humor
devolves from German munitions worker Donald Duck's nightmarish existence under the Nazi regime. The point is, of course, that freedom is pre-
cious and that everyone could be subjected to this sort of oppression if the
Axis prevailed, but it is somewhat unusual for a propaganda short to concentrate almost entirely on the internal affairs of an enemy nation.

Warner Bros.' topical cartoons actually outnumbered the Disney shorts, although Disney produced only half as many shorts in 1943, so his percentage was much higher. Still, 19 of 27 Warner Bros. cartoons released in 1943 had some references to the war, 70 percent in all.

Once again the range of topical references ran from direct war-related themes like *Daffy the Commando* and *Scrap Happy Daffy* to throwaway visual or verbal jokes like the "4-F" sign placed on a little black duck by a predatory vulture in *Corny Concerto* (the duck also metamorphoses into a fighter plane when he pursues the vulture). Cartoons with tangential references to the war outnumber the directly war-relevant cartoons released by Warners, although the dividing line is sometimes hard to discern. For instance, *An Itch in Time* concerns a flea who decides to make a meal of Elmer Fudd's dog (in-joke — Elmer is reading a Bugs Bunny and Porky Pig comic book). There are numerous references to rationing, meatless Tuesdays, air raid shelters, and so on, but the cartoon *could have* existed as a simple flea-dog contest in any period.

One of the best Warner cartoons of 1943 was *Falling Hare*, one of two "gremlin" cartoons made by the company. Disney had purchased the rights to a book called *Gremlin Lore*, but eventually procrastinated and canceled the project. In the meantime, other companies were discouraged from making gremlin cartoons, but WB had already committed to two, although the word gremlin does not appear in the title of either. *Falling Hare* (vastly superior to *Pigs in a Polka* and *Greetings Bait*, the two WB shorts nominated for Academy Awards in 1943) is set at an air base, where Bugs is seen reading *Victory Thru Hare Power* (a parody of the real-life *Victory Through Air Power* which inspired the Disney feature film of the same name), with its tales of sabotage by gremlins. He runs into one of the little creatures and the rest of the short has them battling inside a bomber. Topical gags abound in this cartoon: Bugs nearly falls out of the plane, and his heart beats frantically, displaying "4-F" prominently; the aircraft plunges towards the ground but stops inches short of disaster, out of gas—"You know how it is with these A [gas rationing] cards," Bugs says.

The Warners cartoons were probably the funniest as a group of the 1943 releases, but they also contained more blatantly racist assaults on the enemy than the productions of other companies. *Tokio Jokio*, for instance, is one long anti–Japanese tract (in the guise of a Japanese newsreel made from inferior film stock), outrageous even in the face of prevailing sentiment. Still, the years 1941–1946 were outstanding for Warner Bros., with such talented directors as Frank Tashlin, Bob Clampett, Fred Avery, I. Freleng, and Chuck Jones turning out absolute classics that are as funny today as when first released, despite the raft of practically inexplicable (to today's viewer) topical references.

MGM's cartoons of the period also stand up to the test of time, but for almost the opposite reason: their *lack* of significant topical references. In 1943, for example, 10 of 14 MGM cartoons had one or more topical references, but they were far from the outspoken war themes produced at Disney or Warners. The Academy Award winner for 1943, *Yankee Doodle Mouse*, was a Tom and Jerry short from the Hanna-Barbera team. The standard cat and mouse conflict was given a war-like motif, with Jerry sending back communiqués to Mouse HQ that resemble actual war messages (like "Send More Cats" instead of "Send More Japs") but there was no blatant anti–Axis message. *War Dogs* was one in a seemingly endless string of fighting canine cartoons (practically every company made at least one; features too), but on the whole the topical references in MGM cartoons were more evident in the shorts made by Tex Avery and his crew, rather than the Hanna and Barbera unit. Tom and Jerry cartoons of this period are outstanding examples of characterization, animation, inventiveness and humor, but World War II hardly existed in their world.

Avery, the exception, brought something of Warner Bros. along with him to MGM, and as a consequence topical references show up in a number of his wartime efforts. *Dumb Hounded*, the first Droopy cartoon, is— like many Avery cartoons— basically a one-joke story that keeps repeating (and topping) the same gag, over and over. The topical reference — and very Warners-like it is—comes at the beginning, when the reward for an escaped convict wolf is posted as $5,000 or "one pound of coffee."

The other cartoon producers turned out product of varying quality and with varying numbers of war-related references. At Columbia, for instance, 50 percent of its 1943 releases were topical, but few of these cartoons are shown today, probably because Columbia (made at this time by a wholly owned subsidiary called Screen Gems) had no cartoon "stars" to compete with Bugs Bunny, Donald Duck, or even Mighty Mouse. The Fox and the Crow managed to stay around for a while, but who remembers Willoughby Wren or Professor Small and Mr. Tall?

The supervising chores at Columbia changed hands frequently: Frank Tashlin left in 1943 after about a year's stay and was replaced for four months by Dave Fleischer. After that, the producing chores went out of the control of veteran animators into the hands of Paul Worth (the musical director on some Screen Gems cartoons) and Hugh McCollum, a live-action shorts producer. Only three of Columbia's 1943 cartoons dealt directly with the war: *There's Something About a Soldier*, *The Cocky Bantam*, and *He Can't Make It Stick*, discussed below. Most of the references are much briefer, on the order of a Hitler caricature in *Professor Small and Mr. Tall*, and rationing references in *Plenty Below Zero* and *Nursery Crimes.*

The most notable Columbia cartoon of the year was *He Can't Make It Stick*, a collaboration between the regular Screen Gems animation crew (including directors Paul Sommer and John Hubley) and well-known cartoonist Milt Gross. Gross was at the peak of his popularity in the 1920s with newspaper cartoons and books like *Nize Baby*, which combined outrageous drawings and bizarre, stylized ethnic dialect. Gross had made some early cartoons for the Bray organization and joined MGM briefly in 1939 before making another short-lived stab at the animation business in 1943. Gross cowrote the story for *He Can't Make It Stick*, which portrays the tribulations of "Schicklegruber," a hapless paperhanger trying to hang swastika-studded paper in houses built to resemble occupied countries.[6] But, as the title reveals, this Hitler caricature can't get his paper to stick, and he becomes the butt of ridicule. However, Gross worked only briefly at Screen Gems before moving on to other, nonanimated cartoon work.

Over at Universal, home of the Walter Lantz "Cartunes," 7 of 10 cartoons released in 1943 contained topical references. The Lantz productions were usually nice to look at (until the '50s), but their humor content varied considerably. Woody Woodpecker represented just about the only truly "wild" character they had, with the rest of the shorts opting for milder humor, usually visual rather than verbal. Among the 1943 releases were pleasant cartoons like *Meatless Tuesday*, which starts off with a shot of Andy Panda's mailbox crammed with rationing-related material but swiftly loses sight of the war and turns into a standard, though enjoyable, chase cartoon. There was also a Lantz entry in the "war dog" sweepstakes, *Canine Commandos*. An interesting point about practically every Lantz cartoon, both pre– and post–1943, was their lack of direct wartime assaults on the enemy. There were topical references, but very few Lantz shorts featured caricatures of the enemy (*Pass the Biscuits Mirandy!* was one, showing Nazis and depicting Japanese Emperor Hirohito as a monkey).[7]

One of the best Universal releases of the year was *Ration Bored*, starring Woody Woodpecker. As noted previously, this cartoon shows Woody determined to break the rules about gas rationing. At the outset, when he sees a sign reading "Is This Trip Really Necessary?" Woody devilishly replies, "I'm a necessary evil." This short is very fast-moving and, as with most Lantz films, visually oriented. Woody tries to siphon gas from a police car and winds up compressing, then expanding the cop inside the car, like a balloon. They both crash into fuel storage tanks, at the climax, and are next seen on a cloud, coming out of the "Wing Rationing Board." Not exactly educational or inspirational, but amusing. The Woody Woodpecker of the 1940s is an entertaining, wacky character, a far cry from the quite poor cartoons released in the '50s.

The remaining two companies to commercially release cartoons in 1943 were Paramount and 20th Century–Fox. Seventy-six percent (13 of 17) of the Paramount cartoons (made by the Famous Studios subsidiary) had at least one minor topical reference, sometimes as slight as the fact that Popeye (their star character) was depicted as being in the Navy (*Alona on the Sarong Seas, Too Weak to Work*). While this may seem to be stretching topicality a bit far, prior to the war Popeye was depicted as a sailor, but he was *not* in the United States Navy, and was *not* seen serving on a warship, as he frequently is in these later shorts.

Most Paramount cartoons had more direct references to the war, however, including some with Nazi and Japanese caricatures. *Seein' Red, White 'n' Blue*, for example, opens with Bluto trying to avoid the draft, and concludes in an orphanage, where Japanese spies are disguised as little orphans! Superman, Paramount's other star character in 1943, was left over from the Fleischer days, and the Man of Steel battled the Axis along with assorted monsters in several cartoons before being dropped as a series in midyear. Little Lulu and a noncharacter series called "Noveltoons" took up the slack.

The Paramount cartoons were respectable, technically, in 1943, and while the eccentric Popeye mystique of the '30s was gone — the Famous Studios Popeye was almost a fall guy who just happened to have super

A Nazi submarine "wolfpack" prepares to leave its base in *Jungle Drums* (1943). The Superman cartoons were the only continuing series of dramatic cartoons released during the war.

Main title from the last Superman cartoon, *Secret Agent* (1943).

strength when he ate his spinach — the shorts were generally watchable. *Ration fer the Duration*, for example, is one of the best from this year: Popeye's nephews try to sneak off to go fishing instead of helping with Pop-eye's Victory garden, so Popeye reminds them of the story of Jack and the Beanstalk, and takes a nap while they work. He dreams a giant lives in a castle at the top of the beanstalk that sprouts from the garden (sign on castle: "Bed Vacant for Swing Shift"); the giant hoards sugar, tires, gas-oline, toothpaste tubes, and so on. Stealing mas-sive quantities of the valuable goods, Popeye tumbles to earth, waking up to find his Victory gar-den has grown miraculous

The head Nazi spy of *Secret Agent* (1943) obviously admires his leader, Hitler (frame enlargement).

Henry the rooster joins the Civil Defense corps in *Barnyard Blackout* (1943).

fruit: new tires ("Peaches") and old tires ("Squashes"), tin cans, and so on.

Of 20th Century–Fox's releases of Terrytoons, 10 of 17, or 59 percent, were war-oriented. They ran the gamut, from "straight" patriotic cartoons starring funny animals like *Keep 'Em Growing* (where the song carries the wartime message, while the visuals show farm animals growing crops in unusual ways), to anti–Axis propaganda (in *The Last Round-Up* and *Mopping Up*, Mussolini appears as pig–Hitler's pet monkey), to minor references (Pvt. Gandy Goose and Sergeant Cat in the Army, in the otherwise non-topical

Hitler, depicted as an irate pig, in *The Last Round-Up* (1943).

Aladdin's Lamp). It's easy to find fault with the Terrytoons, particularly in comparison with Warner Bros. or MGM product; the humor, such as it is in these cartoons, results from mild sight gags or knockabout humor. Even the physical comedy in the Terrytoons is conventional: practically nothing goes on in these shorts that couldn't occur in live action (or when it does, as in a number of Gandy Goose cartoons, it is presented in the context of a dream). The deliberate distortions of space, time, and the physical world that make the Warner Bros and MGM cartoons special are all but nonexistent in Terrytoons. There is no verbal humor; the plots are cookie-cutter identical.

To be fair, some Terrytoons are better than others: *Barnyard Blackout* is decent, some of the Gandy Goose "dream" cartoons are imaginative, and the animation and character design is very nice in certain shorts. But basically, Terrytoons — including those starring Mighty Mouse, their most durable character — are an acquired taste.

Finally, the stop-motion animation (as opposed to drawn animation) contribution to the war effort should be noted. With the exception of one short released in 1945 (*The Flying Jeep*), all of the war-relevant works were produced by George Pal and released through Paramount. Of special interest are Pal's "Puppetoons" which addressed Hitler's conquest of western Europe and the resistance of the people of those countries. The "resistance" genre, so prominent in Hollywood's feature films, was virtually absent from wartime animation, with the notable exception of *Tulips Shall Grow* (1942) — nominated for an Academy Award — and *Bravo, Mr. Srauss* (1943), both made by Pal. In the first film, Jan and Janette's courtship in an idyllic land of windmills is interrupted by the nuts-and-bolts "Screwball Army" invasion (= the Nazi invasion of Holland in 1940). The two young people refuse to give in, however. *Bravo, Mr. Strauss* takes place in Vienna, where a statue of composer Johann Strauss comes to life after a Screwball Army tank knocks it over (= the Nazi occupation of Austria, 1938). Appalled by the invaders' barbaric destruction of cultural icons such as books and paintings, Strauss uses his music to lure the goose-stepping fascists to their doom.

As 1943 concluded, the cartoon studios — like America at large — were involved in a total war effort.

7. Slow Fade on the
Home Front: 1944-45

The year 1944 saw a precipitous drop in the number of cartoons with topical references: racial and specific anti–Axis attacks as the central theme of a short were trimmed to almost none, and there were fewer overtly patriotic themes in the cartoons and more passing mentions and minor references. The surge of patriotism of 1942 and the single-minded concentration of 1943 were replaced with a lowered intensity, a dogged determination.

The war was in its third year for Americans, and the popular consciousness of the American people was attuned to the conflict, with all its terms, subjects, and restrictions. To buy bonds was, for many, a natural act on payday, as was the saving of scrap metal, grease and fats, and so on. Rationing and shortages, while not popular, were not novelties. In fact, some may even speculate that by 1944, the American public was becoming almost *used* to the war (though certainly not to the terrible loss of life, the separation from loved ones, or the national upheaval the war had brought about). The same resilience that facilitated the country's rapid conversion to a national war footing may have contributed to a national sense of impatience.

This impatience was evident on the home front in several ways. There were a number of strikes in war-related industries during 1944, actions that would have been almost unthinkable in 1942, when public opinion would have been overwhelmingly negative. Also, many were looking forward, past the current conflict, to the end of the war and beyond — although in doing so they may have overlooked the fact that there were many battles yet to be won. Even General Eisenhower addressed this point — obliquely — after the Allied armed forces had driven into Germany in late 1944. Stating that his men would need plenty of materials to finish off the Axis, the supreme commander of the Allied forces aimed his remarks both at the striking workers and the general population, the bond-buyers and thus the financiers of the war effort.

If an attitude of war-weariness did exist, it may be forgiven to an extent. As noted before, the war was in its third year, and few living Americans had ever seen their country embroiled in a conflict of such duration and immensity. On the war front, the Allies continued to advance into Italy in the early months of the year, but the fighting was extremely heavy at times, and even the establishment of the Anzio beachhead, south of Rome, increased the invasion pace only a bit. On the Eastern Front the Russians were advancing somewhat faster but were also running into staunch opposition. The Pacific Theater saw little decisive action in the early part of the year, with the Japanese invading India but making little progress and having better success in China. The Allies captured the Marshall Islands and kept up the heavy aerial bombing of Japanese possessions. Rome fell to the Allies on June 4; Normandy was invaded on June 6. The Allies captured Saipan, and B-29s began to strike at the Japanese homeland. Also during this month, Hitler's "vengeance" weapons, "buzz-bombs," began to be launched at England.

Fighting in France dragged on throughout the summer; on August 15 the Americans landed in the south of France to start a second drive inland, and Paris was liberated on August 23. After the Allies entered Germany in September, few Americans would have been blamed for feeling optimistic. However, despite the inexorable tide of Allied manpower, and the almost unimaginable aerial might directed at the Nazis, Germany was not easily conquered. In fact, on December 17 the Nazis counterattacked in the Battle of the Bulge, and gave the Allies some tense moments before the offensive was defeated. Also toward the end of the year, MacArthur made good his promise to "return": on October 20, the Americans landed in the Philippines to begin eradicating the Japanese occupation forces.

With the war news generally good though not spectacular (aside from the D-Day landings), one can understand the decision (*if* a conscious decision was made) on the part of the motion picture industry to downplay the war and concentrate on entertainment in pictures. The percentage of cartoons relevant to the war dropped precipitously, from 68 percent in 1943 to only 38 percent in 1944.

Warner Bros., as usual, led with 18 of its 26 1944 releases containing one or more topical references (69 percent). The Warner Bros. cartoon unit underwent some changes during the year, as Leon Schlesinger sold his interest to the parent company and retired. His place was taken by Edward

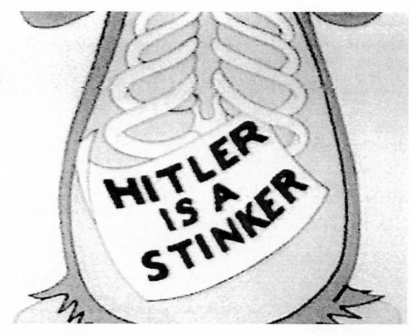

Daffy Duck's "military secret" revealed! From *Plane Daffy* (1944).

Nazi spy Hatta Mari wears telltale earrings. From *Plane Daffy* (1944).

Selzer, a studio administrator, although Selzer's name did not appear on the shorts as producer. Warner Bros. was almost the only company still making strong anti–Axis cartoons in 1944.

Bugs Bunny Nips the Nips and *Russian Rhapsody* are two examples. The first short begins with a standard Bugs Bunny situation: he is floating along in a wooden crate (to the tune of one of the favorite WB songs, "Trade Winds") when he happens upon a Japanese-held island. The wisecracking hare proceeds to wipe out the occupation forces, employing methods he would never have used on Elmer Fudd (hand grenades in ice-cream bars, for example). *Russian Rhapsody*, originally called *Gremlins from the Kremlin*, features Hitler and his "New Odor" bomber taking off to attack Moscow. However, a horde of little Russian-accented gremlins systematically dismantles the plane and drives Hitler nuts.

Other shorts by the Warners crew (1944 directors were Jones, Tashlin, Freleng, and Clampett) focus on the home front and often take satiric aim at women in the workforce. For instance, in the newsreel spoof *The Weakly Reporter*, a long-haired blonde, shown in profile behind the wheel of a taxi, turns to face the camera and reveals tough, masculine features; she smokes a cigar and talks in a deep growl. This short also shows WAACs using their military training to gain an advantage during a department store's sale of nylon stockings! Another home front cartoon is *The Swooner Crooner*, in which Porky Pig runs the Flockheed Eggcraft Company. His dedicated hens produce eggs on an assembly-line basis, until an emaciated

Hitler's "New Order" parodied as The New Odor" in *Russian Rhapsody* (1944).

A mask of Joseph Stalin frightens Adolf Hitler in *Russian Rhapsody* (1944).

singing rooster named "Frankie" (a Frank Sinatra caricature) appears and causes them to become hysterical bobby-soxer "absentees." Absenteeism was in fact a real problem for female war workers, but it was usually due to family responsibilities rather than personal irresponsibility. *Brother Brat* touches on the serious problem of child care, but the lady riveter in the cartoon is portrayed as a *zaftig* eccentric. As a whole, World War II cartoons did not portray the wartime contributions of women or minorities in a favorable manner. The major female characters, such as Olive Oyl in the Popeye shorts and Lois Lane in the Superman series, were generally foils for the male cartoon stars—Lois Lane's primary function was to be rescued by Superman, while Olive Oyl was often the cause of violent romantic rivalry between Popeye and Bluto. African-American characters were occasionally shown in war-oriented activities such as the armed forces (*Coal Black and de Sebben Dwarfs, Boogie Woogie Bugle Boy from Company B*) or civil defense (*Old Blackout Joe*), but these images were fairly rare and were diminished by numerous stereotypes used for quick gags.

MGM's topical output decreased moderately in 1944, to 54 percent from 1943's 71 percent. The real gem of 1944 from MGM was, not surprisingly, a Tex Avery product: *Big Heel Watha*. Nominally a "Screwy Squirrel" effort, this short abounds with rationing and shortages gags, as well as references to blackouts and the draft. That all of this is thrown into

Lobby card for *Coal Black and de Sebben Dwarfs* (1942).

Detail from a model sheet of *Coal Black and de Sebben Dwarfs* (1942), showing some of the dwarfs — including a Stepin Fetchit caricature — now in the Army.

a story about Indians hunting a squirrel is just good cartoon logic (which is to say, no logic at all). Barney Bear was at it again in *Bear Raid Warden*, and there were two one-shot cartoons with some topicality.

However, after WB and MGM, the number of shorts dealing with the war falls off considerably. At Paramount, for instance, only 7 of 21 (33 percent) have significant references, and only one of these (*Yankee Doodle Donkey*) contains more than a slight reference or two. This cartoon deals with a patriotic donkey who tries to join the WAGS (dogs in the army, again), but is rejected since he is not a dog. However, he becomes a hero when the flea army attacks, since his skin is thick enough to qualify him as a "tank." The other Paramount war-relevant cartoons were all Popeye shorts, but on the order of rationing references and the like, rather than being the central themes of the cartoons.

Four of Disney's 12 1944 shorts (33 percent) were topical, including their most "active" (after *Der Fuehrer's Face*, and even that cartoon didn't contain such overtly racist material) entertainment cartoon of the war years, *Commando Duck*. In this short, soldier Donald Duck parachutes onto a Japanese-held island to attack an airfield. He is stalked by concealed Japanese snipers (including one disguised as a slant-eyed tree) who boast that shooting in the back is the traditional way of Japanese warfare. Donald hardly interacts with these enemies at all (he's mostly oblivious to them), and is more concerned about his stubborn rubber raft, which eventually fills up with water and explodes, wiping out the Japanese airfield in a tidal wave.

Five of Columbia's nineteen 1944 releases (26 percent) were war-related, and one of these (*The Disillusioned Bluebird*) was an overtly pacifist tract — a cartoon version of calypso singer Sir Lancelot tells a bluebird that the world won't always be strife-torn. At Universal, only one of eight shorts (13 percent) had war references, and only 20 percent (4 of 20) 20th Century–Fox cartoons contained war references.

One of the Fox shorts, however, is the interesting *My Boy Johnny*, released in May 1944. It shows troops returning from the war and coming back to their families (including Gandy Goose, who has a wife and kids waiting for him); the title song (to the tune of "When Johnny Comes Marching Home") looks forward to the resumption of the production of consumer goods such as refrigerators and washing machines, forecasts construction of superhighways, and concludes with a shot of GIs and their new brides in a church. Put together somewhat haphazardly, with little concern for plot or humor, the short shows that some people felt the end of the war was near. Unfortunately, there was more than a year of hard fighting on all fronts still remaining, and the optimism of *My Boy Johnny* was a little premature.

Hell Bent for Election was another cartoon of interest, directed by Chuck Jones for a fledgling outfit called Industrial Films and Poster Service (which later became UPA). The short was a campaign film for FDR's reelection bid, financed by the United Auto Workers and shown at the Democratic National convention and elsewhere.

There was a conscious decision — at the Disney studios, at least, and possibly elsewhere — to look toward the future, to avoid too many cartoons whose war references would make them useless for such future markets as television. Furthermore, most of the pressing themes (at least those capable of being dealt with in cartoons) had been addressed in the previous two years of production. As noted earlier, by 1944 no one needed to be told about the importance of buying bonds or home defense. It was not a lack of patriotism that led producers to cut back on topical shorts in 1944, but merely a reflection of the feeling of the industry as a whole that American audiences wanted entertainment, even escapism, in 1944.

By mid–1944, the ultimate outcome of World War II was fairly obvious to the participants, although the details and the length of time required to subdue the Axis powers were still unknowable. Thus, in the first months of 1945, Americans were confident that the war would soon be won — it was only a matter of time. Ironically, the last few months of the war saw extremely heavy casualties in the European and Pacific Theaters. The desperate German counterattack known as the Battle of the Bulge was finally squelched in January. The Russians from the east and the Americans and British from the west continued their advance on Berlin. In March, Anglo-American troops crossed the Rhine; in April, Berlin was taken by the Red Army; May 8, 1945, was V-E Day, the cessation of hostilities in Europe.

In the Pacific, fighting continued. Manila was liberated in February, and in April Army and Marine troops landed on Okinawa, but not until June 21 was the island fortress completely subdued, and the Philippines were the scene of fighting until July. President Truman, who had succeeded to the presidency with the death of Franklin D. Roosevelt in April, gave the go-ahead for the use of the atomic bomb, and this weapon was utilized on August 6 and 9. On August 14, the Japanese agreed to "cease hostilities"; on the second day of September, 1945, the surrender agreement was signed. The Second World War was over.

The cartoons considered in this study include those released in 1945 through the month of September. Eighty cartoons were released in this period, and 27 of these, or 34 percent, were war-related. There was a continuation of the trend from 1944, in which direct war references were played down, and most of the relevant cartoons contain topical references along the lines of rationing or shortage jokes, rather than direct war comments.

Top: War worker Cinderella on her way to the plant, in *Swing Shift Cinderella* (1945). *Bottom:* The name of aircraft manufacturer Lockheed Aircraft was frequently parodied in World War II cartoons. Here, it's called "Lockweed Aircraft." From *Swing Shift Cinderella* (1945).

There were several exceptions. In 10 of 15 (67 percent) Warners shorts released from January to September 1945 one finds war references, including the last real anti–Axis cartoon save one, *Herr Meets Hare* (January release). Bugs Bunny, as so often happens, takes an unplanned detour on one of his subterranean trips, and this time winds up in Germany's Black Forest. There he meets and harasses the vainglorious Hermann Göring, and is finally taken back to headquarters as a prize for Hitler. However, Bugs masquerades as Stalin, and this throws the Nazi leaders into a panic.

Draftee Daffy is also quite topical, as the outwardly patriotic Daffy Duck becomes a coward when he receives his induction notice. A cartoon in which the protagonist actively evades the draft was quite rare, and — unlike draft dodger Bluto in *Seein' Red, White 'n' Blue* (1943) — Daffy doesn't change his mind at the conclusion. Instead, hopping onto a rocket labeled "Use in Case of Induction," he blasts off ... straight to Hell!

The other major anti–Axis cartoon released in 1945 was a rarity — an independently produced *and* released cartoon short. Ted Eshbaugh, a former animator and director for Van Beuren in the 1930s, had been making industrial shorts in New York during the '40s. He produced (possibly as early as 1943), a 10-minute color cartoon entitled *Cap'n Cub*.[1] The short was finally released by Film Classics, a sort of clearinghouse distributor for low-budget efforts. Cap'n Cub was a bear cub who — with his animal pals — confronts the Japanese in his little airplane (the short was also advertised as *Cap'n Cub Blasts the Japs*). Unfortunately for Eshbaugh, his timing was off (the short was released in March) and the war ended before a *Cap'n Cub* series could begin. There is also some question as to the economic viability of independently made and released cartoons, especially in those pre-divestiture ruling days when major studios owned a large percentage of theaters, and thus controlled booking. *The Flying Jeep*, a dimensional animation short made by Disney alumni and released by United Artists, also falls into the rare category of independent shorts.

Another noteworthy 1945 cartoon was *When G.I. Johnny Comes Home* (Paramount), which borrows from 1944's *My Boy Johnny* the idea of depicting returning GIs to the tune of "When Johnny Comes Marching Home." This short was released in February, again an indication of the optimism of the producers (and by inference, the public) that the war would soon be over. Terrytoons' *Post-War Inventions* was also reminiscent of *My Boy Johnny*, as Pvt. Gandy Goose and Sergeant Cat dream about the fantastic inventions that will make postwar life wonderful.

Given the time lag between the conception of a cartoon short and its release, it is not surprising that a number of shorts released after the war contained references to the conflict or direct references to the coming of peace. There were not as many of the first type as one might think, since the producers had been sharply reducing wartime references in their cartoons since 1944, but some interesting examples exist.

For instance, Warner Bros. copyrighted *Hollywood Canine Canteen* in December 1945, but did not release this obviously war-related short until April 1946, apparently being unwilling to shelve it permanently. As it is, the cartoon is very dated, caricaturing famous celebrities and bandleaders as dogs ("Boney Goodman" and "Hairy James" for example), with dog soldiers, sailors, and so on being entertained at the servicemen's canteen. *Bacall to Arms* (August 1946), features a Tex Avery-like wolf and some amazing animation (rotoscoped) of Bogart and Bacall in parodied scenes from the feature box office hit *To Have and Have Not* (1944): it begins with a newsreel showing "wartime inventions put to peacetime use" (a man uses radar to warn of his mother-in-law's impending arrival). *Of Thee I Sting* (1946) transposed clichés from war movies to the story of mosquitoes training for a "big raid" on an unsuspecting human (reusing animation from a "Private Snafu" cartoon). In *Nasty Quacks* (December 1945), Daffy Duck angrily stalks out of a house, only to return and say "I forgot — the government doesn't want us to do any nonessential traveling." Elves working in a cobbler's shop in *Holiday for Shoestrings* (February 1946) repair (using a car jack) the fallen arch of a "4-F" shoe, and relabel it "1-A." Following a hiatus of several years, a 1950 Merrie Melody featuring Beaky Buzzard, *Strife with Father*, refers to the London Blitz.

Disney's belated tribute to the United States Coast Guard, *Canine Patrol*, was released on the 1945 anniversary of the Pearl Harbor attack. In this innocuous short, Pluto encounters a little turtle while diligently patrolling a restricted beach area.

Terrytoons' releases also seem to have been scrambled in the 1945–1946 period. Shorts like *Mother Goose Nightmare* (1945) and *The Ghost Town* (1944) feature civilians Gandy Goose and Sourpuss Cat, but a 1946 release such as *The Fortune Hunters* still has them in Army uniforms! Similarly, *Service with a Guile* (Paramount, 1946) depicts Popeye and Bluto as two Navy sailors on leave who help Olive run her gas station.

Nearly a year after the war, certain animosities apparently still lingered with regard to the Japanese. In the 1946 Popeye cartoon *Rocket to Mars*, a buck-toothed Japanese soldier is caricatured behind an "eightball" (a meteor). When Popeye eats his spinach on Mars, an atom bomb is depicted on his bicep. Ironically, the release date of this cartoon, August 9, was the first anniversary of the atomic bombing of Nagasaki.

In later years, cartoon producers would remake their wartime shorts (or "borrow" the plots of other cartoons), leaving out the topical references, or replacing them with new, postwar gags dealing with television, cars, and so forth. Thus, *Booby Hatched* became *The Shell-Shocked Egg* (1948), and *Porky's Pooch* was reworked a number of times (including *Little Orphan Airedale* and *Awful Orphan*, 1947 and 1949). Terrytoons borrowed the plot of Disney's *Chicken Little* for *The Sky Is Falling* (1947). Bugs Bunny's run-in with the gremlin of *Falling Hare* was altered for a Bugs-Yosemite Sam cartoon called *Hare Lift* (1952), and so on.

But for all intents and purposes, when the war ended in 1945, it was the end of the *truly* topical animated cartoon. For the next 20 years, until the demise of the theatrical cartoon in the 1960s, cartoons would rarely be made with the singlemindedness of purpose that was prevalent in Hollywood between 7 December 1941, and 2 September 1945.

8. The Adventures of Private Snafu, or, How to Laugh at the Military While Learning What *Not* to Do

In addition to their regular slate of theatrical shorts, many animation studios produced cartoons for the U.S. government during the Second World War. Some of these shorts were shown in theaters to the general public — Disney's *Out of the Frying Pan, Into the Firing Line,* for instance — but most government-sponsored cartoons were never seen by civilian audiences. These ranged from technical training films to shorts with general educational, informational, and even entertainment content. Though numbering in the hundreds at the very least, many of these films no longer exist or are buried deep in various archives, incompletely or in some cases *un*cataloged. Since government-financed films were, as a rule, not copyrighted (government productions were normally in the public domain), not even this source of information remains to provide a clue about their content.

These government cartoons are not included in this book, with the exception of the few exhibited in regular theaters, and one additional series, the "Private Snafu" cartoons, produced by (in most cases) Warner Bros. for military audiences. Seen by millions of troops, these audacious and even risqué cartoons (SNAFU was wartime slang, an acronym for "Situation Normal — All Fucked Up") were not forgotten after the war. Bootleg 16mm copies began to circulate among collectors and fans within a few years, later appearing on videotape, and recently, on DVD.

The Snafu shorts were black-and-white cartoons (a few may have

The "Private Snafu" logo which begins each cartoon. First seen in *Coming Snafu* (1943).

originally been released in sepiatone), running between two and five minutes in length. They were included in the *Army-Navy Screen Magazine*. Distributed by the U.S. Army Signal Corps, the *Magazine* was a newsreel shown exclusively at military installations. It was produced bi-weekly between June 1943 and early 1946, and by war's end was reaching an average audience of 4.2 million people.[1] Described as a "pictorial report from all fronts," the program opened with a logo which incorporated a large "V" for Victory. The *Magazine* generally included from three to five stories for a total running time of about 20 minutes (two reels). Snafu cartoons appeared about once a month, usually toward the end of the newsreel. A current Hollywood feature film generally followed.

A typical example of the *Army-Navy Screen Magazine* (ANSM) was its 15th "edition," released in November 1943. Three reports precede the Snafu cartoon: "Iron War Horse," depicting the activities of Army railroad battalions in combat areas; "Seized from the Japs," which opens with artwork of a GI smashing a buck-toothed Japanese soldier in the face, followed by captured footage of Japanese military personnel on maneuvers, at forward bases, and so on, while a narrator makes comments like "Rice and fish … no diet for Americans … but it keeps the Nips going"; the third segment was "The Fighting Dutch," chronicling the participation of the

Netherlands in the war effort. Episode 15 of *ANSM* concludes with the Snafu cartoon *The Home Front*—contrary to Pvt. Snafu's belief that his family are slackers, they are actually shown to be diligently doing their bit for the war effort.

The Snafu cartoons were produced by Warner Bros. animators, supervised by Chuck Jones. Jones would direct (without screen credit) nearly half the series, including the opening cartoon, *Coming Snafu*. I. Freleng and Frank Tashlin directed most of the remainder. Theodore (Ted) Geisel (aka author "Dr. Seuss") and Phil Eastman wrote the majority of the Snafu scripts, with Geisel being responsible for the rhyming dialogue that appears in many of the earlier episodes. Carl W. Stalling was the music supervisor and Mel Blanc provided the voice of Pvt. Snafu, a more nasal version of his Bugs Bunny "Brooklynese." Three later Snafu cartoons were made by other units: two by United Productions of America, and one by Hugh Harman, Rudy Ising, and George Gordon. About 25 Snafu shorts were actually shown to troops through September 1945, and a few others were released in the months immediately after the war's conclusion. Produced on a cost-plus basis, the Snafus were made for just under $300,000.

The Snafu segments of *ANSM* open with the Snafu logo, a close-up of the Army private's stupid face (the skinnier version that appears only in *Coming Snafu*), and the words "Private Snafu." As each letter of the latter word appears, a musical note sounds— all together, the brief tune (Pvt. Snafu's "theme song") is known as "You're a Horse's Ass."

Although the Snafu cartoons were not monitored by the Production Code Administration and could therefore include sexual and scatological references not permitted in commercially-released films, the shorts *were* subject to Pentagon approval. At least one wartime Snafu, *Going Home* (1944), was never released, presumably due to a suggestive scene in some bushes between Pvt. Snafu (home on furlough) and a girl.

In addition to the rude connotation of the SNAFU theme, noted above, at least three of the cartoons conclude with the image of Pvt. Snafu actually *changing* into the backside of a horse (*Coming Snafu, Spies,* and *Fighting Tools*). Latrine scenes appear in *Gripes* and *Rumors*, while *The Home Front* includes a humorous scene in which a horse — skipping along on his hind legs— enthusiastically spreads his own manure to fertilize a Victory Garden! And, borrowing directly from the 1942 Popeye cartoon *You're a Sap, Mr. Jap*, an annihilated Japanese task force in the Snafu short *The Outpost* (1944) sinks to the sound of a flushing toilet! *Diarrhea and Dysentery* (1944) includes an even more explicit — and serious— scatological theme. Pvt. Snafu fails to keep his mess kit clean and contracts diarrhea as a result. The cartoon concludes with a shot of a distressed Snafu rushing to the latrine!

The Snafu series is strictly a representation of the white male point of view. Nude pinups appear in barracks in a number of the cartoons, including *The Goldbrick, The Home Front,* and *Pay Day.* Virtually all of the women in the shorts are reminiscent of the Varga and Petty girls regularly featured in popular men's magazines like *Esquire.* These highly stylized representations of the female body, portraying an idealized image of the "girl back home," were quite prevalent in the male-oriented military environment — examples include fetishized or glamour "nose art" on aircraft and other military vehicles, as well as the sexually explicit artwork that often decorated enlisted men's duffle bags.

It is interesting to note that these animated works produced for military audiences are far less propagandistic than their commercial counterparts. There are *no* overt appeals to patriotism and a limited number of scenes demonizing America's enemies: the portrayal of Hitler as a horned devil (*Spies,* 1943) and the buck-toothed and fanged Japanese caricature at the conclusion of *The Goldbrick* (1943) are the most notable exceptions. American iconography is also conspicuous by its absence in the Snafus — for instance, the American flag appears in only a couple of the cartoons. And there is only one ideologically explicit statement in the whole series, occurring in *Snafuperman* (1944), as Pvt. Snafu — in the guise of a rumpled superhero — parodies Superman's oft-cited mission statement and warns the "enemies of democracy" to beware.

Once one gets past the obvious instructional task of the Snafu cartoons, and the sex and vulgarity designed to demonstrate to their military audience that they were seeing a film civilians were "forbidden" to view, it is extremely interesting to see how the highly skilled and motivated animators at Warner Bros. were able to create a subversive subtext. The Snafus reflect the genuine discontent among enlisted personnel in regards to the authoritarian and dehumanizing aspects of military life, in which soldiers sometimes felt they were reduced to mere ciphers, the serial numbers stamped on their dog tags, rather than individual human beings.

The very name of the protagonist, "Snafu," was the soldier's response to military bureaucracy and stupidity. Many American enlisted personnel expressed their frustration with military authority through the liberal use of four-letter words, in countless expletive-laden combinations. Hence, troops in the audience could immediately identify with a "Pvt. Snafu" and his constant grousing and goofing off, although (as the cartoons would show), they would not necessarily want to emulate his actions in real life for fear of the consequences.

Private Snafu is the company jerk who embodies the common sentiments of the audience, chiefly made up of men drafted into the armed
forces. Because Snafu is so obnoxious and outrageous, the typical enlisted
man could on the one hand feel superior to this schlub — nobody could
be that stubborn or stupid — and yet on the other hand, virtually everyone knew of, or had heard of, such a guy in their unit or a buddy's unit.

The purpose of many of the Snafu cartoons was to reinforce the
instructions that GIs had received in their basic training, to remind them
of the potentially fatal consequences inherent in their military service, but
presented in an amusing manner by showing Pvt. Snafu doing exactly the
wrong things. Wartime U.S. military training — buttressed by sanitized
commercial feature films and newsreels— downplayed the realities of combat, minimizing the gory details of traumatic injuries and death. The Snafu
series could be construed as an attempt to ease the military audience into
this reality by suggesting and even portraying the lethal consequences of
going into combat unprepared. Pvt. Snafu's death or capture —for which
his ignorance is primarily responsible — is depicted in several of the cartoons. In *Spies*, his irresponsible consumption of liquor not only results
in an explosive trip to Hell, it also threatens the lives of other Americans
on board a troopship. In *The Goldbrick*, Snafu shirks during basic training, is unable to contribute to his unit's combat effectiveness, and meets
an ignominious death beneath the treads of a Japanese tank. Snafu's neg-
ligence in maintaining his weapons culminates in his imprisonment in a
German POW camp in *Fighting Tools*, and his failure to learn fundamen-
tal battlefield procedures causes Snafu to be blown to bits in *A Lecture on
Camouflage*. *Pvt. Snafu vs. Malaria Mike* even suggests that Snafu's fatal
ignorance might contribute to America losing the war!

Who was Private Snafu supposed to symbolize? He was never specifically identified as a draftee, but he was clearly intended to represent
the millions of men drafted into the U.S. armed forces (particularly the
Army, but by mid–1943, when the series first appeared, the Navy and even
the Marines were conscripting men). However, the only reference to the
draft occurs in *Target Snafu* (1944), when "selective service" is mentioned
during the induction and training of an "enemy"— malarial mosquitoes
who later attack Pvt. Snafu.

Private Snafu was a short, goofy-looking, physically unimpressive
young man whose uniform often seemed ill-fitting. Until the latter half of
1944, Snafu was aggressively ignorant, disgruntled, and sometimes ridicu-
lously obnoxious. In other words, Pvt. Snafu was the diametrical opposite
of the handsome soldier portrayed in Hollywood feature films, in other
media, and on recruiting posters.

Snafu, bathing in a river, presents a tempting target for a mosquito. From *Private Snafu vs. Malaria Mike* (1944).

While Walt Disney's Donald Duck was also depicted as a less-than perfect soldier (in five cartoons released to general audiences in 1942-43) — screwing up during drill, inadvertently wrecking things, unwittingly outraging his sergeant — the volatile fowl enthusiastically embraced his military service. He repeatedly attempts to win the approval of Sgt. Pete and tries to become a useful member of the All-American armed forces "team."

Pvt. Snafu was a dysfunctional, immature, selfish individual with few redeeming virtues. His inflated self-esteem borders on the delusional — he is unable to grasp the realities of military life, which reduces his chance of being a successful soldier (and surviving the war!). The implication is that the soldier who selfishly ignores military rules and training or shirks his duties, betrays his country by placing himself and his fellow soldiers in mortal danger.

Snafu is frequently portrayed griping about something or attempting to avoid his duties—actions not unusual among real soldiers—but the military establishment could hardly condone such behavior. In a few of the shorts, Snafu learns the error of his ways after experiencing a real or imagined disaster. In *Gripes*, Snafu, complaining about KP duty, policing the barracks, and receiving immunization shots, is magically granted the power to command. However, his actions have disastrous results (Snafu gets blown up by a Nazi bomb), which fortunately turns out to be only a fevered reaction to his booster shots, and Snafu (for the time being) quits his bitching. Snafu circumvents military censorship of his mail in *Censored*, and the subsequent leak of information causes the destruction of his entire unit when they attack a heavily fortified Japanese island—but this is again revealed to be just a bad dream.

Although other soldiers sometimes appear in the cartoons, Snafu is an outsider who has no buddy or sidekick—or even a comic nemesis like Sgt. Pete. In *Rumors*, Snafu actually serves as a disruptive force on his base, spreading rumors and believing every wild story he hears, finally winding up insane! The only other continuing character in the series is "Technical Fairy 1st Class," a supernatural creature who represents the voice of experience, like a tough but avuncular "regular Army" veteran who knows how to survive.

American officers only appear in four Snafu cartoons, and are never shown persecuting or even browbeating the enlisted men. In *Gas*, a frustrated officer—irritated by Snafu's poor performance during a gas mask exercise—orders a sergeant to instruct the private in the proper use of the mask; this short and *Coming Snafu* are the only episodes to depict Snafu being punished or reprimanded by NCOs or officers for his incompetence (he usually gets his comeuppance through other means), although he is manhandled by military policemen in *Coming Snafu* and *Rumors*.

The Snafu cartoons were essentially short, animated morality plays. Pvt. Snafu is the "fallen angel," tempted or perplexed by forces which his stubborn refusal to observe regulations have placed beyond his limited capacity to comprehend or control. This key trait is exemplified in two episodes, *Snafuperman* and *Booby Traps*. In the first short, the clueless but cocky Snafu torments his barracks mates—who are diligently trying to study their manuals—but his own ignorance and failure to prepare for combat results in his later hospitalization with severe injuries. Similarly, in the conclusion to *Booby Traps*, the blissfully ignorant Snafu blows himself up and is last seen on a powder-singed cloud, wearing a 14-karat GI halo and plucking a blackened harp.

Sexual issues were obliquely addressed in several Snafu cartoons. *It's Murder She Says* (1945) was ostensibly a short about the prevention of malaria (also discussed in *Pvt. Snafu vs. Malaria Mike* and *Target Snafu*), but it could be construed as a warning about venereal disease and consorting with sex workers. Presented from the point of view of a jaded, aging mosquito prostitute ("Anopheles Annie"), the cartoon does not require much imagination to make the leap from malarial prophylaxis to protection against sexually transmitted diseases. Although the issue of prostitution and venereal diseases had always been a problem for the military, the situation had become particularly acute for the American Army in Europe following the defeat of Nazi Germany in May 1945: large numbers of women were forced to prostitute themselves to survive, and the incidence of sexually transmitted diseases increased significantly.

Spies, while primarily intended to warn military personnel that they were more susceptible to enemy agents while under the influence of alcohol, also points out the negative consequences of consorting with bargirls. In this short, a beautiful woman Pvt. Snafu meets in a bar is actually a Nazi

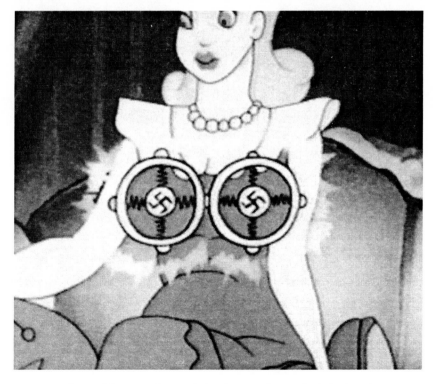

A beautiful woman is revealed to be a Nazi agent in *Spies* (1943).

spy (whose brassiere contains a radio transmitter, and who has a typewriter in her garter!). However, an alternative reading could suggest that bargirls are dangerous in another way — as transmitters of social diseases.

The persona of Pvt. Snafu begins to change in 1944. He is portrayed as more intelligent, although still stubborn. At times he even acts heroically and performs his duties more or less efficiently! It is probably no coincidence that this character modification occurs during the period when the highest number of American ground forces were engaged in combat; the military audience from mid–1944 on thus included more than two million combat veterans and other experienced personnel. They were no longer raw recruits or trainees and didn't necessarily need to be reminded of the basic tenets of being a "good soldier." Reflecting a consciousness of this — and possibly some discomfort with the more negative aspects of the early Private Snafu's character — the War Department refused to release *Going Home* in early 1944.

A transitional Snafu cartoon is *Outpost* (August 1944). In this short, despite his discomfort with duty on a lonely, boring island observation post in the Pacific, Pvt. Snafu successfully carries out his mission — albeit with the assistance of a comic "goony bird" — and provides information which contributes to the destruction of a fleet of Japanese warships. However, at the end of the cartoon, Snafu is shown to be totally clueless as to the significance of the task he has performed.

The "new" cartoons, with their modifications of the central character — Pvt. Snafu's annoying voice is heard less frequently, not only eliminating his gripes and dim-witted comments, but also a source of characterization, as irritating as it was — lose some of their edge.

The final transformation of Pvt. Snafu from a selfish screw-up to a plucky GI occurs in *Operation SNAFU* (October 1945) and *No Buddy Atoll* (November 1945). In the first cartoon, Snafu successfully carries out a mission to steal secret documents from military headquarters in Tokyo; in the latter short, the castaway GI goes head-to-head with another shipwreck survivor, a Japanese admiral, and wins. Breaking with the norm in virtually every one of the previous series entries, neither of these cartoons attempts to teach a lesson to the service personnel in the audience — both episodes are pure entertainment, somewhat reminiscent of Warner Bros. commercial cartoons such as *Bugs Bunny Nips the Nips* (1944, directed by I. Freleng, who also directed *Operation SNAFU*).

No Buddy Atoll was the last Snafu cartoon to be released (Pvt. Snafu himself makes a cameo appearance in *Seaman Tarfu*, 1946, and at least one other Snafu short was completed but shelved). The shorts are still amusing today — as evidenced by their widespread availability — but the series also provides a lot of information about its period. The military's attitude toward the flood of new citizen-soldiers and—conversely—the new troops' attitude toward the military are both visible in the Snafu cartoons. Pvt. Snafu's own transformation from a disruptive, selfish individual to a fully functioning member of the armed forces could be construed as a (rather warped, to be sure) portrait of John Q. Public—drafted into the Army, subjected to regimentation, discipline, and regulations which at times seem pointless; in the end he realizes that *most* of these were necessary measures. Of course, being an American (*and* being an animated cartoon character), even in the final shorts Pvt. Snafu is somewhat wacky, but he gets the job done.

9. That's All, Folks!

And very soon there's bound to be
A "V," a "V," a "V" — For Victory
("We're Working for Defense" from *All Out for V*, 1942)

The spectacle of cute cartoon animals creating and using weapons of war, while cheerfully singing the above lyrics, may seem a little incongruous today, even unsettling. Particularly if, as is often the case, one is viewing cartoons on TV in a time slot designated for "juvenile entertainment." What does a 21st-century child — or an adolescent, or an adult, for that matter — think about such images? The song lyrics, the repetitive verbal and visual use of "V," even the concepts of war production, rationing, the draft, are all components of a language with which most people are unfamiliar.

But what about a contemporary historian? For many, the visual text of motion pictures, and particularly short animated films, may as well be one of the lost tongues of some ancient civilization whose only remaining evidence of its former existence is some potsherds and scattered stones.

Commercially produced animated cartoons throughout their history have often resorted to vulgarity or violent slapstick (indeed, the very term has a violent connotation). If moral, philosophical, or historical concepts are dealt with at all, they are usually approached simplistically, with the world painted in the harshly clashing hues of good and evil. Many American cartoons from the mid–1930s through the mid–1940s — the industry's "Golden Age" — possess a certain nobility. Yet the medium is almost universally maligned as lacking all subtlety or sophistication and is therefore dismissed as politically and historically irrelevant, or condemned as a hotbed of offensive racial stereotypes.

The tragedy is that historians should be fully conversant with their

90

period, but often adamantly refuse to engage in an intellectual dialogue with the surviving celluloid images. Is this a manifestation of professional hubris? We would prefer to think that it may be ignorance; a reluctance to exploit a medium whose historical evidence is admittedly elusive at times, its accessibility so frequently ephemeral.

The animals in *All Out for V*, Popeye, Bugs Bunny, et al., were artistic creations of human beings who were extremely sensitive to the world about them. The audience they attempted to address was of all ages, and the message they delivered was deliberately fabricated to entertain and to appeal to society as they perceived it at the time.

This legacy, 60-odd years later, is not simply a nebulous conglomeration of cartoons that continue to amuse both children and adults, but also a rich audiovisual series of artifacts that beg to be explored — at least 47 percent of the nearly 500 commercial cartoon shorts released in the United States between 1 January 1942 and 30 September 1945 have been identified as containing topical (war-related) material. This is not an inconsiderable number, and what these cartoons say about American culture during World War II is not irrelevant or insignificant.

Popeye's outraged decimation of a Japanese battleship manned by a multitude of craven, sneaky Asian caricatures, concluding with the Rising Sun being literally flushed beneath the sea — this is far more than an example of a series of outrageous images created to entertain the masses six decades ago. It is a document which can be used to develop a better understanding of the popular fears and concerns, the prejudices and humor, of a society — America — at war.

Filmography

Introduction

This filmography contains the most complete and accurate information available on the cartoons discussed in this work. Credits information on animated cartoons is much more difficult to compile than similar information for feature films of the same era; sources used in compiling the credits include the cartoons themselves, copyright deposit information, Office of War Information reports, the World Wide Web (including the Internet Movie Database), and a number of books, including Maltin's *Of Mice and Magic*, Friedwald and Beck's *Warner Bros. Cartoons*, Cabarga's *The Fleischer Story*, and Barrier's *Hollywood Cartoons*. The Walt Disney Archives provided credits for all of the Disney shorts, except for Carl Barks's story credits, which came from an issue of *Funnyworld*. *Mindrot* no. 15 was helpful for Columbia credits information. The plot synopses and coding references came primarily from watching the cartoons, but for shorts not screened the authors utilized the above sources, as well as reviews in *The Film Daily* and *The Motion Picture Herald*.

One reason credits are so hard to find for animated cartoons is the paucity of credit given. Only after 1944 did most companies list more than three or four names onscreen; there is also the pernicious practice of "rotating credits," whereby only one or two animators (or story men) would receive onscreen credit, although the cartoon was actually the work of numerous people. Whenever possible, we have attempted to add names from other sources, if this information can be reasonably verified. In some cases, there were conflicts between sources (especially between copyright data and the onscreen credits), and these discrepancies have been noted.

There also seems to have been a predilection among animator workers to use nicknames or at least variants of their given names. Where possible, we have listed the name that appears onscreen, but some known variations follow:

Gerry (Clyde) Geronimi
Ben (Bugs) Hardaway
Tex (Fred) Avery
Nick (Charles) Nichols
Isadore (I., aka Friz) Freleng
Charles M. (Chuck) Jones
Robert (Bob) Clampett
Isadore (I., aka Izzy) Sparber
Shamus (James) Culhane
Verne (LaVerne) Harding
Tedd (Ted) Pierce
Bill (Vladimir) Tytla

The information for each cartoon in the filmography follows this pattern:

Title (Distribution company — release or copyright (c) date)
    An asterisk (*) before the title means the cartoon is not included
    in the yearly statistics (Appendix A); non-commercial releases,
    clay animation, and feature-length cartoons are in this category.
Producer (If credited)
Director ("Supervisor" on some Warner Bros. cartoons has been
    translated to Director)
Script (usually credited onscreen as "Story")
Animators, Layout, etc.
Music

Voice credits have usually been omitted, since this specialty was rarely credited during the war years. Some notable names in this area include Mel Blanc (Bugs Bunny, Private Snafu, many other Warner Bros. characters); Arthur Q. Bryan (Elmer Fudd); Bill Thompson (Droopy); Pinto Colvig (Goofy, others); Clarence Nash (Donald Duck); Jack Mercer (Popeye); Bud Collyer (Superman); and Berneice Hanson.

The Roman numerals below each entry represent the authors' judgment as to the degree of topicality present in the 1942–1945 cartoons. "I" denotes a short with significant wartime content; "II" indicates a short with peripheral or minor references to the war. These totals appear in Appendix B.

The code terms following most entries provide readers with a quick subject reference to the topical references found in each cartoon. These terms, in some cases combined into broader categories, are tabulated in Appendix C. Appendix D is an index to series characters appearing in cartoons included in the filmography (only starring characters with two or more cartoons are listed). Appendix E is the "Ambiguous List," cartoons whose war relevancy was questionable.

The authors would like to stress that the filmography entries for cartoons we were unable to screen personally are based on "reconstructions" from secondary sources. Although every effort to provide an accurate description of these cartoons was made, some errors or omissions are, unfortunately, possible.

1939

1 *Gulliver's Travels (Paramount —12/20/39)
Producer: Max Fleischer; *Script:* Dan Gordon, Cal Howard, Tedd Pierce, I. Sparber, Edmond Seward; *Music and Lyrics:* Ralph Rainger and Leo Robin; *Atmosphere Music:* Victor Young; *Scenics:* Erich Schenk, Robert Little, Louis Jambor, Shane Miller; *Directors of Animation:* Seymour Kneitel, Willard Bowsky, Tom Palmer, Grim Natwick, William Henning, Roland Crandall, Tom Johnson, Roberto Leffingwell, Frank Kelling, Winfield Hoskins, Orestes Calpini; *Animators:* Graham Place, Arnold Gillespie, Otto Feuer, Nicholas Tafuri, Alfred Eugster, James [Shamus] Culhane, David Tendlar, George Germanetti, Joseph D'Igalo, Nelson Demorest, Reuben Grossman, Abner Kneitel, Frank Endres, Joseph Oriolo, Stan Quackenbush, Harold Walker, Lod Rossner, Joe Miller, Lou Zukor, Frank Smith, Ben Clopton, James Davis, Bill Noland, Edwin Rehberg, Stephen Muffati, Irving Spector, Sam Stimson, Ted Dubois, Edward Smith, Tony Pabian, George Moreno, Thurston Harper, William Sturm, Robert Bentley; *Song:* "It's a Hap-Hap-Happy Day" (Sammy Timberg, Al Neiberg, Winston Sharples)

This was Paramount's answer to Disney's *Snow White and the Seven Dwarfs* (1937). Loosely adapted from the classic satire by Jonathan Swift and released during the Christmas season, this feature-length cartoon alluded to contemporary world problems. The inhabitants of Lilliput are on the verge of war with the kingdom of Blefuscu because the two countries' monarchs cannot agree on the song to be sung at the wedding of their children. Comic "spies" try to sow further discord until Gulliver, the giant from a land across the sea (the United States?) is discovered on the beach one night. He is able to abort an invasion by King Bombo, restore peace, and reunite the prince and princess with parental blessings.
War Allegory; Spies

2 Naughty Neighbors (Warner Bros.—11/4/39)
Director: Robert Clampett; *Script:* Warren Foster; *Animator:* I. Ellis; *Music:* Carl W. Stalling

Released in November 1939, after the outbreak of the Second World War in Europe. An opening title states the story takes place in "Kaintucky ... where in contrast to the troubled outside world the simple folk live in peace and harmony."

A newspaper headline features a photograph of Porky Pig and Petunia, and announces "Leaders of Two Feudin' Sides Sign Non-Agression Pact" (a reference to the Nazi-Soviet Non-Agression Pact?). This idyllic bliss is soon disrupted when fighting breaks out once more between the Martins and the McCoys. The whole countryside is mobilized — even little chicks who have just hatched keep the tops of their shells as "helmets"— and Porky's romance with Petunia is jeopardized. In a final desperate effort to end the conflict, Porky tosses a "feud pacifier" grenade down into the valley, where a full-scale battle is in progress. When the smoke clears, everyone is smiling and some are even dancing around a maypole.

War Allegory; Pacifism

3   Old Glory (Warner Bros.— 7/1/39)

Producer: Leon Schlesinger; *Director:* Charles M. Jones; *Animator:* Robert McKimson; *Music:* Carl W. Stalling

Beneath a waving U.S. flag, Porky Pig— in this film portrayed as a schoolboy pig rather than an adult — is trying to memorize the Pledge of Allegiance from a history book. After several failed attempts, he gives up and promptly falls asleep. Porky dreams he meets Uncle Sam (voice of John Deering), who tells the little pig how Americans won their freedom from "tyranny ... [and] injustice." Beginning with Paul Revere's ride, Uncle Sam relates the story of America's struggle for independence and growth as a new nation, concluding with Abraham Lincoln's Gettysburg address. Porky awakens, quickly memorizes the pledge and recites it as he salutes the flag. An unusual, non-humorous Warner Brothers' cartoon, specifically commissioned to accompany its two-reel live-action patriotic films (e.g. *Sons of Liberty*, 1939). It is interesting to note that Great Britain is never identified as the "tyrannical" country which America had to fight to achieve freedom (even Paul Revere shouts "To arms!" rather than the traditional "The British are coming!"). Three years earlier, in *I Haven't Got a Hat*, Porky Pig had trouble reciting "Paul Revere's Ride."

Historical American Figures; Armed Forces

4   Peace on Earth (MGM —12/4/39)

Producer: Hugh Harman; *Director:* Hugh Harman; *Music:* Scott Bradley; *Voice:* Mel Blanc

This pacifistic work was released during the Christmas season of 1939. The snow-covered ruins of a town are shown; it can be seen that animals have fashioned homes out of the debris of war (helmets, etc.). Three little squirrels, singing "Peace on Earth" beneath a lamp made from a bayonet, are joined by their grandpa, who sings "Good will to men." The squirrels ask Grandpa to explain what "men" are. He tells them men no longer exist — they were the "orneriest, cussedest, dagnabbed tribe of varmints I ever did see." As a montage of battle sequences is shown, including gas warfare, Grandpa says the human race fought itself into extinction many years before. When the last two soldiers killed each other, the animals gathered together to hear the advice of a wise old owl, who tells them to "rebuild the old wastes." *Peace on Earth* was remade as *Good Will to Men* (1955).

War Allegory; Terror Weapon; Pacifism; Armed Forces

5   Peaceful Neighbors (Columbia — 1/30/39)

Producer: Charles Mintz; *Director:* Sid Marcus; *Animators:* Art Davis, Herb Rothwill; *Music:* Joe DeNat

"A short as timely as this morning's newspapers" was how Columbia marketed this "Color Rhapsody" in the trade journals. It is a war allegory with certain similarities to *What Price Porky?* (Warner Bros., 1938). Two rival families of chickens, led by aggressive roosters, become involved in a territorial dispute. Several doves in a nearby tree watch the squabble escalate to open warfare, with the chicks of both families used as "troops." They fight with tanks, aircraft, and machine guns; there is even a suicide squadron consisting of a chick with a shell tied to its back. The doves decide to restore peace, secretly replacing poison gas with perfume in gas bombs, and stuffing cannon shells with flowers and candy. In the midst of battle, the combatants—showered with these treats—stop fighting and begin eating. Soon they are rebuilding their homes and playing games together. The roosters shake hands and make up. Up in the tree, the doves are shown wearing laurel wreaths as they congratulate themselves on their peacemaking. Released less than eight months before the outbreak of war, this cartoon is ironically far more optimistic than its 1935 predecessor, *Neighbors*.

War Allegory; Armed Forces; Pacifism

1940

6   Africa Squeaks (Warner Bros — 1/27/40)

Producer: Leon Schlesinger; *Director:* Robert Clampett; *Script:* Dave Hoffman; *Animator:* John Carey; *Music:* Carl W. Stalling

A cartoon following the adventures of Porky Pig, on safari in "darkest Africa." Porky meets Stanley (who talks like Spencer Tracy, the star of *Stanley and Livingstone*, a 1939 feature film), who initially confuses the pig with Dr. Livingstone. After spot gags about wildlife — including a Brooklyn gorilla — an evil, black bird of prey spots three grazing fawns. The narrator states: "It's a giant condor ... despised attacker of the weak, the jungle's most ruthless killer." When the bird attacks like a dive bomber, the baby deer take cover in the bush; a moment later, the vegetation parts—one deer cranks a siren and shouts "Air Raid!" as his two companions, now wearing steel helmets, man an anti-aircraft gun. The menacing bird is hit and crashes in flames to the earth. This gag was reworked with bunnies instead of baby deer for *Crazy Cruise* (1942), q.v. (The notorious German air force unit that fought beside Franco's fascist forces during the Spanish Civil War was called the Kondor Legion.)

Armed Forces — Germany; Blacks; World War II; Spanish Civil War?

7   Ali Baba Bound (Warner Bros. — 2/10/40)

Producer: Leon Schlesinger; *Director:* Robert Clampett; *Script:* Melvin Millar; *Animator:* Vive Risto; *Music:* Carl W. Stalling

In this remake of *Little Beau Porky* (1936), Foreign Legionnaire Porky Pig is stationed in the Sahara Desert, where it is so hot "even the fan dancers use electric

fans." A sleazy George Raft caricature (Warner Bros. cartoons frequently lampooned celebrities), leaning against a palm tree and flipping a coin with his big toe, slips Porky a note reading "Confessions of a Nasty Spy" (in 1939, Warners had produced the first unequivocal anti–Nazi feature film in Hollywood, *Confessions of a Nazi Spy*). The note warns of an impending attack on the desert outpost where Porky is stationed. The stuttering pig thanks the "nasssty spy" and heads for the fort on a rented baby camel. When Porky arrives, he learns the other Legionnaires have "gone to [a] convention in Boston." Porky and the little camel — aided by Mama Camel — have to fight off "Ali Baba and his dirty sleeves" by themselves.
Spies; Nazis

8   Ants in the Plants (Paramount — 3/15/40)

Director: Dave Fleischer; *Script:* George Manuel; *Animators:* Myron Waldman, George Moreno; *Music:* Sammy Timberg

A colony of ants is diligently preparing and storing munitions in their fortress-like mound against the day of invasion by their arch enemy, the anteater. When he appears, the mobilized ants — in military units led by their snail-riding queen — go into action. But the anteater is not easily defeated, and the ant brigade suffers many casualties. Eventually the ants abandon modern tactics and the "Sewer Side Squad" angrily swarms over their opponent. Released during the height of the so-called "phony war" on the Western Front, this short may have been making allusions to France's defensive Maginot Line.
War Allegory; Armed Forces — Army

9   Ceiling Hero (Warner Bros. — 8/24/40)

Producer: Leon Schlesinger; *Director:* Fred Avery; *Script:* Dave Monahan; *Animator:* Rod Scribner; *Music:* Carl W. Stalling

The title parodies the 1936 Warner Bros. feature *Ceiling Zero*. The narrator says the audience will see the "latest developments in the science of modern aviation." These include a yellow, slant-eyed "China Clipper" (Pan Am's famous Trans-Pacific airliner), and the newest camouflage developed by Army engineers for our "combat planes" (only the pilots' heads are seen, flying through the air). The final sequence features an unflappable test pilot making a dangerous high-altitude run in an experimental plane. His flight jacket bears the logo "Test Pilot — from the Picture of the Same Name" (a reference to MGM's 1938 feature film).
Armed Forces — Air Corps

10   Fightin' Pals (Paramount — 7/12/40)

Producer: Max Fleischer; *Director:* Dave Fleischer; *Script:* Joseph E. Stultz; *Animators:* Willard Bowsky, Robert E. Bentley; *Music:* Winston Sharples, Sammy Timberg

Popeye's pal Dr. Bluto departs on an expedition to Africa. Time passes, and Popeye finally hears over the radio that his friend is lost. He immediately jumps into a rowboat and heads across the Atlantic Ocean. Popeye's route is traced on a map — as his boat nears the Iberian peninsula, a series of explosions emanates

from the rim of the then-troubled European continent. The little vessel veers sharply away and crashes into the North African coast.
World War II

11 *Invasion of Norway (Cartoon Films Ltd.—6/40?)

Producer: Lawson Haris; *Director:* Paul Fennell; *Narrator:* Thomas Freebain-Smith
Over nine minutes in length, this "War Graphs" uses poster-style art, graphs, and "pull-through" animation to depict the German conquest of Norway, which began in April 1940. This is instructional anti–Nazi propaganda delivered in a "March of Time" format.
Armed Forces— Germany; Nazi; World War II; Norway

12 Of Fox and Hounds (Warner Bros.—12/7/40)

Producer: Leon Schlesinger; *Director:* "Draft No. 412" (Fred Avery); *Script:* "Draft No. 1312"; *Animator:* "Draft No. 6102"; *Music:* "Draft No. 158 (Too Bad)"
Dim-witted foxhound Willoughby (who acts and talks like "Lenny" from *Of Mice and Men*) attempts to capture wily fox George. The contemporary relevance of this cartoon is limited to the credits (see above). The first number drawn in the Selective Service Lottery on 29 October 1940 was 158, hence the parenthetical comment "Too Bad." At least two other Warner Bros. cartoons, both released in 1942, feature a variation on this—*Sergeant* Dave Monahan is credited with the stories of *Lights Fantastic* and *Saps in Chaps*. *Of Fox and Hounds* was re-released in spring 1944.
Draft

13 Porky's Poor Fish (Warner Bros.—4/27/40)

Producer: Leon Schlesinger; *Director:* Robert Clampett; *Script:* Melvin Millar; *Animator:* David Hoffman; *Music:* Carl W. Stalling
Porky Pig leaves his Pet Fish Shoppe for lunch, and a hungry cat sneaks in to help himself. After a turtle mounts a seahorse and shouts "To arms!" the fish mobilize to repel the invader. The tuna's eggs hatch with shell "helmets," the flying fish launch from their aquarium and attack in military formation, etc.
War Allegory; Blacks

14 Recruiting Daze (Universal —10/28/40)

Producer: Walter Lantz; *Director:* Alex Lovy; *Script:* Ben Hardaway; *Music:* Hughie Prince
Probably the first fictional film to refer to the draft. Punchy, an Ed Wynn caricature, joins the Army when he hears the country needs "67½ billion men." The officers, thoroughly engrossed in a tic-tac-toe game, pay little attention to Punchy as he wanders aimlessly around the camp pushing a wheelbarrow loaded with munitions. Various implements of modern warfare are lampooned, including a unit of mechanized Indians and a fighter plane cutting slices from a "sausage" dirigible. Punchy tries to load a shell into a "Big Bertha" cannon but falls into the barrel himself and is propelled to a distant planet when the gun is fired. In Technicolor.
Draft; Armed Forces— Army

15   Swing Social (MGM — 5/18/40)

Producer: Fred Quimby; *Directors:* Rudolf Ising, William Hanna and Joseph Barbera (uncredited); *Music:* Scott Bradley

A black deacon discovers a man fishing on Sunday, and tells him the black bass don't bite because that's the day they attend their weekly social. Underwater, the deacon's fish counterpart talks and sings the "Social Sunday Morn." He introduces "Franklin D. Roosevelt Jones," a baby bass in a clamshell stroller who holds up his lollipop like a microphone and states: "My friends, as I've said before … I'se hates war!" Various musical routines follow, utilizing familiar black stereotypes and caricatures of performers like Fats Waller. (On several occasions during the 1940 presidential election campaign, in an attempt to reassure the voters that he was not going to deliberately involve America in the expanding world war, President Roosevelt said "I hate war.")

Blacks; FDR; World War II; Neutrality

16   Wacky Wildlife (Warner Bros. — 11/9/40)

Producer: Leon Schlesinger; *Director:* Fred Avery; *Script:* Dave Monahan; *Animator:* Virgil Ross; *Music:* Carl W. Stalling

Spot gags about wildlife. Near the end of the cartoon, the offscreen narrator observes a group of armed hunters surrounding a little duck sitting on a pond. The narrator anxiously asks the duck: "Why don't you fly away?" The fowl smirks and turns to reveal an American flag painted on his side. Note: since America was still neutral in 1940, the U.S. merchant marine painted large Stars and Stripes on the sides of its ships in an attempt to avoid being torpedoed by German U-boats.

Neutrality; World War II

1941

17   All This and Rabbit Stew (Warner Bros. — 9/13/41)

Producer: Leon Schlesinger; *Director:* Fred Avery [uncredited]; *Script:* Dave Monahan; *Animator:* Virgil Ross; *Music:* Carl W. Stalling

A lethargic, slow-witted black hunter is Bugs Bunny's opponent in this short. Pointing his shotgun at the rabbit, the hunter says (in heavy black dialect): "Okay Mr. Rabbit …come out with hands up … or else I'll blitzkreig you." Rarely screened today due to the black stereotype, this was one of *four* similar Bugs Bunny cartoons released in 1941 alone. The others were *Hiawatha's Rabbit Hunt* (a dumb Indian hunter tries to get Bugs), *The Heckling Hare* (a dumb dog chases Bugs), and *Wabbit Twouble* (with Elmer Fudd as the hunter).

Armed Forces — Germany; Blacks; World War II

18   *Any Bonds Today? (Warner Bros. for U.S. Government — 12/41)

Producer: Leon Schlesinger; *Director:* Robert Clampett; *Animators:* Bob McKimson, Rod Scribner, Virgil Ross

This post–Pearl Harbor release was sponsored by the government. The one-minute, plotless cartoon opens with Bugs Bunny — briefly attired as Uncle Sam —

dancing and singing "Any Bonds Today?" ("The tall man with the high hat and whiskers on his chin/Will soon be knocking at your door and you'd better be in..."). Bugs then does an Al Jolson imitation in blackface (cut in some current prints) and sings "Any Stamps Today?" ("Here comes the freedom man, can't make tomorrow's plan/Not unless you buy a share of freedom today..."). In the final scene, the fat version of Elmer Fudd (in Army fatigues) and Porky Pig (in sailor's garb) join Bugs. As part of America's prewar mobilization, Defense Bonds had been on sale for several months. In the spring of 1942 they were re-named "War Bonds." The Irving Berlin song which inspired this cartoon was also used in a "Soundies" short starring Barry Wood.

Bonds; Armed Forces — Army, Navy; Blacks

19   Boogie Woogie Bugle Boy of Company B (Universal — 9/1/41)

Producer: Walter Lantz; *Director:* Walter Lantz; *Script:* Ben Hardaway, Lowell Elliott; *Animators:* Alex Lovy, Verne Harding; *Music:* Hughie Prince (song); *Music Arrangement:* Darrell Calker

Black trumpeter "Hot Breath" Harry is drafted into the Army. Rushed through his physical at "Draft Board 13," he is dumped out of a chute — already in uniform — at camp. The tough sergeant hands Harry a bugle and tells the agitated draftee he is "now de new bugle boy of Company B." When Harry tries to leave camp he is informed he has a choice of playing Reveille or Taps! At 5:00 a.m., Harry blows his bugle but a disgruntled listener splits his instrument with a cleaver. Switching to trumpet, he plays the title tune, accompanied by a chorus. Three young women wearing red, white and blue outfits show up and boogie with the soldiers, and even the sergeant gets caught up in the beat. "Boogie Woogie Bugle Boy of Company B," sung by the Andrews Sisters, was a hit song from Universal's top-grossing feature film of 1941, *Buck Privates*. Lantz made a number of cartoons with "boogie woogie" themes, including *Boogie Woogie Sioux* (1942), *Cow Cow Boogie* (1943) q.v., and *Boogie Woogie Man* (1943), the latter featuring black ghosts in zoot suits. *Boogie Woogie Bugle Boy of Company B* was the first Lantz cartoon nominated for an Academy Award.

Draft; Blacks; Armed Forces — Army

20   *Broken Treaties ("This Changing World" series) (Cartoon Films Ltd./Columbia — 8/1/41)

Producer: Lawson Haris; *Director:* Paul Fennell; *Music:* Clarence Wheeler; *Narrator:* Raymond Gram Swing

Noted author and radio commentator Raymond Gram Swing had been making bi-weekly broadcasts of "American commentary" to Great Britain since 1940. He appears in a live-action introduction and then narrates this eight-minute pro-interventionist cartoon (in "Dunningcolor"). After a shot of the globe, there is a dissolve to Hitler going to bed, then hands crushing Austria and Czechoslovakia on the globe. Hitler and Mussolini meet and talk, but with their fingers crossed behind their backs! Hitler next makes a deal with Stalin and the Russian bear (the Nazi-Soviet Pact of August 1939). With the unholy alliance between communists and fascists in place, tanks roll into Poland the following month. Britain and

France have little choice but to declare war on Germany on 3 September 1939. The destruction of Poland is depicted in a montage sequence. As the film concludes, Uncle Sam is shown watching over America.

Mussolini; Hitler; Stalin; Austria; Czechoslovakia; Poland; World War II; Brit; Fr

21   The Bug Parade (Warner Bros.—10/21/41)

Producer: Leon Schlesinger; *Director:* Fred Avery; *Script:* Dave Monahan; *Animator:* Rod Scribner; *Music:* Carl W. Stalling

A comic examination of the peculiarities of various insects. At one point the commentator discusses the cootie and says the bug has been around countless camps during many wars. A little cootie spots a sign for a "U.S. Army Training Camp," then turns to the audience and gleefully shouts: "Millions and millions of soldiers, and they're all mine!" A similar routine (but with a dog and trees) appears in *Cross Country Detours* (1940).

Armed Forces — Army

22   A Coy Decoy (Warner Bros.—6/7/41)

Producer: Leon Schlesinger; *Director:* Robert Clampett; *Script:* Melvin Millar; *Animator:* Norm McCabe; *Music:* Carl W. Stalling

Another "what happens after-hours in a store" cartoon; cf. *I Like Mountain Music* (1933) and *It's an Education* (1938). In "Le Booke Shoppe," Daffy Duck starts out on the cover of "The Ugly Duckling," then is lured out of "Swan Lake" by a cute duck decoy placed there by a "Wolf from Wall Street." Daffy desperately tries to dissuade the wolf from eating him, listing a plethora of defects concluding with "Why, even the Army don't want me!" (as he shows a draft registration form stamped "REJECTED"). The wolf is not deterred, and blocks Daffy's "Escape" (an anti–Nazi book filmed by MGM in 1940) and chases him over the "Bridge of San Luis Rey." Daffy finally opens the book "Hurricane" and the wind blows the wolf into "The Mortal Storm" (another anti–Nazi work filmed by MGM in 1940). A white flag flies from the battered wolf's tail as he lies in front of "For Whom the Bell Tolls" (Hemingway's 1940 novel about the Spanish Civil War).

Draft; Nazis; Germany; Spanish Civil War

23   The Cute Recruit (Columbia — 5/21/41/)

Director: no credit; *Script:* Art Davis; *Animator:* Sid Marcus; *Music:* Eddie Kilfeather, Joe DeNat?

In this Columbia "Phantasy Cartoon," a little boy walking down the street spots an Army recruiting poster which promises to "Make a Man Out of You." After scrutinizing a competing Navy poster, the boy imagines being in both services, while the rival recruiters vie for his attention. Finally, the boy's mother arrives to hustle him away.

Armed Forces — Navy, Army

24   *Dumbo (Walt Disney/RKO — 10/31/41)

Producer: Walt Disney; *Director:* Ben Sharpsteen; *Script:* Joe Grant, Dick Huemer
Story Director: Otto Englander; *Sequence Directors:* Norman Ferguson, Wilfred

Jackson, Bill Roberts, Jack Kinney, Sam Armstrong; *Animation Directors:* Vladimir Tytla, Fred Moore, Ward Kimball, John Lounsbery, Arthur Babbitt, Wolfgang Reitherman; *Story Development:* Gill Peet, Aurelius Battaglia, Joe Rinaldi, George Stallings, Webb Smith; *Character Designers:* John P. Miller, Martin Provensen, John Walbridge, James Bodrero, Maurice Noble, Elmer Plummer; *Art Directors:* Herb Ryman, A. Kendall O'Connor, Terrell Stapp, Donald DaGradi, Al Zinnen, Ernest Nordli, Dick Kelsey, Charles Payzant; *Animators:* Hugh Fraser, Howard Swift, Harvey Toombs, Don Towsley, Milt Neil, Les Clark, Hicks Lokey, Claude Smith, Berny World, Ray Patterson, Jack Campbell, Grant Simmons, Walt Kelly, Joshua Meador, Don Patterson, Bill Shull, Cy Young, Art Palmer; *Backgrounds:* Claude Coats, Albert Dempster, John Hench, Gerald Nevius, Ray Lochrem, Joe Stahley; *Music:* Oliver Wallace, Frank Churchill; *Lyrics:* Ned Washington; *Orchestration:* Edward H. Plumb

A feature-length film about a little circus elephant who is mocked because of his oversized ears. After he learns to use his ears to fly, Dumbo is accepted and even becomes a celebrity. Following his aerial debut, a newspaper montage is shown — next to a photograph of the flying elephant, a headline reads "Bombers for Defense." There is also a reference to "fireside chats."

National Defense; Blacks; FDR

25 The Fighting 69½th (Warner Bros.—1/18/41)

Producer: Leon Schlesinger; *Director:* I. Freleng; *Script:* Jack Miller; *Animator:* Gil Turner; *Music:* Carl W. Stalling

The title parodies the feature *The Fighting 69th* (Warner Bros., 1940). A red ant and a black ant are both attracted to a sumptuous picnic lunch which has been spread out on a blanket. They come to blows over an olive, and war is declared. Each side mobilizes its armed forces (including the Royal Flying Ants, a reference to the Royal Air Force, Britain's famed service). A red ant officer brief his troops for an attack on a hot dog, but the raiding party is subsequently ambushed by its opponents. The blacks go on the offensive, tossing some Limburger cheese into the red ants' trench. The red ants respond to the "gas attack" by covering up the cheese with dirt. Eventually, a dark shadow passes over the "battlefield"—a woman gathers up the blanket and the food, but as she leaves a small cake falls to the ground. The commanders of the rival ant armies, resplendant in their heavily bemedaled uniforms, finally agree to a peace conference to divide the cake, but when they cannot reach an agreement, fighting breaks out once more.

War Allegory; Blacks; Armed Forces — Army; Armed Forces — RAF?

26 The Flying Bear (MGM —11/1/41)

Producer: Rudolf Ising; *Director:* Rudolf Ising; *Music:* Scott Bradley

For Barney Bear's second stint in the armed forces, he is a mechanic in the Army Air Corps. Tired of merely repairing engines, Barney builds his own personal airplane, a smiling, anthrophomorphized contraption. The bear and his "friend" take to the air, but after some playful flying, the little plane gets cocky and zooms past a slow-moving pelican. A dogfight with the irritated bird results in the loss of the plane's propeller. Barney and his craft land in the cockpit of a fighter plane, and Barney's frantic efforts as a pilot wreak havoc on the airfield. The fighter falls apart, and Barney and his plane crash into a building, winding up in traction in the base hospital.

Armed Forces — Air Corps

27   Flying Fever (20th Century–Fox — 12/26/41)

Producer: Paul Terry; *Director:* Mannie Davis; *Script:* John Foster; *Music:* Philip A. Scheib

Gandy Goose's first appearance in the Army. Impressed by a hard-boiled flight commander (a rooster), soldier Gandy joins the air corps. After a series of tests (with dubious results), Gandy goes on his first solo flight but gets caught in a storm and crashes. The rooster tells Gandy he is now "qualified to jump with full equipment," but the reluctant goose has to be kicked out of the airplane by a mechanical boot. He lands on the flight commander, and both of them plunge through the earth and wind up in China!

Armed Forces — Air Corps, Army

28   The Home Guard (20th Century–Fox — 3/7/41)

Producer: Paul Terry; *Director:* Mannie Davis; *Script:* John Foster; *Music:* Philip A. Scheib

Jenny, the girlfriend of Gandy Goose, falls for pompous Rufus Rooster, captain of the home guard, prompting the rustic Gandy to join up (as "You're in the Army Now" plays on the soundtrack). Gandy is assigned to guard duty and warned to "keep your eyes open for the fifth column." As he puzzles over this instruction, the fifth column of the headquarter's building starts to inch toward him. Gandy seizes the ambulatory column and takes it to the captain; a vulture pops out of the column and chases the home guard across the parade ground. Rallied by a bugler, the citizen-soldiers man a machine-gun and an egg-crate tank, firing eggs at the vulture. Gandy flies a broom-and-box "airplane" into combat against the vulture and his cohort; the two evil birds collide and plunge to the earth in flames. A heroic Gandy is reconciled with Jenny. This cartoon contains one of the earliest uses of the "V" as a symbol of anti-totalitarianism.

Armed Forces — Army; Fifth Column; "V"; Home Defense

29   *How War Came (Cartoon Films Ltd./Columbia — 11/1/41)

Producer: Lawson Haris; *Director:* Paul Fennell; *Narrator:* Raymond Gram Swing

The second film (see *Broken Treaties*, 1940) in Columbia's "This Changing World" series. It was based on commentator Raymond Gram Swing's 1939 book of the same title, written about his experiences as a journalist reporting from Germany. Swing blames the war on the failure of the League of Nations to stop the "lawlessness" of certain countries, beginning with Japan's seizure of Manchuria in 1931. A litany of chicanery and aggression by the militarist states during the 1930s follows. A Hitler caricature rants: "Today we own only Germany, tomorrow the whole world." Interestingly enough, mention of Soviet misdeeds are omitted, but Stalin's aid to Republican Spain is mentioned. Swing concludes this tendentious, 8½ minute cartoon with this statement: "We in America have seen our own gangsters use just these methods, and we know the only way to meet them. It takes preparedness, power, and courage." Perhaps as more of a reflection upon the times rather than for its artistic merit, *How War Came* was nominated for an Academy Award.

> *Russia; Japan; Mussolini; Hitler; Nazis; Spanish Civil War; League of Nations; World War II*

30   Hysterical High Spots in American History (Universal — 3/31/41)

Producer: Walter Lantz; *Director:* Walter Lantz; *Script:* Ben Hardaway; *Animators:* Alex Lovy, Verne Harding; *Music:* Darrell Calker

An off-screen narrator announces "This is draftee #158 bringing you high spots in American history.... Is draftee #192 in the house?" As he speaks, a couple of dumb-looking guys in uniform poke their heads out through the credits. Various blackout gags about American history follow. As Minutemen march in response to Paul Revere's call to arms during the American Revolution, two ugly sisters put out a "Detour" sign to divert the men to their house. In the final sequence, the narrator announces the adoption by the United States in 1940 of "peacetime conscription — millions of men report for registration." As the legs of massed soldiers are shown marching, the two ugly sisters reappear and put out their "Detour" sign again. The title of this cartoon may have been inspired by Universal's "Hysterical History Comedies," a series of shorts made in the 1920s which burlesqued famous historical events and prominent personages.

> *Draft; Historical American Figures; Armed Forces — Army*

31   *Jim Dandy in the Gay Knighties (Paramount — 8/22/41)

Producer: George Pal; *Director:* George Pal

A "Madcap Models" Puppetoon which begins with a closeup of a printed storybook. The text reads "Once upon a time, long, long ago ... B.C. (Before Conscription)." During the medieval era, a giant ogre is terrorizing a kingdom, but wandering minstrel Jim Dandy discovers the monster loves music and tames him.

> *Draft*

32   Meet John Doughboy (Warner Bros. — 7/5/41)

Producer: Leon Schlesinger; *Director:* Robert Clampett; *Script:* Warren Foster; *Animators:* Virgil Ross, Vive Risto; *Music:* Carl W. Stalling

Porky Pig, in a World War I "doughboy" uniform, is introduced to a theatre audience as "Draftee No. 158¾." He tells them they will see some "sensational movies full of military secrets," and asks any "fifth columnists" to leave the theatre as a newsreel parody begins. References to "America's defense effort," "blitz warfare," and the RAF are made. A newspaper montage reads: "Nazis Order Sub Attacks Off U.S.," "Draft Debates," and "Draft Passes." Scenes of boot camp follow, with footage of armaments our soldiers will be using, including seige guns drawn by horses "from South America" (who start dancing the conga). A new "land destroyer" flashes by — when it stops, Jack Benny (in uniform) and Rochester are revealed in Benny's old jalopy (the Maxwell). Finally, the narrator queries: "Are we safe from air attack? Supposing one day a fleet of enemy bombers appeared over the horizon..."

A squadron of planes heads toward the New York skyline, but the Statue of Liberty spots them, pulls out a spray-gun full of insecticide, and gasses the invaders. The planes crash into the harbor as the statue resumes her stately pose.

Draft; Fifth Column; Blacks; Armed Forces — Army, RAF; Nazis; "V"; South America; Britain

33   The Mighty NaVy (Paramount — 11/14/41)

Producer: Max Fleischer; *Director:* Dave Fleischer; *Script:* William Turner, Ted Pierce; *Animators:* Seymour Kneitel, Abner Matthews

The capital "V" in the title of this film was a clear reference to Britain's "V for victory" symbol, introduced in January 1941 by the BBC. Popeye appears for the first time as a member of the U.S. Navy, and is seen on an armed naval training vessel. After he belly-flops a plane off a catapult into the sea, he is exiled to peeling potatoes. Soon afterwards, his ship is encircled by a hostile fleet whose battleship coyly flies a banner reading—"Enemy (Name Your Own)". Popeye responds to the challenge and sinks the aggressor's battleships, then downs several planes—whose wings bear markings which resemble swastikas—launched from a carrier. The "mother" carrier, after losing her brood, makes an about-face and speeds off, yelping. Popeye spots a super battleship heading straight for his ship, guns blazing. He gulps his spinach and turns himself into a human torpedo, ramming into the enemy craft. When the smoke clears, the skeleton of the battleship is seen slowly sinking beneath the waves. Popeye is decorated for his efforts.

Armed Forces — Navy; "V"; Nazis?

34   The One Man Navy (20th Century–Fox — 9/5/41)

Producer: Paul Terry; *Director:* Mannie Davis; *Script:* John Foster; *Music:* Philip A. Scheib

Gandy Goose, after receiving his "Greetings" draft notice — with "love and kisses from Uncle Sam," as "You're in the Army Now" is heard on the soundtrack — dutifully reports to his local draft board, but returns to the barnyard despondent after being rejected. The goose decides to join the Navy, but in his own way and with his own equipment. For example, he induces the hens to lay eggs loaded with dynamite. After recruiting a crew from his fellow farm animals, Gandy sets sail in a little row boat, searching for enemy submarines. One is eventually sighted and a battle begins; the enemy attacks, but Gandy and his mates are able to neutralize or deflect all incoming missiles, sending them back at the sub. With the added help of his homemade munitions, Gandy succeeds in routing the submarine (marked with a skull and crossbones). The U.S. Navy arrives on the scene and a (rooster) admiral pins a metal on the heroic goose, to the tune of "Columbia, Gem of the Ocean."

Armed Forces — Navy; Draft; Armed Forces — Army

35   Porky's Pooch (Warner Bros. — 11/1/41)

Producer: Leon Schlesinger; *Director:* Robert Clampett; *Script:* Warren Foster; *Animator:* I. Ellis; *Music:* Carl W. Stalling

A Brooklyn-accented mongrel dog, riding in a chauffeur-driven limousine, picks up a down-and-out Scottie dog (who speaks with a brogue and looks like Fala, President Roosevelt's dog). The mongrel relates his success story in flashback. The dog storms into Porky Pig's penthouse and alternately demands and begs to be adopted. At one point he dramatically states: "I'm a dog without a country — a ref-u-geee!" This short is similar to *Little Orphan Airedale* (1947) in which "Charlie Dog" tries to browbeat Porky into adopting him.

   World War II; Refugees

36   Porky's Preview (Warner Bros. — 4/19/41)

Producer: Leon Schlesinger; *Director:* Fred Avery; *Script:* Dave Monahan; *Animator:* Virgil Ross; *Music:* Carl W. Stalling

   Porky Pig screens his homemade animated cartoon for a barnyard audience. The ticket girl dons a gas mask when a skunk appears, but he walks away, unable to pay five cents for a ticket (because he has only one "scent"). The cartoon — comprised of crudely-drawn stick figures— includes a self-portrait of Porky (an arrow indicates this is "Me") is labeled "draft No. 6⅞" (another arrow indicates this is "Funny").

   Draft; Blacks

37   Porky's Snooze Reel (Warner Bros. — 1/11/41)

Producer: Leon Schlesinger; *Director:* Robert Clampett, Norman McCabe; *Script:* Warren Foster; *Animator:* John Carey; *Music:* Carl W. Stalling

   Porky Pig presents the "Passé News" (a parody of the Pathé newsreel). The second half of the reel is largely devoted to "national defense." Scenes include the Army's "new tank trap" (a giant mousetrap), a jellyfish swallowing one of the Navy's most advanced mines, and a "dogfight" between two "interceptor planes" (they viciously gnaw at each other, then fly off in opposite directions, yelping). The newsreel spoof had been used since the silent era — the 1920 cartoon *Nooze Weekly* (Fox) featured Mutt and Jeff traveling across the globe to report on world events.

   National Defense; Armed Forces — Army, Navy, Air Corps?

38   Red Riding Hood Rides Again (Columbia — 12/5/41)

Director: Sid Marcus; *Animators:* Bob Wickersham, Bill Hamner; *Music:* Eddie Kilfeather

   In this "Color Rhapsody," the Wolf spots Red Riding Hood traveling through the forest on a motor scooter. He puts on a police-dog disguise and tries to catch her, but she's too fast, so he hops in a plane and beats her to Grandma's house. Grandma goes out dancing with her boyfriend, leaving the way clear for the Wolf to impersonate her. Red arrives and the wolf is preparing to pounce, but a messenger arrives with a telegram for him: "YOU ARE DRAFTED No. 786. Report for Military Training Immediately!" In the final scene, the wolf receives some stern military discipline at the hands of an officer.

   Draft; Armed Forces — Army

39   *The Reluctant Dragon (Walt Disney/RKO — 6/20/41)

Producer: Walt Disney; *Directors:* Ford Beebe, Jasper Blystone, Jim Handley,

Hamilton Luske, Erwin L. Verity, Alfred L. Werker; *Script:* Ted Sears, Al Perkins, Larry Clemmons, William Cottrell, Harry Clork, Robert Benchley, Kenneth Grahame, Erdman Penner, T. Hee, Joe Grant, Dick Huemer, John P. Miller; *Photography (Live action):* Bert Glennon, Winton Hoch; *Film Editors:* Earl Rettig, Paul Weatherwax; *Special Effects:* Ub Iwerks, Joshua Meador; *Animators:* Jack Campbell, Walt Kelly, Ward Kimball, Fred Moore, Milt Neil, Wolfgang Reitherman, Claude Smith, Bud Swift, Harvey Toombs

This part–Technicolor episodic feature combines live-action and animation. In the framing story, humorist Robert Benchley visits the Disney studio to pitch his idea for a cartoon about a shy dragon. He wanders off from the studio tour and meets Disney's animation staff (including at least one "ringer," Alan Ladd) and animated characters (such as Donald Duck and Goofy). Benchley observes a storyboard session for a proposed cartoon about child prodigy "Baby Weems"— the young genius has his portrait painted by Salvador Dali, tells Albert Einstein the theory of relativity is incorrect, and is introduced by President Franklin D. Roosevelt (shot from behind) during a "fireside chat" as the child who can explain "how to solve our greatest problem." The animated episode about the titular dragon could be construed as a pacifist-interventionist allegory, since the reluctant beast (voice of Barrett Parker) has to be goaded into action.

FDR; Pacifist?

40 *Rhythm in the Ranks (Paramount—(c) 12/26/41)

Producer: George Pal; (no other credits)

Red-white-and-blue wooden soldiers emerge from their box and come to life in this George Pal "Puppetoon," part of the "Madcap Models" series. Little Jan wakes up late and has to rush to join his comrades for inspection; because he is last, Jan is assigned to haul the cannon. The marching soldiers pass a mirror "lake" upon which a beautiful Dutch girl doll is skating. Jan abandons the cannon and joins her. When Colonel Planck discovers this, he demotes Jan and orders him to paint the barracks. After the regiment departs, a messenger brings an "Operagram" from General Nutt of the Screwball Army (the Screwball Army would reappear in *Tulips Shall Grow* [1942], q.v.). The message musically declares war on the "parasites." Colonel Planck and the soldiers are attacked by the Screwballs and flee, but Jan, standing firm, is able to demoralize and rout the invaders.

Armed Forces; Netherlands

41 Robinson Crusoe, Jr. (Warner Bros.—10/25/41)

Producer: Leon Schlesinger; *Director:* Norman McCabe; *Script:* Melvin Millar; *Animator:* Vive Risto; *Music:* Carl W. Stalling

After his schooner is shipwrecked on a tropical island, sailor Porky Pig is enthusiastically welcomed by his very own Man Friday (wearing a stovepipe hat). Their island paradise is later disrupted by the arrival of cannibals. As Porky and his pal escape on a motorboat that Porky chopped out of a log, the pig unfurls a large American flag and the cannibals stop tossing their spears at the fugitives. Friday smiles and waves a "V" for Victory banner.

Armed Forces— Merchant Marine; Blacks; "V"; World War II

42 The Rookie Bear (MGM — 5/17/41)

Producer: Rudolf Ising; *Director:* Rudolf Ising; *Music:* Scott Bradley

An article in *Strife* magazine is headlined "Conscription Bill Passed; Draft Numbers Drawn." Number 158 is drawn from a fishbowl, followed by No. 0000. Soon, a bugle-blowing messenger awakens a hibernating Barney Bear, singing "You're in the Army Now." Barney arrives in camp; during his physical, the off-screen narrator remarks, "Flat feet like these used to be a sure-fire exemption, but not any more" (Barney's feet are pumped up with air, like automobile tires). A WPA (Works Progress Administration) crew performs "bridgework" on the bear's mouth, and "Government Inspected" is stamped on his butt. He's issued a uniform, gas mask, and assorted other equipment, which is all piled on his back (topped off with an American flag) as Barney embarks on an extended march under a blazing sun. As he nurses his popping corns, Barney is suddenly awakened by a hot coal which explodes in his fireplace — he's really in his own home, dreaming. However, a telegram arrives, ordering him to report to his local draft board, with a P.S.: "and this time, buddy, it ain't no dream."

Draft; Armed Forces — Army

43 Rookie Revue (Warner Bros. — 10/25/41)

Producer: Leon Schlesinger; *Director:* I. Freleng; *Script:* Dave Monahan; *Animator:* Richard Bickenbach; *Music:* Carl W. Stalling

A narrator invites the audience to join the Army for a day, to "get a glimpse of military life" in "typical" training camp Fort Nix (a reference to real-life Fort Dix, New Jersey). It's just before dawn, so the sleeping soldiers can be heard snoring to the tune of "You're in the Army Now." A uniformed bird emerges from a cuckoo clock and blows Reveille, awakening the real bugler, who inserts a nickle in a juke box, which then plays Reveille for the whole camp. Elmer Fudd makes a cameo appearance as the last man out of his tent, belatedly discovering he is wearing only his underwear. The mess tent features a Tex Avery caricature among the infantry and the "Suicide Squad" eating hash. Out in the field there are invisible ("camouflage") troops and makeshift tanks, including a requisitioned "Good Rumor" ice cream truck (such a truck also appears during military maneuvers in 1941's *Meet John Doughboy*, q.v.). In the final sequence, a general meticulously plots the coordinates for a coastal defense gun's target; the information is relayed to the gun via telephone, the giant cannon fires, and the general's headquarters are reduced to rubble!

Armed Forces — Army; Draft?

44 Salt Water Daffy (Universal — 6/9/41)

Producer: Walter Lantz; *Director:* Walter Lantz; *Script:* Ben Hardaway, Lowell Elliott *Animators:* Alex Lovy, Lester Kline; *Music:* Darrell Calker

As the narrator states that the Navy is one of the pillars of the nation's defense, a silly recruit is shown entering a naval training station. After a physical and intensive instruction, the sailor is sent to a naval base. Various elements of the fleet are depicted, including "over-age destroyers" (the term referred to World War I-vintage "four-stackers" and became associated with the destroyer-bases deal with Great Britain, concluded in September 1940) in reserve with "skeleton crews." Just as the trainee is finally getting his sea legs, he is shipped off for maneuvers, during which a cuckoo clock provides the timing as a gun crew methodically tracks its target. After a thunderous barrage (in which a hapless bird is caught), the captain says "last one home is a rotten egg."

Armed Forces — Navy; Britain

45   Timber (Walt Disney/RKO — 1/10/41)

Producer: Walt Disney; *Director:* Jack King; *Script:* Carl Barks; *Layouts:* Bill Herwig; *Animators:* Ed Love, Ray Patin, Judge Whitaker, Dick Lundy, Hal King, Volus Jones, Paul Allen

Hobo Donald Duck is hiking along a railroad track when he spots food through the window of a nearby logger's shack. Caught by foreman Pierre as he attempts to steal the food, Donald is put to work chopping down trees. The irascible duck, struggling with the chore, mutters "I might just as well be in a concentration camp." Donald's incompetence leads to friction with Pierre, and when Donald cuts a tree and it falls on the burly lumberjack, the chase is on.

Concentration Camps

46 $21.00 a Day (Once a Month) (Universal — 12/1/41)

Producer: Walter Lantz; *Director:* Walter Lantz; *Script:* Ben Hardaway, L.E. Elliott *Animators:* Alex Lovy, Frank Tipper; *Music:* Felix Bernard; *Music Arranger:* Darrell Calker

The Maybe So Department Store's Toyland Army Department is the home of various military toys, mostly in animal form. A uniformed bird emerges from a cuckoo clock to awaken the elephant bugler. A puppet band plays "You're in the Army Now," which segues into the title song, as performed by various toys, including helmet-wearing penguins. Woody Woodpecker makes a cameo appearance, as does Andy Panda, who blows a bugle in front of the paymaster's tent, summoning the happy recruits to receive their monthly pay — the actual draftees' wage.

Armed Forces — Army; Draft

47   We the Animals Squeak (Warner Bros. — 8/9/41)

Producer: Leon Schlesinger; *Director:* Robert Clampett; *Script:* Melvin Millar; *Animator:* I. Ellis; *Music:* Carl W. Stalling

Porky Pig emcees this parody of a contemporary radio program. He introduces Kansas City Kitty (a cat version of radio character Molly McGee, from "Fibber McGee and Molly"). Kitty says she was once a proud mouse catcher and the loving mother to her son, Patrick. But she didn't know a group of "rats [was] hatchin' the devil's own plan." As the gangster-rats sketch out plans to kidnap Patrick, their leader doodles a Hitler moustache and hairstyle on a crude drawing of their enemy "the Kat!"

Hitler

1942

48   Ace in the Hole (Universal — 6/22/42)
Producer: Walter Lantz; *Director:* Alex Lovy; *Script:* Ben Hardaway, Milt Schaffer; *Animator:* George Dane; *Music:* Darrell Calker

Woody Woodpecker (in an early, thick-legged incarnation) is grooming horses at an Army camp, under the watchful eye of his sergeant. Absorbed in the aerobatics of a fighter plane, Woody shaves a loop-the-loop design in one horse's hide. The sergeant obliges Woody's desires to fly, winding up his tail-feathers and launching him into the air. The woodpecker boards an empty "PU-2" airplane and takes off, crashing back to earth with disastrous consequences for himself, the plane, and the sergeant. As the film concludes, Woody is confronted with an endless row of horses which need grooming, as the wheelchair-bound sergeant watches him with a shotgun.

II; *Armed Forces— Air Corps, Army*

49   Air Raid Warden (Universal—12/21/42)
Producer: Walter Lantz; *Director:* Alex Lovy; *Script:* Ben Hardaway, Milt Schaffer; *Animator:* George Dane; *Music:* Darrell Calker

Air raid warden Andy Panda receives a phone call announcing a blackout, so he runs out to sound the siren mounted on his porch (until a goat eats it). After dousing their lights, several cars crash; the goat, grazing among the debris, eats a traffic signal, which continues to function from within the animal's stomach. Trying to shut off the offending light, Andy pursues the goat into a partially-constructed building. An anti-aircraft battery's searchlight spots them on a girder and they are mistaken for an enemy airplane. As the film concludes, a heavily-bandaged Andy chases the similarly-injured goat out of his bed with a stick.

I; *Air Raid Warden; Armed Forces— Army*

50   All Out for "V" (20th Century–Fox — 8/7/42)
Producer: Paul Terry; *Director:* Mannie Davis; *Script:* John Foster; *Music:* Philip A. Scheib

A peaceful forest is bombed as war is declared. A "War Production Office" is established in a log cabin and the woodland creatures are exhorted via radio to participate, as the song "We're Working for Defense" is heard. Among other things, a rabbit collects for the Red Cross, a chick stamps eggs with a "V," a goat collects scrap to be converted to rifles, and a mouse uses paint to black out windows (and the moon). A lookout bird warns his companions of invading "Beetles!" (There is some indication the word "Japanese" was edited out of existing prints of this cartoon; the beetles are only briefly seen, but are Japanese caricatures.) The pests infest a nearby patch of flowers, but are repulsed by the forest animals and flee to a nearby pond. Trying to escape on leaf-boats, they are quickly sunk. There is a dissolve to three battleships sailing in "V" formation, as an endless stream of bombers flies overhead; this shot subsequently dissolves to a golden "V" which fills the screen. This Academy Award-nominated cartoon was the first of several wartime Terrytoons featuring animals working for defense (see also *Keep 'Em Growing* and *Shipyard Symphony*, both 1943).

I; *Armed Forces — Navy; Japanese Caricatures; Production; Scrap Metal; "V"; Bonds*

51   Alona on the Sarong Seas (Paramount — 9/4/42)

Director: I. Sparber; *Script:* Jack Ward, Jack Mercer; *Animators:* Dave Tendlar, Abner Kneitel

The title of this cartoon parodies *Aloma of the South Seas*, a 1941 Dorothy Lamour film released by Paramount. As the cartoon opens, Popeye and Bluto are sailors on an American battleship anchored in a tropical lagoon. Popeye dreams of a sarong-clad Princess (Olive Oyl), so he and Bluto jump ship to find her. The usual romantic competition follows, with Bluto winding up plugging an active volcano.

II; *Armed Forces — Navy*

52   Andy Panda's Victory Garden (Universal — 9/7/42)

Producer: Walter Lantz; *Director:* Alex Lovy; *Script:* Ben Hardaway, Milt Schaffer; *Animator:* Lester Kline; *Music:* Darrell Calker

The opening credits feature Andy Panda standing inside a "V" made of vegetables. Andy and his dog "Bomber" take a wheelbarrow and tools into the yard to prepare a Victory Garden. The ground is so hard Andy uses a hand drill to bore holes for the seeds, disturbing a mole in the process. Bomber chases off this pest, then pursues a rooster which is eating the seeds as fast as Andy can plant them. The dog and rooster destroy most of the garden in their tussle, but overturn a special fertilizer which causes everything to begin growing at an outstanding rate. The media campaign promoting "Victory Gardens" suggested gardening was a form of "combat" on the home front.

I; *Victory Garden; "V"*

53   The Army Mascot (Walt Disney/RKO — 5/22/42)

Producer: Walt Disney; *Director:* Clyde Geronimi; *Script:* Carl Barks; *Animators:* George Nicholas, Claude Smith, Nick Nichols, Norman Tate; *Layouts:* Bruce Bushman; *Music:* Frank Churchill

Pluto the dog sniffs his way into "Camp Drafty," where he enviously watches various mascots (including a bulldog named Winston) receiving healthy rations. He decides to join up and — thinking it is food — gobbles down Gunther the goat's chewing tobacco, with nauseous results. Gunther attacks Pluto but misses the dog, crashes into an explosives storehouse, and is blown into the sky where he becomes embedded in the fuselage of a passing Yankee Clipper plane. The next day, a recovered Pluto — the new mascot of the "Yoo Hoo" Division — answers mess call and uses his ears to salute as the meat truck delivers his meal.

I; *Armed Forces — Army; Shortages; Draft; Churchill?*

54   Baby Wants a Bottleship (Paramount — 7/3/42)

Producer: Max Fleischer; *Director:* Dave Fleischer; *Script:* Jack Ward, Jack Mercer; *Animators:* Al Eugster, Joe Oriolo

Olive Oyl leaves SweePea in a stroller on the dock where Popeye's battleship — the *Pennsyltucky*— is tied up so she can go shopping. While Popeye is distracted, SweePea escapes down a ramp (which deploys like a landing craft) from his stroller and crawls up the battleship's gangplank. Popeye frantically attempts to capture the wandering infant. In a scene reminiscent of Chaplin's *Modern Times* (1936), Popeye is caught up in the gears in one of the gun turrets. Hit in the head with an anchor, Popeye mutters "It should happen to Hitler." When SweePea launches himself down the dock on a torpedo dolly (Lou Costello takes a similar ride in Universal's 1941 film *Keep 'Em Flying*), Popeye is forced to eat his spinach to save the child. SweePea isn't pleased at being rescued, and is only appeased when he is allowed to steer the massive warship.

II; *Armed Forces— Navy; Hitler*

55   Barney Bear's Victory Garden (MGM — 12/26/42)

Producer: Fred Quimby; *Director:* Rudolf Ising; *Music:* Scott Bradley

Attempting to plant a Victory Garden, Barney Bear is frustrated by the rock-hard soil; spotting some Army Air Corps planes overhead, Barney quickly creates a caricature of Hitler on his lot (using an old tire for an ear), and the pilots "plow" up the garden with bombs, the neat furrows resembling the American flag. The bear sows the seeds for various crops, including a rubber plant (a reference to the rubber shortage), but as he prepares for the harvest, an intruding gopher begins devouring the vegetables. As the rodent reaches for an Italian squash (which briefly resembles Mussolini's face), Barney swings at him with a shovel, but only succeeds in demolishing the squash. A mad chase ensues, resulting in the total destruction of the garden. In 1942, 16.5 million Victory Gardens were planted in the United States.

I; *Victory Garden; Armed Forces— Air Corps; Hitler; Mussolini; Shortages; Italy*

56   Barnyard WAACS (20th Century–Fox — 12/11/42)

Producer: Paul Terry; *Director:* Eddie Donnelly; *Script:* John Foster; *Music:* Philip A. Scheib

When the hens leave their nests to join the WAACs and participate in Red Cross activities, the rooster has to remain home and protect their chicks from marauding cats. However, the felines overwhelm the rooster and are absconding with the chicks (and the henhouse too!) when the WAACs return and save the day. In real life, the Women's Auxiliary Army Corps was authorized in May 1942; in 1943, the organization was given military status as the Women's Army Corps.

I; *Armed Forces— Army, Women; Home Front*

57   Blitz Wolf (MGM — 8/23/42)

Producer: Fred Quimby; *Director:* Tex Avery; *Script:* Rich Hogan; *Animators:* Ray Abrams, Irv Spence, Preston Blair, Ed Love; *Music:* Scott Bradley

The MGM pressbook for this version of the Three Little Pigs calls it "pro-democracy propaganda." The two lazy pigs have become isolationists and the third— Sgt. Pork (a reference to World War I hero Sgt. York, the subject of a 1941 Warner Bros. feature film)— espouses preparedness. "Colossal Stinker" Adolf Wolf (voiced by Pinto Colvig) violates the non-aggression pact he signed with the pigs and uses his "Mechanized Huffer und Puffer" to blow down the pigs' houses of straw and wood. Sgt. Pork welcomes his two fugitive brothers to his fortified home (which sports a sign reading "No Japs Allowed"), and the pigs fire a huge cannon — the shell lands on Tokyo, collapsing the Rising Sun seen in the background. Adolf attacks the pigs in his "Stinka Bomber PU" (a reference to Germany's JU-87 Stuka dive bomber), but is shot down by a myriad of shells labeled "Defense Bonds." After the villain crashes and goes straight to Hell, the cartoon concludes with two printed titles: "The end of Adolf" and "If You'll Buy a Stamp or Bond — We'll Skin That Skunk Across the Pond!" Academy Award nominee.

I; *Home Defense; Historical American Figures; Hitler; South America; Japan; Bonds; Armed Forces — Army; Isolationism; Shortages; World War I*

58   Blunder Below (Paramount — 2/13/42)

Producer: Max Fleischer; *Director:* Dave Fleischer; *Script:* Bill Turner, Tedd Pierce; *Animators:* Dave Tendlar, Harold Walker

Popeye and his fellow sailors (who are drawn in a more realistic fashion, somewhat resembling Fleischer's Superman character) on a battleship receive a lecture on the operation of an anti-submarine gun. After Popeye inadvertently destroys both the target and the ship towing it while trying to master the weapon, he is exiled below decks. A real enemy submarine appears and the ship's crew fires on it with no effect; a periscope (with slanted eyes) peeks through a porthole into the boiler room where Popeye is working, but he punches it and it withdraws. The sub fires a torpedo at the ship, but Popeye lifts up the ship's hull (like a woman's skirts), allowing the missile to pass harmlessly beneath it. Eating his spinach, Popeye swims to the enemy "skunk-marine," which vainly attempts to torpedo him (a buck-toothed Japanese officer wearing eyeglasses— i.e., a typical caricature of the period — sticks his head out of the torpedo tube and says "So sorry"). Popeye subdues the vessel and hauls it to the deck of his ship like a prize marlin, causing the Rising Sun to turn white. Released during the height of racial antagonism on the West Coast, *Blunder Below* probably contains the earliest anti-Japanese reference in a Hollywood cartoon. The punishment and redemption-by-valor routine appeared in at least two other Popeye cartoons, *The Might NaVy* (1941) and *Scrap the Japs* (1942), both q.v.

I; *Armed Forces — Navy; Japanese Caricatures; "V"; Armed Forces — Japan*

59   Bugs Bunny Gets the Boid (Warner Bros. — 7/4/42)

Producer: Leon Schlesinger; *Director:* Robert Clampett; *Script:* Warren Foster; *Animator:* Rod Scribner; *Music:* Carl W. Stalling

A mama buzzard sends her offspring after fresh meat. Her dopiest son reluctantly goes after Bugs Bunny, but the wily hare easily outwits the nerdy bird. Two minor topical references appear in this cartoon: Bugs "talks" the flying buzzard down to earth by stretching an antenna between his ears and talking into a microphone ("Come in, B-19"), and a tussle between the rabbit and the bird turns into a jitterbug dance to the tune of "Don't Sit Under the Apple Tree," a wartime hit. The dopey buzzard, who speaks with a Mortimer Snerd–like voice, was later dubbed "Beaky Buzzard" and appeared in other cartoons.

II; *Armed Forces — Air Corps*

60   The Bulldog and the Baby (Columbia — 7/3/42)

Producer: Frank Tashlin (Production Supervisor); *Director:* Alec Geiss; *Script:* Jack
Cosgriff; *Animator:* Volus Jones; *Music:* Paul Worth

A bulldog named Butch is left to watch the baby when the infant's black
nursemaid goes into a store to shop. When the baby's carriage rolls off, the dog
frantically tries to retrieve his charge. A sign reading "Buy War Bonds Now" is
briefly glimpsed on a wall.

II; *Bonds; Blacks*

61   The Bulleteers (Paramount — 3/26/42)

Producer: Max Fleischer; *Director:* Dave Fleischer; *Script:* Bill Turner, Carl Meyer;
Animators: Orestes Calpini, Graham Place; *Music Arr:* Sammy Timberg

A criminal mastermind uses the super "Bullet Car" to destroy police headquarters and demands the contents of the city's treasury or dire consequences will
follow. The mayor refuses to comply, so the Bullet Car transforms into a rocket-
propelled weapon and begins attacking important municipal buildings. The police
and military vainly try to stop the criminal and his diabolical machine. Superman appears, saves the captive Lois Lane, and destroys the flying Bullet Car. Afterwards, as Clark Kent and Lois Lane return to the Daily Planet building, they pass
a folding display sign with a "Buy Defense Bonds" poster (this sign is obscured
on some prints of the cartoon). Released soon after America's entrance into World
War II, this cartoon's portrayal of a menacing criminal and his gang using a weapon
of mass destruction could be construed as an oblique reference to Hitler and the
Nazis' terror bombing of civilian populations.

II; *Armed Forces — Army; Bonds*

62   Cat Meets Mouse (20th Century–Fox — 2/20/42)

Producer: Paul Terry; *Director:* Mannie Davis; *Script:* John Foster; *Music:* Philip
A. Scheib

A cat creates a box trap which he labels "Concentration Camp," and uses this
to capture various mice in the house where he lives. An alarm goes out, and the
rest of the mice organize into military units (some are dressed in what appear to
be Royal Canadian Mounted Police uniforms, but this is probably not intentional)
to attack the aggressor cat by land, sea, and air. Finally, the battered feline is
confined in his own prison and flies the white flag of surrender.

I; *Concentration Camp; War Allegory*

63   Cholly Polly (Columbia — 12/18/42)

Producer: Dave Fleischer; *Director:* Alec Geiss; *Script:* Jack Cosgriff; *Animator:* Chic
Otterstrom; *Music:* Paul Worth

A parrot observes a dog and cat sleeping peacefully, side by side. He remarks
that it is unnatural for the two to be friends, and reads a book entitled *Mein Kramp*
(a reference to Hitler's *Mein Kampf*) for suggestions on how to break up the friend-
ship. The book suggests such tactics as "Sow Suspicion" and "Divide and Conquer." (At one point an inter-title is inserted reading "Mein Kramp — Try a Stab
in the Back.") The parrot finally provokes an argument between the dog and cat,

but the book falls to the floor and his scheme is exposed, resulting in the bird's eviction from the household. This cartoon is somewhat similar in theme to *Chicken Little* (1943), q.v., although in that short the fox has a purpose in creating discord, whereas here the parrot is simply spiteful.

I; *Hitler; Fascist*

64 Cinderella Goes to a Party (Columbia — 5/3/42)

Producer: Frank Tashlin; *Director:* Alec Geiss (or Bob Wickersham); *Script:* Jack Cosgriff; *Animator:* William Shull; *Music:* Paul Worth (The screen credits for this film indicate Cinderella is "escorted by Frank Tashlin," etc.)

A topical version of the traditional fairy tale. Cinderella's fairy godmother has a magic wand labeled "AFL" (American Federation of Labor). She produces a gown (and stockings!) for Cinderella, and the young woman's pots and pans are converted into a bomber, which flies her to the ball, which in this cartoon is Prince Charming's USO Party, featuring "Hot Music — Frozen Prices." At the stroke of midnight, Cinderella's bomber reverts to its former state and she flees. The Prince (a Jerry Colonna caricature) launches a frantic search for her, offering $10,000 in war bonds as a reward. The story has a happy ending as Cinderella is found riveting tail assemblies at Lockheed. This is probably the earliest cartoon reference to women in defense work, and a similar gag appears in *Swing Shift Cinderella* (1945), q.v.

I; *Armed Forces — Air Corps; Shortages; Bonds; Women in Labor Force; Blacks; South America; Home Front; Production*

65 Coal Black and de Sebben Dwarfs (Warner Bros.—12/26/42 or 1/16/43, sources differ)

Producer: Leon Schlesinger; *Director:* Robert Clampett; *Script:* Warren Foster; *Animator:* Rod Scribner; *Music:* Carl W. Stalling

A little girl asks her mammy to tell her the tale of "So White." The Wicked Queen is a fat, ugly hoarder (of tires, sugar, etc.) and Prince Chawmin' is a flashy, zoot-suited stud who drives a fancy car (however, due to the rubber shortage, the tires are made out of shoes). So White is a sexy laundress who catches the Prince's eye. The jealous Queen orders "Murder Incorpolated" (who advertise they kill "Japs for free") to "black out" So White but the gangsters free the young woman in exchange for some kisses. She goes looking for her friends, the "sebben" [sic] dwarfs, and discovers they are now in the Army, prompting her to sing "I'm Wacky Over Khaki Now." The Queen gives So White a poisoned apple, and even Prince Chawmin's powerful kiss can't revive her; instead, the littlest dwarf does the job (causing So White's pig tails to spring upright and fly American flags). The Office of War Information analysis of this cartoon referred to it as a "vulgar parody ... [with] some excellent boogie-woogie background music."

I; *Armed Forces — Army; Blacks; Shortages; Japan; Home Defense*

66 Confusions of a Nutzy Spy (Warner Bros.—12/26/42 or 1/23/43 (sources differ)

Producer: Leon Schlesinger; *Director:* Norman McCabe; *Script:* Don Christensen; *Animator:* I. Ellis; *Music:* Carl W. Stalling

Constable Porky Pig and his lethargic bloodhound Eggbert try to capture the "Missing Lynx," a wolf-like spy with a German accent who eludes his pursuers by donning various disguises. When Porky's dog discovers a mask of Hitler, he tosses it away as if it smelled bad. The Lynx plants a time bomb (marked "Made in Berlin") on a bridge, but Eggbert finds it and returns it to the saboteur. The Lynx flees, but the dog constantly catches up to him and tries to give back the bomb. Finally, it appears the bomb is a dud, and the Lynx is tossing it around angrily when it explodes. He's blown into the air and jubilantly shouts "It worked! Sieg Heil!" The last shot of the cartoon shows his feet—forming a "V"—sticking out of a cloud. Porky Pig had earlier encountered a "mad bomber" in *The Blow Out* (1936), which bears some similarities to this cartoon.

I; *Hitler; Spies; "V"; Armed Forces—Army; Germany; Home Front*

67   Conrad the Sailor (Warner Bros.—2/14/42)

Producer: Leon Schlesinger; *Director:* Charles M. Jones; *Script:* Dave Monahan; *Animator:* Ben Washam; *Music:* Carl W. Stalling

Conrad (a cat) is a sailor on a battleship; while swabbing the decks, Conrad's bucket of soap-and-water is switched for one full of red paint by stowaway Daffy Duck. Conrad chases Daffy throughout the ship — periodically stopping to salute a diminutive admiral as he strolls by, oblivious— until the duck takes shelter inside one of the ship's big guns. Daffy is blasted into the air astride a shell, shouting "Look at me, I'm a dive bomber!" Returning to the warship, Daffy and Conrad are both pursued around the deck by the errant shell.

II; *Armed Forces—Navy*

68   Crazy Cruise (Warner Bros.—2/28/42)

Producer: Leon Schlesinger; *Director:* Fred Avery [and Bob Clampett, uncredited]; *Script:* Michael Maltese; *Animator:* Rod Scribner; *Music:* Carl W. Stalling

A spoof of movie travelogues with many topical gags. The "u" in "cruise" has been replaced by a "V," for example. The narrator states: "Because of unsettled world conditions, all ships are camouflaged," and the invisible U.S.S. *Yoohooty* passes by (this joke is based on a story about comedian Jerry Colonna, who mispronounced the name of violinist Yehudi Menuhin when the latter failed to appear for a performance, and became a running gag for something nonexistent or invisible). A "central European" oilfield is shown — its product is the "lifeblood of mechanized warfare" that an "aggressor nation ... sorely needs to run some of its stalled mechanized units," but only a single drop of oil is produced by the massive drilling machinery. The cartoon concludes as a black vulture (with the Rising Sun painted on its wings) attacks three innocent little bunnies. However, the rabbits quickly man an anti-aircraft gun as "We Did It Before and We Can Do It Again" is heard on the soundtrack. Bugs Bunny (wearing a doughboy-style helmet) appears and tells the audience "Thumbs up, Doc!" His ears form a "V" and the signature three dots and a dash from Beethoven's Fifth Symphony are heard. This final sequence seems likely to have been a last-minute (post–Pearl Harbor) addition to the cartoon, since the other gags aren't very specific.

I; *Japanese Caricatures; "V"; Armed Forces—Navy; World War I; Armed Forces—Germany?*

69   The Daffy Duckaroo (Warner Bros.—10/24/42)

Producer: Leon Schlesinger; *Director:* Norman McCabe; *Script:* Melvin Millar; *Animator:* Cal Dalton; *Music:* Carl W. Stalling

On his way to attend a rodeo, Daffy Duck, a Hollywood crooner, stops off at an Indian village to woo a cute (duck) squaw. This makes her burly Indian chief boyfriend (Beethoven's Fifth is heard when he arrives) jealous, and the chase is on. After the chief shoots arrows at him, Daffy replies by making a "gun" out of his fingers and "firing" back, explaining to the audience "We don't use any ammunition, folks, we save it all for the Army." Daffy, heading back to Hollywood, is surrounded in the Petrified Forest by a war party of Indians who steal the tires from his wagon, but then return them because "no fit-um putt-putt." The chief drives by on a motor scooter bearing the sign "Keep 'um under 40, U.S.A." (this was a reference to the new, lowered national speed limit).

II; *Shortages; "V"; Armed Forces—Army*

70   Daffy's Southern Exposure (Warner Bros.—3/2/42)

Producer: Leon Schlesinger; *Director:* Norman McCabe; *Script:* Don Christensen; *Animator:* Vive Risto; *Music:* Carl W. Stalling

Daffy Duck decides to forego the annual migratory flight to the South. A mother duck departs, followed by her ducklings towing a sign reading "Keep 'Em Flying" (also the title of a 1941 Universal feature film about military training), as the popular wartime song "We Did It Before and We Can Do It Again" is heard on the soundtrack. Daffy begins to regret his decision when his lake freezes and he is caught in a blizzard. Drawn by the smell of food, he takes refuge in a rustic cabin (a poster on the wall has a drawing of a Revolutionary War Minuteman and reads "Buy Defense Bonds Today") inhabited by a fox and a weasel. Since they're growing tired of their diet of beans, they welcome the duck as their "guest" and invite him for dinner. Daffy figures out *he* is on the menu, and rapidly departs for the South. In the final scene, Daffy admires the "South American way" from his perch in the fruity headdress of a Carmen Miranda–like singer. This cartoon has certain similarities to *Pantry Panic* (1941), a Universal cartoon starring Woody Woodpecker.

II; *Bonds; South America; World War I; Shortages*

71   Destruction, Inc. (Paramount—12/25/42)

Director: I. Sparber; *Script:* Jay Morton; *Animators:* Dave Tendlar, Tom Moore, Steve Muffati; *Music Arrangement:* Sammy Timberg

When the body of the elderly night watchman of the Metropolis Munitions Works is discovered, an organized gang of saboteurs is suspected. Clark Kent, posing as another old man, is hired as the new watchman, while Lois Lane joins the factory work force as a stenciller. She is caught eavesdropping on the saboteurs and is locked inside an experimental torpedo scheduled to be test-fired. The saboteurs also plant dynamite under one of the plant's shops. Superman rescues Lois just before the torpedo hits its target, disables the dynamite, and also prevents a truck loaded with explosives from crashing into the factory.

I; *Production; Spies; Women in the Labor Force; Armed Forces—Navy*

72 Ding Dog Daddy (Warner Bros.—12/12/42)

Producer: Leon Schlesinger; *Director:* I. Freleng; *Script:* Tedd Pierce; *Animator:* Gerry Chiniquy; *Music:* Carl W. Stalling

A dumb mutt (whose voice resembles Disney's Goofy) mistakes the bronze statue of a female dog ("Daisy") for a real animal and falls in love with it. When he kisses her, Daisy is struck by lightning and the real dog is impressed by the power of her kiss. However, a "Scrap Metal for Victory" truck arrives and Daisy is carted off. The love-struck mutt follows the truck to an armaments factory (the smokestacks puff Beethoven's Fifth), where Daisy is converted into an artillery shell. The dog wanders among the stacks of thousands of shells searching for his beloved, and finally finds one marked "Daisy." He runs out of the factory with the shell in his arms and kisses it. An explosion ensues, and the dog gleefully shouts "Wow! She hasn't changed a bit!"

I; *Scrap Metal;* "*V*"; *Production*

73 Doing Their Bit (20th Century–Fox—10/30/42)

Producer: Paul Terry; *Music:* Philip A. Scheib (no other credits available)

The second of two "Nancy" cartoons (based on the comic strip by Ernie Bushmiller), following *School Daze* (1942), q.v. Nancy is the dynamic force behind a neighborhood campaign to collect money for the U.S.O. Sluggo and her friends employ every possible means to extract money from their elders; after they win over Officer O'Toole, a makeshift amusement park is set up. Business is booming when a rich Civil War veteran appears and decides to spend his money to help out the servicemen. The kids, loaded down with donations, march to U.S.O. headquarters singing its song.

I.; *Armed Forces; Home Front; USO*

74 Donald Gets Drafted (Walt Disney/RKO—5/1/42)

Producer: Walt Disney; *Director:* Jack King; *Script:* Carl Barks; *Animators:* Paul Allen, Judge Whitaker, Ed Love, Ray Patin, Retta Scott, Jim Armstrong; *Music:* Leigh Harline (song), Paul Smith

Donald Fauntleroy Duck receives his notice and heads for local Draft Board No. 13, located at the corner of Soldiers Walk and Generals Drive. On his way, as the song "The Army's Not the Army Any More" is heard, Donald sees various recruiting posters glamorizing the Army and the Air Corps. After undergoing his physical and receiving his ill-fitting uniform (which shrinks to fit after someone dumps a bucket of water on the new soldier), Donald reports to Sgt. Pete (the spitting image of Disney cartoon villain Pegleg Pete, except without the peg-leg) for training. However, Donald is repeatedly distracted by the aircraft flying overhead, and eventually close-order drill and the manual of arms turn into a disaster (and Sgt. Pete winds up in a tree). Donald is last seen behind bars, surrounded by an enormous pile of potatoes that needs peeling.

I; *Draft; Armed Forces— Army, Air Corps*

75 The Draft Horse (Warner Bros.— 5/9/42)

Producer: Leon Schlesinger; *Director:* Charles M. Jones; *Script:* Tedd Pierce; *Animators:* Robert Cannon, Ken Harris (uncr.); *Music:* Carl W. Stalling

An oafish but patriotic plowhorse (closely resembling one seen in 1941's *Porky's Prize Pony* and 1943's *Super Rabbit*), spots a billboard advertising for Army horses, and dashes off to the local draft board to sign up. However, an extensive physical results in the enthusiastic horse receiving a "44-F" classification. Depressed that Uncle Sam doesn't want him, the horse wanders off, right into the middle of realistic, live-fire maneuvers. Barely escaping with his life, the horse runs home and contributes to the war effort by knitting "Bundles for Blue Jackets"— his first effort is a sweater with a large "V" for Victory on the back. The song "We Did It Before and We Can Do It Again" is heard once again in this cartoon. A soldier briefly seen grooming the horse strongly resembles Private Snafu.

I; *Draft;* *"V";* *Armed Forces— Army, Navy; Home Front; World War I*

76   The Ducktators (Warner Bros.— 8/1/42)

Producer: Leon Schlesinger; *Director:* Norman McCabe; *Script:* Melvin Millar; *Animator:* John Carey; *Music:* Carl W. Stalling

The credits are superimposed over a rotten egg labeled with a swastika; the cartoon itself begins in a German barnyard, as a little Hitler-like duckling hatches from a black egg who "heils" Papa Duck. When he reaches "duckhood," the budding ducktator begins delivering political diatribes to the other fowl, impressing one squat, black, balding duck who looks like Mussolini. Turning to the audience, Mussolini-duck says "He's a smart-a fellow with brains, like-a me." After delivering his own speech, he holds up an "Applause" sign as a cue for his (literally) captive audience, a little bird chained to the ground. Hitler-duck and his stormtroopers go on the march; when the Dove of Peace sets up a peace conference, Hitler-duck pushes Mussolini-duck aside and signs the treaty, then tosses it into a paper shredder. A buck-toothed Japanese duck (singing a parody of "Japanese Sandman" with the words "I'm a Japanese Sap-Man") arrives and is beaten up by a turtle; he screams he is "very, very sorry" and displays an "I am Chinese" button to try to deflect his opponent's anger. The Dove tries to stop the trio of fascist ducks with platitudes, but— after he is trampled by the marching storm troopers— joins forces with a rabbit (a Jerry Colonna caricature) to thrash the ducktators. As originally released, this cartoon ends with a printed title: "If you want this to be true, this is all you have to do— Buy War Stamps and Bonds."

I; *Hitler; Mussolini; Japanese Caricature; Blacks; Nazis; Bonds; World War I; FDR?*

77   The Early Bird Dood It (MGM — 8/29/42)

Producer: Fred Quimby; *Director:* Tex Avery; *Script:* Rich Hogan; *Animators:* Irv Spence, Preston Blair, Ed Love, Ray Abrams; *Music:* Scott Bradley

A bird carrying a "Worm Ration Book" chases a worm who acts and talks like Lou Costello. The worm allies himself with a cat who is after the bird. The cat finally gobbles up the bird, but too late for the worm, who's already been eaten by the bird.

II; *Rationing*

78   Eatin' on the Cuff (Warner Bros.— 8/15/42)

Producer: Leon Schlesinger; *Director:* Robert Clampett; *Script:* Warren Foster; *Animator:* Virgil Ross; *Music:* Carl W. Stalling

A live-action pianist introduces the story of "The Moth Who Came to Dinner." The happy moth celebrates his impending marriage by rapaciously devouring various articles of clothing on his way to the altar. At one point he savors the cuffs of a man's trousers, commenting, "And pre-war cuffs, too!" He demolishes a fox-fur stole on a mannequin — all that remains when he is finished is a denuded fox with a Hitler moustache. A big, ugly black widow spider tries to capture the moth by donning a Veronica Lake-style blonde wig. The moth's fiancée, a pretty bee, hears his calls for help and flies to the rescue ("BEE-19" is marked on her wings). The spider and the bee have a duel of stingers, and the bee wins.

I; *Hitler; Shortages; Blacks; Armed Forces — Air Corps*

79   The Eleventh Hour (Paramount — 11/20/42)

Director: Dan Gordon; *Script:* Carl Meyer, William Turner; *Animators:* Willard
   Bowsky, William Henning; *Music Arranger:* Sammy Timberg

Reporters Clark Kent and Lois Lane have been interned in Yokohama, Japan. They are under house arrest in a hotel; each night at 11:00 p.m., Kent becomes Superman and flies to a nearby shipyard where he destroys nearly-completed war ships. In response, the Japanese authorities post a warning that any further sabotage will result in the execution of the American woman reporter. The next night, Superman wrecks another ship, but is knocked out by a falling beam. When he recovers, he reads the Japanese warning. Lois has been arrested by the Japanese (portrayed as either ominous shadows or buck-toothed caricatures mouthing gibberish) and is standing in front of a firing squad when Superman flies in and rescues her. The impressions of the OWI analyst are worth quoting: "It seems to me to have a bad influence. The Japs are not to be beaten by a mythical Superman, but by the men of the United Nations."

I; *Japanese Caricatures; Armed Forces — Japan; Atrocities*

80   Fleets of Stren'th (Paramount — 3/13/42)

Producer: Max Fleischer; *Director:* Dave Fleischer; *Script:* Dan Gordon, Jack Mercer; *Animators:* Al Eugster, Tom Golden

Popeye, a sailor on a battleship, is reading a Superman comic book when he is ordered to load a torpedo onto a mosquito boat. His unorthodox methods result in a reprimand. When the ship comes under aerial attack, Popeye hops into the little craft and fires back; the enemy plane drops its bombs and flees to its carrier, whistling for assistance. A swarm of airplanes responds; one uses its landing gear to pick up and crush Popeye's boat. Blown into the air by a torpedo, Popeye is saved when enemy bullets rip open his can of spinach; fortified by the miracle vegetable, the sailor becomes a human "B-17." Flying through the air, Popeye destroys the enemy squadron (the one pilot who is glimpsed has a monkey face), sending the ruined planes crashing onto the carrier. The final scene shows Popeye sitting on the deck of the captured enemy ship — "tears" are dripping from its anchor holes, and a "V" for Victory and the three dots and a dash are cut into the hull. Popeye blows the theme from Beethoven's Fifth Symphony on his pipe as the cartoon concludes.

I; *Japanese Caricatures?; Armed Forces — Navy, Air Corps; "V"*

81   Foney Fables (Warner Bros. — 7/18/42)

Producer: Leon Schlesinger; *Director:* I. Freleng; *Script:* Michael Maltese; *Animator:* Richard Bickenbach; *Music:* Carl W. Stalling

The pages of a book of "Foney Fables" are flipped, introducing parodies of various familiar stories, many with war-relevant content. For example, when the industrious ant criticizes the lazy grasshopper, the latter smiles and flashes several $100 war bonds. The wolf in sheep's clothing is described by the narrator as "the fifth columnist of his day." The goose that *used* to lay golden eggs proudly displays its "Ever Wear Aluminum" eggs (while the "V" theme from Beethoven's Fifth Symphony plays), then dumps a whole nest-full of the shiny eggs into an aluminum scrap pile. The goose (sounding suspiciously like Daffy Duck) says "I'm doin' my bit for national defense." Old Mother Hubbard goes to the cupboard to get her dog a bone, but the cobweb-covered shelves are bare. However, the dog knows better — he opens the other side of the cupboard, exposing shelves overflowing with food, screaming "Food hoarder!"

I; *Bonds; Fifth Column; Shortages-Rationing; "V"; World War I*

82   Fresh Hare (Warner Bros. — 8/15/42)

Producer: Leon Schlesinger; *Director:* I. Freleng; *Script:* Michael Maltese; *Animator:* Manuel Perez; *Music:* Carl W. Stalling

Elmer Fudd is a Mountie pursuing the notorious Bugs Bunny through the snow-covered wilds of Canada. As Elmer tracks the fugitive rabbit, he passes several trees bearing wanted posters reading "Wanted by the Mounted Police — 'Bugs' Bunny — Dead or Alive (Preferably Dead)." The posters are all defaced with graffiti, but on the fourth poster, Bugs's picture has been given a Hitler moustache and hairstyle.

II; *Hitler; Blacks*

83   Goodbye, Mr. Moth (Universal — 5/11/42)

Producer: Walter Lantz; *Director:* Walter Lantz; *Script:* Ben Hardaway, Chuck Couch; *Animators:* Alex Lovy, Verne Harding; *Music:* Darrell Calker

A black maid shakes out a rug, dispossessing a hobo-moth. Strolling down the street, the moth spots a wool suit in the window of Andy Panda's Tailor Shop. (The government had placed sharp restrictions on the use of wool for civilian clothing in January and April.) The moth forces his way into the shop for a feast. Proprietor Andy discovers the damage when he arrives and begins to remove clothes from a bin — a shirt has "Buy Defense Bonds" gnawed into it, and "V ···–" has been chewed out of a pair of pants. Andy ultimately destroys his shop with a shotgun as he tries to eliminate the pest.

II; *Bonds; Blacks; "V"*

84   The Hare Brained Hypnotist (Warner Bros. — 10/31/42)

Producer: Leon Schlesinger; *Director:* I. Freleng; *Script:* Michael Maltese; *Animator:* Phil Monroe; *Music:* Carl W. Stalling

Elmer Fudd reads a book on hypnotism and tries to mesmerize his eternal rival, Bugs Bunny, but Bugs turns the tables and makes Elmer think *he* is a rabbit.

The animalistic Elmer temporarily gets the best of his long-eared opponent, but eventually the status quo is restored. As the cartoon concludes, Bugs looks at his watch and says "I'm overdue at the airport, I'm the B-19," then flies off into the sky as Beethoven's Fifth Symphony's "V" theme is heard.

II; *"V"; Armed Forces — Air Corps*

85 A Hull of a Mess (Paramount — 10/16/42)

Director: I. Sparber; *Script:* Jack Ward, Jack Mercer; *Animators:* Al Eugster, Joe Oriolo; *Music:* Winston Sharples

Popeye and Bluto are rival defense contractors bidding for a naval contract. The contract will be awarded to whoever completes the construction of a battleship first. The competitors, in adjoining shipyards, work frantically, both using novel methods— Bluto makes portholes with an acetylene torch and his fist; Popeye "knits" anchor chains. Popeye finishes first. In a dubious gesture of wartime unity, Bluto puts nitroglycerine in the champagne bottle to be used for the ship's christening, ruining Popeye's craft. Amid the rubble, Popeye eats his spinach and rapidly builds a whole fleet of battleships. As the cartoon concludes, Popeye is atop the mast of the lead ship, and a sunlit "V" appears behind him.

I; *Armed Forces — Navy; "V"; Production*

86 Japoteurs (Paramount — 9/18/42)

Director: I. Sparber; *Script:* Joe Morton; *Animators:* Myron Waldman, Graham Place; *Music:* Sammy Timberg (The copyright information for this cartoon conflicts with the on-screen credits. Seymour Kneitel is listed as director, Bill Turner and Carl Meyer as scripters, and Nicholas Tafuri as an animator instead of Place.)

A sinister Japanese agent reads *The Daily Planet* story headlined "World's Largest Bombing Plane Finally Completed." He rises and bows to a picture of the Statue of Liberty as it converts into the Rising Sun. At the airfield, last-minute preparations for a test flight are being made. Reporter Lois Lane stows away on the craft to get an exclusive story, unaware the head Japanese spy and two henchmen are also on board. The spies take control of the bomber and head for Tokyo, but Lois radios for help before she is caught. The stolen plane drops a bomb on the airport's runaway, preventing fighters from taking off in pursuit. Superman reaches the craft, and saves Lois— who is seconds away from being dropped out the bomb bay — but the head spy wrecks the plane's controls and sends it into a dive toward Metropolis. Superman takes Lois to safety and then catches the craft before it can crash.

I; *Japanese Caricatures; Spies; Armed Forces — Air Corps*

87 *Jasper and the Haunted House (Paramount — (c)10/23/42)

Director: George Pal

Part of the "Madcap Models" series of Technicolor Puppetoons (puppet animation). Jasper, a little black boy, appeared in 20 shorts between 1942 and 1947, usually in a bucolic setting. The other continuing characters in the series were pumpkin-headed Professor Scarecrow (voiced by Roy Glenn) and the Black Crow, two bragging schemers who constantly try to get Jasper in trouble. In *Jasper and the Haunted House*, Jasper is sent by his mother to deliver a gooseberry pie to Deacon Jones. The scarecrow and the crow, hoping to take possession of the pie, misdirect Jasper to the local haunted house. When Jasper protests that he's scared of ghosts, they assure him all the ghosts have been drafted: "They was all 1-A born."

II; *Armed Forces — Army; Blacks; Draft*

88   Kickin' the Conga Round (Paramount — 1/17/42)

Producer: Max Fleischer; *Director:* Dave Fleischer; *Script:* Bill Turner, Ted Pierce; *Animators:* Tom Johnson, George Germanetti

Sailors Popeye and Bluto get shore leave when their battleship docks in a South American port. When they visit the famous dancer Olivia Oyla, Bluto impresses her with magic tricks; a jealous Popeye retaliates with a trick of his own (he puts his handkerchief over Bluto's face, then punches him! Afterwards, he removes the cloth and exclaims, "Look, a blackout!"). Later, open warfare breaks out between the two rivals in a nightclub, when both of them want to dance the conga with Olivia. The Shore Patrol arrives and puts a stop to their shenanigans.

II; *Armed Forces — Navy; South America; Home Defense*

89   King Midas, Junior (Columbia — 12/18/42)

Producer: Dave Fleischer; *Directors:* Paul Sommer, John Hubley; *Script:* Jack Cosgriff; *Animator:* Volus Jones; *Music:* Paul Worth

As this "Color Rhapsody" begins, the narrator says King Midas XIII will receive the magic touch on his 21st birthday, soon to arrive. An eager crowd of his subjects gathers as the "touch" arrives via Western Union. However, the touch turns everything to rubber instead of gold — a doughnut, for example, becomes an automobile tire. People in the little kingdom are in great distress until they learn rubber has become the scarcest commodity in the world.

II; *Shortages*

90   Lights Fantastic (Warner Bros. — 5/23/42)

Producer: Leon Schlesinger; *Director:* I. Freleng; *Script:* Sgt. Dave Monahan; *Animator:* Gil Turner; *Music:* Carl W. Stalling

The gags in this cartoon revolve around the animated neon signs on Broadway. A theatre marquee announces "Caught in the Draft with Selected Shorts" (*Caught in the Draft* was a 1941 Paramount feature film starring Bob Hope). An interesting sidelight to this cartoon is that the bright lights of Times Square and Broadway were soon shut down by blackout restrictions; this indirectly brought animator Otto Messmer back into the cartoon industry, since he had been working in the neon sign field and went to work for Paramount when this business was shut down for the duration.

II; *Draft; South America*

91   Lights Out (20th Century–Fox — 4/17/42)

Producer: Paul Terry; *Director:* Eddie Donnelly; *Script:* John Foster; *Music:* Philip A. Scheib

A witch invites Army private Gandy Goose (who talks like Ed Wynn) and Sergeant Cat (who talks like Jimmy Durante) to a party "for all the boys in the service." The party is held in a haunted house, and all of the other guests are ghosts. When Gandy asks Sgt. Cat if he thinks their hostess is a little strange, the cat replies "I'm in the Army now, I'm not supposed to think!" However, it's all a dream, and when Gandy wakes up in his tent, Sgt. Cat orders him to "leave me out" of further dreams. This was the first of several cartoons depicting Gandy as a soldier—*Night Life in the Army* (1942), q.v., was also a "dream sequence" story.

II; *Armed Forces—Army*

92   Malice in Slumberland (Columbia—11/20/42)

Producer: Dave Fleischer; *Director:* Alec Geiss; *Animator:* Ray Patterson; *Music:* Eddie Kilfeather

After a busy day of war-related activities, a dog is trying to get some sleep, but a leaky faucet disturbs his rest. His patriotic schedule includes "Home Front work, War Relief work, Auxiliary Police practice, Air Raid Warden tour...." Trying to stop the drip, the dog eventually destroys his entire house.

II; *Home Front; Air Raid Warden*

93   Many Tanks (Paramount—5/15/42)

Producer: Max Fleischer; *Director:* Dave Fleischer; *Script:* Bill Turner, Carl Meyer; *Animators:* Tom Johnson, Frank Endres

Army private Bluto is restricted to camp. In order to sneak out for a date with Olive Oyl, Bluto lures his pal Popeye onto the base, beats him up, steals his sailor's uniform, and departs. Popeye, dressed in Bluto's oversize Army uniform, is ordered to drive a tank during maneuvers. With the aid of his spinach, Popeye drives the tank to Olive's house and roughly retrieves his own clothes from Bluto. Bluto would appear as a G.I. in one other wartime cartoon, *Spinach-Packin' Popeye* (1944), q.v. The music score of this cartoon includes "You're in the Army Now," "Yankee Doodle Dandy," and a conga beat.

II; *Armed Forces—Army, Navy*

94   *The New Spirit (Walt Disney/U.S. Treasury Department—(c) 1/21/42)

Producer:: Walt Disney; *Directors:* Wilfred Jackson, Ben Sharpsteen; *Music:* Oliver Wallace, Cliff Edwards

This cartoon, produced by Disney for the U.S. Treasury, was released through the War Activities Committee. It had a record 11,700 bookings in the six weeks prior to 15 March (tax day). Donald Duck listens to a radio broadcast which tells him "Your whole country is mobilizing for total war.... Your country needs you." One patriotic act would be to pay one's taxes promptly—when Donald mutters "What's the hurry?" the radio replies—"Your country need taxes to beat the Axis!" This inspires Donald to quickly complete the new simplified tax form and rush to deliver his $13 check. As stacks of coins mount next to tax forms, they become factory smoke stacks and munitions plants. The narrator says the money will be used to "blast the aggressors from the seas," and a warship bearing the Rising Sun logo explodes and sinks, as Beethoven's Fifth Symphony "V" theme is heard. A swastika-marked bomber goes down in flames. The narrator continues: "Taxes ... to beat to earth the destroyer of freedom and peace." A monster Nazi war machine (somewhat reminiscent of Tchernabog from Disney's feature *Fantasia*) looms over a city but a montage of American military might reduces it to rubble. "God Bless America" is heard as the narrator invokes President Roosevelt's "Four Freedoms." Ironically, this cartoon's $80,000 cost drew charges of "war profiteering" in Congress!

    I; *Home Front;* "*V*"; *Armed Forces — Japan; Germany; FDR; Production; Nazi*

95   Night Life in the Army (20th Century–Fox — 10/12/42)

Producer: Paul Terry; *Director:* Mannie Davis; *Script:* John Foster; *Music:* Philip A. Scheib

    Private Gandy Goose's sleepwalking and vivid dreams disturb his tent-mate, Sgt. Cat. In one fantasy sequence, Gandy and Cat are in the clouds; Gandy asks his pal if he would like to learn to fly and "get a commission" (Air Corps pilots were officers) but the sergeant says he would rather have "straight salary." They begin to swoop through the sky like birds, but collide and plunge to earth, waking up on the floor of their tent. Although Sgt. Cat orders Gandy to leave him out of future dreams, he peeks into the goose's next dream and sees him kissing a beautiful girl (goose). "I would give a month's pay to have that guy's dream," says Sgt. Cat, and soon he has joined Gandy in slumberland. The cat is in the backseat of a car with a sexy girl (cat), but chauffeur Gandy rams them into a speeding train, and they both wake up. Partial remake of *String Bean Jack* (1938).

    II; *Armed Forces — Army*

96   Nutty News (Warner Bros. — 5/23/42)

Producer: Leon Schlesinger; *Director:* Robert Clampett; *Script:* Warren Foster; *Animator:* Virgil Ross; *Music:* Carl W. Stalling

    Another Warners newsreel spoof, cf. *Porky's Snooze Reel* (1941), q.v. The credits appear upside down, and the narrator has a speech impediment (pronouncing "r" as "w"). Among the numerous war-oriented gags are fireflies being forced to "black out" their glow, the battleship U.S.S. *California* (which always sails in bright sunshine), and a barber getting a little boy to sit still in the chair by frightening him with an "Adolf-in-a-box."

    II; *Hitler; Armed Forces — Navy; Home Defense*

97   Old Blackout Joe (Columbia — 8/27/42)

Director: Paul Sommer, John Hubley; *Script:* Ford Banes; *Animator:* Jim Armstrong; *Music:* Paul Worth

    An air raid warden stationed at Harlem's Post 13 tries to enforce a "totalitarian blackout," but is frustrated by the persistence of a little gas flame that refuses to go out. The warden puts it under his helmet and even swallows it, but only the "all clear" signal (allowing the lights to go back on), relieves him of his burden (and then he discovers he has a burning stick of dynamite to contend with!). Assistant director of the Office of Civilian Defense, during the early months of the war,

Eleanor Roosevelt had assiduously lobbied for the participation of African Americans in the civil defense program.

I; *Blacks; Air Raid Warden*

98 Olive Oyl and Water Don't Mix (Paramount — 5/8/42)
Producer: Max Fleischer; *Director:* Dave Fleischer; *Script:* Jack Mercer, Jack Ward; *Animators:* Dave Tendlar, Abner Kneitel

Sailors Popeye and Bluto, whose battleship is docked in port, agree to have nothing to do with trouble-making "female women." However, when Olive Oyl comes aboard and asks to be given a tour of the ship, the two men frantically compete for her attentions. She is ignorant of ships, and largely unaware of Popeye and Bluto's rivalry; spotting the "Powder Room," Olive goes in to powder her nose, lights a match because it is dark and ... boom! Some time later, a heavily-bandaged Popeye and Bluto reaffirm their belief that "women are trouble-makers." This was Bluto's belated wartime debut, possibly delayed because of confusion about how to retain the character's negative aspects (as Popeye's rival and enemy) without making him seem unpatriotic, a situation that nonetheless occurs in *A Hull of a Mess* (1942), q.v.

II; *Armed Forces — Navy*

99 *Out of the Frying Pan, Into the Firing Line (Walt Disney/War Production Board —(c)7/24/42)
Producer: Walt Disney; *Director:* Jack King; *Animators:* Josh Meador, Marvin Woodward, John Lounsbery, Les Clark, Norman Tate, Andy Engman, George Rowley, George Nicholas, Nick Nichols, Jack Hanna

A three-minute cartoon made for the War Production Board. Minnie Mouse is about to pour her bacon grease into Pluto's bowl when a voice from the radio admonishes: "Don't!! Housewives of America, one of the most important things you can do is save your waste kitchen fats.... We and our Allies need ... fats ... to make glycerin [for] explosives...." Pluto is aggravated, but the announcer says meat drippings will help "crush" the Axis as scenes of a munitions factory are followed by footage of enemy ships being sunk. Pluto salutes (with his ear) a photograph of Mickey Mouse in an Army uniform (the only time during the war that Mickey was so portrayed); following instructions about how to prepare the grease, Pluto takes a can of it to the local butcher shop, and is rewarded with a string of hotdogs (as opposed to cash, which most people would receive). His tail proudly flies the American flag as he departs.

I; *Home Front; Armed Forces — Army, Navy, Germany, Japan*

100 The Outpost (20th Century–Fox — 7/10/42)
Producer: Paul Terry; *Director:* Mannie Davis; *Script:* John Foster; *Music:* Philip A. Scheib

Gandy Goose and tough Sgt. Cat (aka Sourpuss, in pre-war cartoons) are stationed on a Pacific island when Japanese bombers attack. Using a coconut-firing palm tree as an anti-aircraft gun, Gandy downs one of the planes; another drops its bombs and retreats to a carrier, with Gandy and Sgt. Cat pursuing in a row-boat. The carrier's crew consists of a large number of squealing pigs, with buck teeth and slanted eyes. (This was the first of several Fox and Paramount cartoons portraying the Japanese as animal-like creatures, cf. *Scrap the Japs* and *Somewhere in the Pacific*, both 1942, q.v.) The two Americans board the Japanese warship and after a wild melee (Sgt. Cat smokes a booby-trapped Japanese cigar and says "Ya can't trust those Japs") succeed in blowing it up; the Rising Sun sinks as Gandy and Sgt. Cat escape in their dinghy and give the "V" for Victory sign.

I; *Japanese Caricatures; "V"; Armed Forces — Army, Japan*

101   Pigeon Patrol (Universal — 8/3/42)

Producer: Walter Lantz; *Director:* Alex Lovy; *Script:* Ben Hardaway, Milt Schaffer; *Animator:* Ralph Somerville; *Music:* Darrell Calker

Homer Pigeon (a caricature of Red Skelton's Clem Kadiddlehopper charac-ter, here in his screen debut) decides to join the Signal Corps after his erstwhile girlfriend Mazie Day swoons over some handsome carrier pigeons. At headquar-ters, Home passes signs reading "Uncle Sam Needs Birds Like You" and "Buy Defense Bonds," but is rejected because he is flat-chested. On his way home, he spots a Japanese buzzard downing a carrier pigeon; the wounded bird gives Homer his message to deliver. The buzzard steals the message from Homer, who becomes infuriated, shouting "Remember Pearl Harbor and Singapore! And a kick in the Axis for Hitler!" The enemy bird is knocked down by a passing plane; Homer retrieves the message, delivers it, and wins back Mazie's affections.

I; *Armed Forces — Army, Navy; Bonds; Japanese Caricatures; Hitler; Pearl Harbor; Britain*

102   Saps in Chaps (Warner Bros. — 4/11/42)

Producer: Leon Schlesinger; *Director:* I. Freleng; *Script:* Sgt. Dave Monahan; *Animator:* Manuel Perez; *Music:* Carl W. Stalling

A series of sight gags about the conquest of the American West and cowboy life in general. A running joke concerns the attempt of a Pony Express rider to mount his horse. A reference to "when the West was young" is accompanied by a shot of Mount Rushmore in which the famous Americans depicted are all youth-ful. "We Did It Before and We Can Do It Again" is heard on the soundtrack, and a rodeo sequence includes a horse named "Sabotage."

II; *World War I; Historical Americans*

103   School Daze (20th Century–Fox — 9/18/42)

Producer: Paul Terry; *Script:* Ernie Bushmiller; *Music:* Philip A. Scheib

A class of elementary school children tries to convince their teacher that "Nancy" comic books can "show you the way" better than boring textbooks. When they open their comics, Nancy and her pals come to life. After Civic Pride Week and an anti-noise campaign, Nancy and Sluggo are inspired by a Defense Bonds poster to start their own "home defense guard." In the next scene, the children (including a little Chinese boy), armed with toy rifles, march to defend "da most important joint in town," the Candy and Ice Cream Parlor.

II; *Bonds; Home Defense; China*

104 Scrap the Japs (Paramount-11/20/42)

Director: Seymour Kneitel; *Script:* Carl Meyer; *Animator:* Tom Johnson, Ben Solomon

Popeye is doing punishment duty on a carrier after jumping out of his plane without a parachute. When a "cloud" appears and drops bombs, Popeye leaps into his plane to investigate. The "cloud" is artificial, and attached to a Japanese plane piloted by a slant-eyed, buck-toothed caricature. After firing a shell that merely bounces off Popeye's head, the enemy flees. Popeye calls him a "storm trooper" (a linkage between Germany and Japan) and destroys the plane. He then lands on a barge labeled "Jap Scrap Repair Ship" and engages the enemy; after eating his spinach (and briefly changing into the Statue of Liberty), Popeye sinks the craft. A battleship appears and — as "Yankee Doodle" is heard — Popeye defeats the crew, tossing them through the superstructure to form a "V," and uses a piece of railing as a "can opener" to rip open the hull. As the cartoon concludes, Popeye is towing the barge behind his plane; the captive Japanese are in a cage on the barge, squealing like mice in a trap. Note: in one scene, Popeye remarks "I never seen a Jap that wasn't yeller." The term "yellow" was rarely used in the pejorative sense to refer to the Japanese, because this could also reflect badly on our Asian allies, the Chinese.

I; *Japanese Caricatures; Armed Forces — Navy, Japan; Scrap Metal; "V"*

105 Sham Battle Shenanigans (20th Century–Fox — 3/20/42)

Producer: Paul Terry; *Director:* Connie Rasinski; *Script:* John Foster; *Music:* Philip A. Scheib

The first cartoon featuring Gandy Goose and Sgt. Cat in the Army. Private Gandy relates his experiences during some recent war games to a radio audience. Gandy and Sgt. Cat, members of the Blue Army, were sent in their jeep to capture the town of Castor Oil. When the cat is "killed," the dumb goose tries to bury him. Later, they have to cope with a gas attack.

I; *Armed Forces — Army*

106 Sky Trooper (Walt Disney/RKO — 11/6/42)

Producer: Walt Disney; *Director:* Jack King; *Script:* Carl Barks; *Animators:* Dan MacManus, Judge Whitaker, Charles Nichols, Jack King, John McManus, Ed Love, Paul Allen, Ray Patin, Walter Scott, James Armstrong, Ed Aardal, Don Towsley, Josh Meador; *Music:* Frank Churchill; *Layouts:* Bill Herwig

Army private Donald Duck observes bombers passing over the Mallard Field Air Training Base and wishes he could fly; Sgt. Pete allows him to apply for training, but only after he peels a huge pile of potatoes. Passing his tests, Donald is given a parachute and taken up in a plane, but balks when Pete orders him to jump out. A wild scramble inside the plane follows, and eventually the sergeant and Donald both plunge out of the craft, holding onto a bomb! The bomb makes a direct hit on the general's headquarters and as the cartoon ends, a bandaged Donald and Sgt. Pete are peeling potatoes as punishment.

I; *Armed Forces — Army, Air Corps*

107 Somewhere in the Pacific (20th Century–Fox — 12/25/42)

Producer: Paul Terry; *Director:* Mannie Davis; *Script:* John Foster

On their tropical island base, commandos Sgt. Cat and Private Gandy Goose receive orders (from a kangaroo messenger) to attack an enemy stronghold. Setting out in a little boat, the two Americans run into a fleet of "Jap" subs but sink them all, causing the crews (squealing pigs) to abandon their doomed vessels. A Japanese carrier appears (the commanding admiral is another pig, wearing eyeglasses); Gandy shoots down several airplanes and Sgt. Cat rams the warship and sinks it. The crew (more pigs) swim to a nearby island. Sgt. Cat and Gandy land there and are confronted by knife-wielding Japanese pig-soldiers, but seal their enemies up in a cave and replace the Rising Sun flag with the Stars and Stripes. As they tow the island back to headquarters, an off-screen chorus sings "Glory, glory, hallelujah, the Yanks go marching on."

I; *Armed Forces — Army, Japan; Japanese Caricatures; Ally-Australia (?); South America*

108 Song of Victory (Columbia — 9/4/42)

Producer: Dave Fleischer; *Supervisor:* Frank Tashlin; *Director:* Bob Wickersham; *Script:* Leo Salkin; *Layout:* Zack Schwartz; *Color:* Clark Watson; *Animators:* Howard Swift, Phil Duncan, Bernard Garbutt; *Music:* Eddie Kilfeather

As the "V" theme from Beethoven's Fifth Symphony is heard, a printed title states: "Any similarity between the Vulture, Gorilla, and Hyena ... to certain dictators, either living or dead (we hope) is purely intentional...." A peaceful forest is "invaded" by a Hitler-vulture, a loutish Mussolini-gorilla, and a buck-toothed Hirohito-hyena, who enslave the cute animal inhabitants. The Vulture makes a speech (in German double-talk) to the animals, his body contorting into a swastika and other shapes as he talks. The dictators set up housekeeping in a cave and force the other animals to provide food for them. Resistance flares up after the Gorilla and Hyena sadistically beat a little chipmunk. The animals use the "V"— the letter (formed by geese in the sky and fireflies' glow, among other things) and the three dots-and-a-dash Morse code — to terrify the Vulture and his henchmen. Skunks force the villains to leave their stronghold, and the forest creatures pursue them to the edge of a cliff; the tortured chipmunk steps forward and blows a derisive "raspberry" at the Vulture, Gorilla, and Hyena, who— yellow streaks on their backs— topple off the edge in terror. The cartoon concludes with Beethoven's Fifth Symphony on the soundtrack as the rays of the sun form a blazing "V" in the sky. The OWI report said: "It is important to note that the invaded ... oppose [the invaders] ... not with force, but with symbolism — and triumph" (by destroying the invaders' morale).

I; "*V*"; *Hitler; Mussolini; Hirohito; Atrocities*

109 A Tale of Two Kitties (Warner Bros. — 11/21/42)

Producer: Leon Schlesinger; *Director:* Robert Clampett; *Script:* Warren Foster, Tedd Pierce?; *Animators:* Robert McKimson, Rod Scribner; *Music:* Carl W. Stalling

Dopey cats Babbitt (voiced by writer Tedd Pierce) and Catstello (voice of Mel Blanc)—caricatures of Abbott and Costello—attempt to catch Tweety Bird (although he is not given a name in this, his cartoon debut), whose nest is high atop a spindly tree. At one point, Babbitt is shown working in a Victory Garden, whistling "We Did It Before and We Can Do it Again." Babbitt uses a giant slingshot to launch the pudgy Catstello— outfitted with artificial wings— into the air. As he flies, Catstello says "I'm a Spitfire!" Tweety puts on an oversized air raid warden's helmet and calls "Interceptor Command" to report the airborne intruder — searchlights flash across the sky and Catstello is promptly shot down. Back on the ground, air raid warden Tweety criticizes the two exhausted and bug-eyed cats for violating the blackout.

II; *Victory Garden; Britain; Air Raid Warden; World War I; Home Defense; Armed Forces— RAF*

110   Tire Trouble (20th Century–Fox — 7/24/42)

Producer: Paul Terry; *Director:* Eddie Donnelly; *Script:* John Foster; *Music:* Philip A. Scheib

Gandy Goose and Sourpuss the Cat are driving along in their dilapidated car when they hear a radio broadcast predicting they will soon be walking. Immediately afterwards, they have a flat. The tires are all heavily patched and attempts to make repairs prove futile (Gandy tries to inflate the tire, claiming he is an "air warden," but fails). At a tire shop, all Gandy can find are substitutes made of doughnuts, baloney, and funeral wreaths; he buys a baloney tire but after he puts it on the car, dogs come along and eat it! Sourpuss states: "We gave up tires to help in the war, so get out and walk, cause there ain't any more." The cat and goose shake hands and walk off together. (Tires were one of the first items to be restricted during the war; gas rationing was enforced mostly to save rubber, not gasoline.)

II; *Shortages; Home Defense*

111   Toll Bridge Troubles (Columbia — 11/27/42)

Producer: Dave Fleischer; *Director:* Bob Wickersham; *Script:* Leo Salkin; *Animators:* Lou Schmidt, Howard Swift, Phil Duncan; *Music:* Ed Kilfeather

The Crow sets up a tower — labeled "Sucker Detector"— equipped with sound detectors near a bridge. When he spots the Fox approaching on a motor scooter, the Crow switches the "Free Public Bridge" sign for one reading "Toll Bridge." The Fox, unwilling to pay the Crow's price, takes the inner tube out of a tire (marked "Priority 467") and unsuccessfully tries to float across. Several attempts later, an airborne Fox is caught by searchlights during a blackout and brought down. He finally pays the two-dollar fee; the Crow squawks "Sucker!" as his victim plunges off a dead-end into the water.

II; *Shortages; Home Defense*

112   *Tulips Shall Grow (Paramount — 6/26/42)

Producer: George Pal

This Puppetoon features some of the same characters as *Rhythm in the Ranks* (1941), q.v. Dutch boy Jan is courting Janette, and they are dancing together in front of her windmill home when thunder rolls and ominous music begins to play. Horror-struck, the two young people observe the mechanical "Screwball Army" (the soldiers are literally made of nuts and bolts) swarming over the horizon, the goose-stepping troops trampling the tulips in their path. Bat-like planes drop bombs, hitting the church and other buildings; tanks float down on parachutes, chasing and separating the lovers. Jan goes to the damaged church and prays; as tears fall from his eyes, the camera tilts up — past "V"-shaped beams — to the sky. Clouds gather and raindrops fall; the robotic Screwballs scatter. One gives the fascist salute, then rusts into immobility and topples over. A tank rolls over a fallen soldier and is then swallowed up in the mud (this is similar to the "ice" scene in Eisenstein's 1938 Russian feature *Alexander Nevsky*). Jan and Janette are reunited, and as they dance through their rebuilt village, they look up to see puffs of smoke form a huge "V" in the sky as Beethoven's Fifth Symphony plays. The end title reads "Tulips Shall Always Grow." Academy Award nominee.

I; *"V"; War Allegory; Netherlands; Nazis*

113   The Vanishing Private (Walt Disney/RKO — 9/25/42)
Producer: Walt Disney; *Director:* Jack King; *Script:* Carl Barks; *Layouts:* Bill Herwig; *Animators:* Paul Allen, Ed Love, Hal King, Art Scott, Judge Whitaker, Charles Nichols, Bill Tytla, Woolie Reitherman; *Music:* Oliver Wallace; *Song:* Leigh Harline ("The Army's Not the Army Anymore")
      Army private Donald Duck is criticized for "camouflaging" a cannon by painting polka dots on it. Sgt. Pete informs him that the purpose of camouflage is to *hide* an object (to which Donald sheepishly replies, "Oh, I didn't know"). Donald uses some experimental "Invisible Paint" which, predictably, makes the whole gun vanish. The sergeant thinks a "fifth columnist" has stolen the cannon, but then runs into the invisible weapon. Donald, inside the invisible cannon, is blown into the bucket of paint by Sgt. Pete, and becomes invisible himself. The irascible sergeant, armed with grenades, chases Donald around the camp — when they run into a general, Pete's explanation that he is chasing an invisible duck is not accepted. As the cartoon concludes, a now-visible Donald walks guard duty outside the padded cell where Sgt. Pete is confined.

I. *Armed Forces — Army; Fifth Column*

114   The Wabbit Who Came to Supper (Warner Bros. — 3/28/42)
Producer: Leon Schlesinger; *Director:* I. Freleng; *Script:* Michael Maltese; *Animator:* Richard Bickenbach; *Music:* Carl W. Stalling
      The fat version of Elmer Fudd learns he has inherited $3 million from his Uncle "Wooie," on the condition that he harm no animals. Like Monty Woolley in the feature film *The Man Who Came to Dinner* (1942), Bugs Bunny — armed with knowledge of Uncle Wooie's will — becomes an obnoxious houseguest who refuses to leave. However, Elmer receives a telegram from his lawyer: after various taxes (including a "Defense Tax") have been deducted from his inheritance, he actually *owes* $1.98.

II; *Home Front*

115   Wacky Blackout (Warner Bros. — 7/14/42)
Producer: Leon Schlesinger; *Director:* Robert Clampett; *Script:* Warren Foster; *Animator:* Sid Sutherland; *Music:* Carl W. Stalling

A yokel announcer introduces the audience to a farmyard where all the animals have adjusted to wartime conditions. The spitz (dog), in Civil Defense attire, spits to put out fires; a cow has increased her milk production; a woodpecker is now a Lockheed riveter; a turtle thinks he is a "tank," and caterpillars are proud of their "retreads." A dog fakes a blackout to steal a kiss from his girlfriend. Finally, a couple of elderly pigeons in the barn are shown; when the announcer recalls their service in World War One as messengers, the old birds are rejuvenated and sing "We Did It Before and We Can Do It Again," which is accompanied by a dissolve to a live-action shot of the American flag.

I; *Home Front; Rationing; Production; Air Raid Warden; World War I*

116   The Wacky Wabbit (Warner Bros. — 5/2/42)

Producer: Leon Schlesinger; *Director:* Robert Clampett; *Script:* Warren Foster; *Animator:* Sid Sutherland; *Music:* Carl W. Stalling

The fat version of Elmer Fudd goes into the desert, prospecting for gold. He passes a "Defense Bonds" sign as he sings "Oh, Susanna, oh don't you cry for me, I'm gonna get me lots of gold, 'V' for Victory." Wearing a cow skull on his head, Bugs Bunny appears and harmonizes along. After endless persecution by the rabbit, Elmer finally gets gold — a tooth yanked from his own mouth.

II; *"V"; Bonds*

117   Who's Who in the Zoo (Warner Bros. — 1/31/42)

Producer: Leon Schlesinger; *Director:* Norman McCabe; *Script:* Melvin Millar; *Animator:* John Carey; *Music:* Carl W. Stalling

A comic tour of the Azusa Zoo, including several scenes with zookeeper Porky Pig. The zoo's inhabitants include the "Missing Lynx," a bald eagle who wears a toupee, and a black panther who tosses his supper bowl into a pile marked "Aluminum for National Defense." Later in the cartoon, a haggard rabbit surrounded by baby bunnies mutters: "I can't do it! There's a limit!" He holds up a notice reading "The Government Hereby Notifies You to INCREASE YOUR PRODUCTION 100%"

II; *Scrap Metal; Production*

118   Wild Honey (MGM — 11/7/42)

Director: Rudolf Ising; *Script:* Henry Allen; *Animators:* Michael Lah, Rudy Zamora, Don Williams; *Music:* Scott Bradley

After reading "How to Get Along Without a Ration Book," Barney Bear heads into the forest in search of wild honey as a sugar substitute. He decoys the bees away from their hive, using a sexy mechanical queen bee that resembles Veronica Lake. The bees follow her in a conga line, but when they discover the deception, go after Barney with a vengeance. They form a bomber-like formation and drop "bombs" (more bees) on the hapless bear. Taking refuge in a nearby lake, the bee-stung Barney reads the last page of the book , which contains a picture of a sugar ration card and the advice — "Next time use your ration book!"

I; *Rationing; South America*

119   Wolf Chases Pigs (Columbia — 4/20/42)

Producer: Frank Tashlin; *Directors:* Paul Sommer, John Hubley; *Animator:* Bob
Wickersham; *Music:* Paul Worth (Copyright information credits Tashlin, Wickersham, Leo Salkin, Hubley, and Sommer but does not specify their roles.)
  Learning the three little pigs have joined the Army, the Wolf reports to
Recruiting Office 13 and does the same. However, he discovers they are sergeants,
and thus his plans to keep chasing them are foiled; it is only "Open Season for Japs."
Eventually, Private Wolf becomes a model soldier, serves his hitch, and is mustered
out. When he spots the pigs, also discharged and back in civilian clothes, the Wolf
resumes his pursuit ("Can I help it if I love pork?"). This cartoon was probably produced prior to Pearl Harbor, since otherwise it is difficult to explain why characters would be shown *leaving* the armed forces in the midst of a national emergency.
  II; *Armed Forces — Army; Japanese*

120   Woodsman Spare That Tree (Columbia — 7/2/42)

Director: Bob Wickersham; *Script:* Jack Cosgriff; *Animator:* Phil Duncan; *Music:*
Eddie Kilfeather
  The title of this cartoon refers to Henry Russell's popular 19th-century song,
"Woodman, Spare That Tree." The Fox, who works for the "Victory Lumber Com-
pany" (a sign on the office reads "Buy Defense Stumps"), tries to cut down a tree
but runs afoul of the Crow, who lives there. The two tangle repeatedly, with the
Crow always foiling the Fox's attempts, until the Fox lays railroad tracks up to the
base of the trunk and rams a locomotive into the Crow's domicile at full speed.
  I; *"V"; Bonds*

121   Yankee Doodle Swing Shift (Universal — 9/21/42)

Producer: Walter Lantz; *Director:* Alex Lovy; *Script:* Ben Hardaway, Milt Schaffer;
Animator: Harold Mason; *Music:* Darrell Calker
  The "Zoot Suit Swing Cats" jazz band learns "all brass [is] to be salvaged" for
the war effort. In fact, the long arm of Uncle Sam reaches onto the screen and
snatches up their instruments. The dejected cats go to work, after a fashion, on
the swing shift in a defense plant. One worker rolls gunpowder in paper (as if he
was making a cigarette) to form a "MacArthur bullet." When swing music begins
to play, the workers and machines begin functioning to its rhythm, converting all
sorts of scrap metal into guns, tanks, etc. The final shot features the American flag.
  I; *Home Front; Scrap Metal; Production; MacArthur*

122   You're a Sap, Mr. Jap (Paramount — 8/7/42)

Director: Dan Gordon; *Script:* Jim Tyer, Carl Meyer; *Animators:* Jim Tyer, George
Germanetti; *Music:* Winston Sharples, Sammy Timberg
  This cartoon opens as an off-screen quartet sings the title song (copyrighted
December 7, 1941), which warns "Mr. Jap" that he is "a sap ... to make a Yankee
cranky," because "Uncle Sam is gonna spanky." Popeye, on patrol in his little boat,
investigates a fishing vessel; two buck-toothed Japanese crewmen wearing oversized glasses and kimonos invite him on board. They offer him a "peace treaty,"
but hit him from behind when he signs it. As Popeye chases the "fishermen," their

boat rises out of the water, revealing a huge battleship attached underneath. Popeye eats his spinach, invokes "V" for Victory, and attacks the "double-crossin' Japansies." Fashioning a giant pair of pliers from an anchor, he "extracts" the barrels from a gun turret, which briefly transforms into a groaning, toothless face. The last surviving Japanese — an officer below decks— says he must "save face," so he drinks gasoline and eats firecrackers. Observing the enemy has "gas on his stomach," Popeye escapes to his boat and watches the Japanese ship explode. The Rising Sun flag sinks beneath the swirling waters as the sound of a flushing toilet is heard on the soundtrack! The OWI report on this cartoon criticized it as "propaganda on the absurd side ... it laughs at the enemy in such a way as to discredit their real danger." *You're a Sap, Mr. Jap* was the first "Famous Studios" cartoon to be released, after Paramount took over the Fleischer studios in 1942. The last official Max Fleischer production was *Terror on the Midway* (8/30/42).

I; *Armed Forces— Navy, Japan; Japanese Caricatures; "V"*

1943

123   Aladdin's Lamp (20th Century–Fox —10/22/43)
Producer: Paul Terry; *Director:* Eddie Donnelly; *Script:* John Foster; *Music:* Philip A. Scheib

After Private Gandy Goose reads a book about Aladdin and his lamp, the goose and Sgt. Cat are magically transported to the Middle East. The two soldiers are wined and dined by Aladdin and a coterie of dancing girls, but eventually wake up back in their tent in camp. The armed forces setting is merely a framework for the Oriental story, but Gandy and Sgt. Cat twice drink toasts to China, an Allied power. This cartoon is not to be confused with the 1947 Mighty Mouse film with the same title and production credits but an entirely different story.

II; *Armed Forces— Army; Ally–China*

124   Barnyard Blackout (20th Century–Fox — 3/5/43)
Producer: Paul Terry; *Director:* Mannie Davis; *Script:* John Foster; *Music:* Philip A. Scheib

This cartoon opens with a parade of air raid wardens, including Gandy Goose and Sourpuss Cat, as a rather catchy song is heard: "When the bombs are bursting all around, / And explosions shake the very ground, / You'll find us on the job and unafraid, / We're the air raid wardens on parade!" Despite his wife's entreaties, Henry the rooster hasn't prepared for the upcoming blackout. When the sirens sound, he rushes around his house madly, trying to cover the windows and turn out the lights. Gandy and Sourpuss are wardens on duty: "What's the matter with you? Are you a fifth columnist? Get those lights out!" Finally, the clumsy and befuddled Henry winds up battered and bruised, so his wife breaks out her first aid supplies. When he recovers, Henry agrees to build an "air raid room" in his house and proudly joins the air raid wardens himself. One of the better Terrytoons of the period, *Barnyard Blackout* has a moral, a peppy tune, and even some humor (a rather rare commodity in Terrytoons).

I; *Air Raid Warden; Fifth Column; Home Front*

125   *Bravo, Mr. Strauss (Paramount — 2/26/43)
Producer-Director: George Pal (no other credits available)

The peaceful city of Vienna is invaded by the Screwball Army. A statue of Johann Strauss, Sr.— toppled by an enemy tank —comes to life and lures the Screwballs to their doom in a lake by playing the "Radetzky March." Pal's Puppetoon version of the Nazis, the Screwball Army, also appeared in *Rhythm in the Ranks* (1941) and *Tulips Shall Grow* (1942), both q.v. The OWI information sheet on this cartoon characterizes the Screwballs as "destroyers of culture and religion"— they goosestep, give the fascist salute, and burn books by Freud, Einstein, Thomas Mann, and others (a fairly rare cartoon reference to Nazi anti–Semitism). They tear down or destroy famous paintings like the Mona Lisa. The unseen narrator says this cartoon was a dream of his and refers to the enemy's "cruelties and ruthless persecutions" and their "pompous, goose-stepping general." But at the end he says, "Things have a way of working themselves out."

I; *Nazis; Austria; War Allegory; Jew; Armed Forces — Germany*

126   Camouflage (20th Century–Fox — 8/27/43)
Producer: Paul Terry; *Director:* Eddie Donnelly; *Script:* John Foster; *Music:* Philip A. Scheib

Pvt. Gandy Goose and Sgt. Cat are stationed on a island in the Pacific; Gandy does such a good job camouflaging their base that he and the cat decide to fly to Tokyo and lure some Japanese back. They bring back "thousands of 'em" and wipe them out. Few Terrytoons dealt with the military aspects of the war (most of their war-oriented shorts focused on the home front) but *Camouflage, Mopping Up* (1943), q.v., and a few others were this company's answer to the more "active" Warner Bros. and Paramount product.

I; *Armed Forces — Army, Japan; Japanese Caricatures*

127   Canine Commandos (Universal — 7/28/43)
Producer: Walter Lantz; *Director:* Alex Lovy; *Script:* Ben Hardaway, Milt Schaffer; *Animator:* Verne Harding; *Music:* Darrell Calker

A humorous look at the duties of dogs in the war effort (one of a number, from various studios), including "para-pups," and a "ski pooch." Andy Panda makes a cameo appearance as a dog trainer. At the cartoon's conclusion, a dog says "Bonds Buy Bones" (which doesn't seem likely to make the audience contribute wildly).

I; *Armed Forces — Army; Bonds; Draft*

128   Cartoons Ain't Human (Paramount — 9/3/43)
Director: Seymour Kneitel; *Script:* Jack Mercer, Jack Ward; *Animators:* Orestes Calpini, Otto Feuer

Popeye makes his own animated cartoon, entitled "Wages of Sin (Less 20%)." The 20% refers to the wartime amusement tax. The animation is mostly stick figures, but there are many topical references in the cartoon-within-a-cartoon. Olive is shown on a farm, practicing first aid on a cow; Popeye arrives in a car with no tires, and says "Olive, me little cup of sugar," to which she replies, "Popeye, my retreaded lover." During a chase scene, Popeye pulls out his can of spinach, which is labeled "17 Points." The cartoon also includes some peripheral references, such as a drawing Popeye makes while "inspired" by a Vargas-style girlie calendar — a huge hand stamps it "CENSORED." During the inserted cartoon, Popeye wears a sandwich-sign reading "See Newt for a Zoot Suit." For a short which does not directly address any aspects of the war, *Cartoons Ain't Human* is loaded with topical references. This was the last black-and-white Popeye cartoon.

II; *Shortages; Rationing; Home Defense*

129   Chicken Little (Walt Disney/RKO — 12/17/43)

Producer: Walt Disney; *Director:* Gerry Geronomi; *Animators:* Ward Kimball, Norman Tate, Milt Kahl, Ed Aardal, Ollie Johnston, George Rowley, Andy Engman, John Lounsbery; *Layout:* Charles Philippi; *Music:* Oliver Wallace

Foxy Loxy can't penetrate the farmyard's fine defenses to steal some chickens, so he decides to use psychology. After reading a book (originally intended to be identified as *Mein Kampf*), he tries out maxims such as "To influence the masses, aim at the least intelligent" (which happens to be Chicken Little), and "undermine the faith of the masses in their leader" (Cocky-Locky, who loses his stature after a smear campaign spear-headed by the duped Chicken Little). Foxy-Loxy tricks Chicken Little into leading his flock into the fox's cave — and the fox is last seen surrounded by a graveyard full of chicken bones! The rather shocking ending (especially for a Disney cartoon) reinforces the film's warning about rumors and enemy propaganda. Most, if not all of the blatant anti–Nazi symbolism was dropped in favor of an oblique approach to the subject. This cartoon was produced under contract with the Coordinator of Inter-American Affairs. *Chicken Little* was "remade" (uncredited, of course) by Terrytoons as *The Sky is Falling* (1947).

I; *Collaborators; Anti-Fascist*

130   The Cocky Bantam (Columbia — 11/12/43) (aka *Black and Blue Market*)

Producer: Dave Fleischer; *Director:* Paul Sommer; *Script:* Sam Cobean; *Animators:* Volus Jones, Basil Davidovich; *Music:* Eddie Kilfeather

Freddy Falcon's ration card has run out, so he's forced to buy a chicken at Hirohito's Black Market. However, as Freddy is preparing to cook his illicit purchase, the chicken reveals himself to be Richard Rooster of the "Federal Bureau of Indignation." The falcon and the black marketeer — a Japanese agent — wind up in jail.

I; *Rationing; Japanese Caricature; Black Market; Hitler; Hirohito; Spy-saboteur*

131   A Corny Concerto (Warner Bros — 9/25/43)

Producer: Leon Schlesinger; *Director:* Robert Clampett; *Script:* Frank Tashlin; *Animator:* Robert McKimson; *Music:* Carl W. Stalling

This parody of Disney's *Fantasia* (1940) begins with a seedy-looking Elmer Fudd introducing "Tales from the Vienna Woods." Bugs Bunny, Porky Pig, and a dog chase each other to the music. The second selection is "The Blue Danube." A little black duck wants to join Mama Swan and her graceful offspring, but is consistently rejected. A buzzard (with an Ish Kabibble haircut) snatches the baby swans, but puts the duck back, sticking a "Rejected 4-F" sign on him. Mama Swan faints when she discovers her offspring are missing, but the little duck goes into action, roaring into the sky like a seaplane, and briefly metamorphosing into a Flying Tiger–style fighter. He eradicates the buzzard and is invited to join the swan family at last.

II; *Draft; Armed Forces — Air Corps*

132   Cow Cow Boogie (Universal — 1/3/43)

Producer: Walter Lantz; *Director:* Alex Lovy; *Script:* Ben Hardaway, Milt Schaffer; *Animator:* Hal Mason; *Music:* Darrell Calker

Part of the "Swing Symphony" series. On a cattle ranch, the cowboys sing a lugubrious version of "Home on the Range" as the steers play gin rummy and knit. The ranch foreman, after unsuccessfully trying to balance the books and disgustedly examining a poorly-patched innertube, shouts at his workers: "You gotta stop singin' that song — it's slowin' down production." A little black man riding on a mule appears singing "Cow Cow Boogie" (by Don Raye and Gene de Paul); he's lassoed by the foreman, who puts him in front of a piano. The ensuing boogie woogie rejuvenates the ranchhands, who start rounding up the herd and branding them "Grade A" (although one crazy steer is stamped "Jerky Beef"). As the song continues, the cheerful cattle are herded to the train station and loaded onto the "Super Beef" for the trip to market.

II; *Blacks; Production; Shortages*

133   Daffy — the Commando (Warner Bros — 10/30/43)

Producer: Leon Schlesinger; *Director:* I. Freleng; *Script:* Michael Maltese; *Animator:* Ken Champin; *Music:* Carl W. Stalling

Nazi officer Von Vulture receives a telegram from the "Apes of Wrath" (Hitler, Mussolini, and Hirohito depicted in the "see no evil, hear no evil, speak no evil" poses), warning him that his "ka-rear" will be in danger if one more Allied commando sneaks through. Von Vulture (also called "Von Limburger" and "Lederkrantz" at times) and his diminutive assistant Schultz spot commando Daffy Duck parachuting behind their lines. After a chase through the trenches, Daffy escapes in a German airplane, and causes a "mess of Messerschmitts" to shoot each other down. When his plane is wrecked by Von Vulture, Daffy hides in a "cave" that turns out to be the barrel of a giant cannon. Daffy is shot into the air, wearing a "Human Cannon Ball" outfit and carrying an American flag in each hand. He lands on a podium next to a realistic-looking (rotoscoped?) Hitler and smashes him in the head with a mallet. Von Vulture and Adolf Wolf (from *Blitz Wolf*, 1942, q.v.) share certain similarities and even a telephone gag (based on the "Myrt and Marge" radio show). In one scene, Von Vulture salutes and says "Heil Hitler" as a skunk walks by, then looks at the audience and shrugs. There is some suggestion that Daffy is intended to be a *British* commando, since he is introduced wearing a British-style helmet and singing a music-hall song with a cockney accent.

I; *Hitler; Mussolini; Hirohito; Armed Forces — Army, Germany; Nazis; AF-British?*

134 *Defense Against Invasion (Walt Disney/Coordinator for Inter-American Affairs—(c) 8/5/43)

Producer: Walt Disney; *Director:* Jack King; *Animators:* Josh Meador, Marvin Woodward, Hal King, Milt Neil, Judge Whitaker, Paul Allen; *Music:* Charles Wolcott

Sponsored by the Coordinator for Inter-American Affairs, *Defense Against Invasion* was not released through normal commercial distribution channels to theaters. Others in the series included *The Winged Scourge* (about malaria) and *The Grain That Built a Hemisphere*. This short combines live-action and animation. Four young boys are waiting at their doctor's office to be vaccinated. To calm their fears, the doctor says the body is like a city: a defenseless body is overwhelmed by invading germs, but a vaccination provides munitions to repel the invaders. The boys agree to be vaccinated. "V for Vaccination and Victory, victory over invasion" the narrator concludes.

II; *"V"*

135   Der Fuehrer's Face (Walt Disney/RKO —1/1/43)

Producer: Walt Disney; *Director:* Jack Kinney; *Script:* Dick Huemer; *Animators:* John Sibley, Bill Justis, Milt Neil, Andy Engman, George Nicholas, Robert Carlson, Hugh Fraser, Les Clark; *Layout:* Don DaGradi; *Music:* Oliver Wallace

Donald Duck, a citizen of the Third Reich, lives in a Hitler-shaped house, wakes up to a Hitler cuckoo clock and — after an *ersatz* breakfast — is escorted to his job in a munitions factory by an Axis marching band (including a Japanese member) playing the title song. Donald tightens fuses on shells passing by on a conveyor belt, while simultaneously "heiling." Even a "vacation" (exercises in front of a painted backdrop of the countryside) doesn't help — Donald finally goes berserk. He wakes up in his good old American bed and hugs a model of the Statue of Liberty: it was all a bad dream. The title song, sung in the film by Cliff Edwards, was a commercial hit for Spike Jones. Winner of the Academy Award for Best Cartoon.

I; *Hitler; Nazis; Japanese Caricatures; Mussolini; Göring*

136   Dizzy Newsreel (Columbia — 8/27/43)

Producer: Dave Fleischer; *Director:* Alec Geiss; *Script:* Sam Cobean; *Animators:* Chick Otterstrom, Grant Simmons; *Music:* Paul Worth

Spot gags in newsreel format include horse races ("The Filet Mignon Sweepstakes"), a boxing match, hog callers, etc. The final sequence is datelined "Wattarat, Japan: Captured Pictures Show Launching of New Giant Vulture," a Japanese invention that doesn't fly.

II; *Japanese Caricatures; Shortages*

137   Donald's Tire Trouble (Walt Disney/RKO —1/29/43)

Producer: Walt Disney; *Director:* Dick Lundy; *Animators:* Tom Palmer, Don Towsley, Robert Carlson, Ray Patterson; *Layout:* Ken O'Connor; *Music:* Oliver Wallace

Speeding through the countryside, Donald gets a flat tire. The inner tube has been patched many times with odd pieces of rubber (including gloves), but Donald finally gets a patch on it and with great difficulty replaces the tire on his car. As he drives off, all four of his tires go flat! At one point Donald says "Doggone rubber shortage," the only overtly war-oriented reference in this short, which otherwise could have been produced at almost any time.

II; *Shortages*

138   Dumb-Hounded (MGM — 3/20/43)

Producer: Fred Quimby; *Director:* Tex Avery; *Music:* Scott Bradley

The first screen appearance of Droopy (although he wasn't called this yet; the character was inspired by "Wallace Wimple" on the "Fibber McGee and Molly" radio show, and voiced by Bill Thompson, who played the radio role). Droopy is assigned to catch a wolf who escaped from Swing-Swing Prison; the wolf goes to extraordinary lengths to evade his pursuer, but the little dog is always one step ahead of him. The only topical reference occurs early in the cartoon — the reward for the wolf is $5,000 or "one pound of coffee," a reference quite relevant to 1943 movie audiences. *Northwest Hounded Police* (1946) is a reworking of the same basic idea, also featuring Droopy and the fugitive wolf.

II; *Shortages*

139   Duty and the Beast (Columbia — 5/28/43)

Producer: Dave Fleischer; *Director:* Alec Geiss; *Animator:* Grant Simmons; *Music:* Paul Worth

The duties of a hunting dog are described, although the on-screen example isn't exactly the hunter's ideal helpmate. When the hunter shoots down a Japanese airplane by accident, there is a cut to a cash register ringing up a "Zero."

II; *Armed Forces — Japan; Japanese Caricature*

140   Education for Death (Walt Disney/RKO —1/15/43)

Producer: Walt Disney; *Director:* Gerry Geronimi; *Assistant Director:* Ralph Chadwick; *Original Book:* Gregor Ziemer; *Animators:* Norman Tate, George Rowley, Bill Tytla, Ward Kimball, Frank Thomas, Milt Kahl, John Lounsbery, Dan MacManus; *Layout:* Charles Philippi, Herbert Ryman, Ken O'Connor; *Music:* Oliver Wallace

Based on a book by Gregor Ziemer, also used as the source for the feature film *Hitler's Children* (RKO, 1943), this cartoon shows how Nazis indoctrinate their citizens, especially their youth. The life of young Hans is controlled from the moment of his birth. In school, he is told the story of Sleeping Beauty — while most of the short is drawn in a semi-realistic style, this section features a comic Hitler as Prince Charming (the caricature of Hitler as a knight in armor was probably inspired by Hubert Lanzinger's well-known portrait of Hitler in this costume, prominently displayed by the Nazis in 1937) and a grossly overweight "Germania" as Sleeping Beauty (who sings "Heil Hitler" to the music from Richard Wagner's "Die Walküre," the second opera in his "Der Ring des Nibelungen" series). Later, Hans learns about the law of nature: a fox catches and eats a rabbit; rebuked by his teacher for expressing pity for the rabbit, Hans changes his ways and shouts "I hate it — it is a coward!" He grows up to be a mindless Nazi soldier who burns books, sacks churches, and despises culture. *Education for Death* contains a reference to the Nazi policy of euthanasia for "defectives" — when Hans falls ill, his mother is warned that a sickly child won't be tolerated by the Third Reich. There are also references to anti–Semitism.

I; *Hitler; Nazis; Goebbels; Göring; Jew; Armed Forces — Germany; Churchill; FDR*

141   The Egg Cracker Suite (Universal — 2/22/43)

Producer: Walter Lantz; *Directors:* Ben Hardaway, Emery Hawkins; *Script:* Milt Schaffer; *Animator:* Lester Kline; *Music:* Darrell Calker

Oswald the Rabbit's Easter Egg factory mass-produces gaily-painted eggs to a musical beat "conducted" by Oswald. The eggs go from chicken to finished product, and are dropped by parachute to people everywhere. At one point, an obviously rotten egg is detected: a rabbit worker pulls the "Gas Alarm" switch and a disposal truck roars up and carts off the offending egg. The "Gas Alarm" gag and a general ambience of wartime production (the rabbits march up to the factory gates to begin their shift) are the only topical aspects. *The Swooner Crooner* (1944), q.v., also depicts an "egg factory."

II; *Production*

142   Fall Out, Fall In (Walt Disney/RKO — 4/23/43)

Producer: Walt Disney; *Director:* Jack King; *Animators:* Ray Patterson, Paul Allen, Judge Whitaker, John McManus, Milt Neil, Hal King; *Music:* Paul Smith

Army Private Donald Duck and his platoon set off on a grueling march through rain, snow, ice, and desert heat. At the end of the day Donald has to pitch his tent, a task which takes almost all night. Finally, the dawn arrives and an exhausted Donald is forced to resume the march once more. Donald Duck was Disney's star in the war years, appearing quite frequently as a soldier, although the only "hard" propaganda shorts he appeared in were *Commando Duck* (1944) and *Der Fuehrer's Face* (1943), both q.v.

I; *Armed Forces — Army*

143   Falling Hare (Warner Bros—10/23/43)

Producer: Leon Schlesinger; *Director:* Robert Clampett; *Script:* Warren Foster; *Animator:* Rod Scribner; *Music:* Carl W. Stalling

At an Army airfield, Bugs Bunny is reclining on a "block buster" bomb and reading the book *Victory Thru Hare Power*. He is amused by its description of sabotage by gremlins, until he is disturbed by a little creature attempting to set off the bomb by hitting it with a hammer. Could this be a gremlin? "It ain't Wendell Wilkie!" (the politician and statesman who lost the presidential election to Franklin D. Roosevelt in 1940). Bugs and the gremlin wind up going aloft in a bomber; out of control, the plane plunges toward the earth, stopping just inches from the ground — it's out of gas ("You know how it is with these 'A' cards," Bugs remarks. "A" gas ration cards were the lowest priority.) One of two gremlin cartoons from Warner Bros. (See also *Russian Rhapsody*, 1944.); the gremlin — both humorous and creepy — is reputedly a caricature of director Clampett. Scenes from this cartoon appear in *His Hare-Raising Tale* (1951), sans gremlin. Remade as *Hare Lift* (1952), with Bugs in the gremlin role and Yosemite Sam as the dupe.

    I; *Armed Forces — Air Corps; Sabotage; Rationing*

144   The Fifth Column Mouse (Warner Bros — 2/6/43)

Producer: Leon Schlesinger; *Director:* I. Freleng; *Animator:* Gil Turner; *Music:* Carl W. Stalling

    A bunch of cute mice are playing in the kitchen when a hungry cat bursts in — an air raid warden mouse shouts "Lights out!" The cat manages to catch one dopey-looking mouse, and tells him he can have "all the cheese you want" if he cooperates (at this point, "oriental" music is heard on the soundtrack and the cat briefly becomes a Japanese caricature). Giving the cat the fascist salute, the ratty mouse convinces his fellow mice — to the tune of "Blues in the Night" — that the cat only "wants to protect us from the ones who wrecked us." The mice agree to appease the cat, but when the feline dictator later decides he'd like a "nice fat mouse" for dinner, the mice organize to fight back. As "We Did It Before and We Can Do It Again" plays, the mice mobilize (wearing bottle caps as helmets, and so on). At one point a diagram of the cat is shown, marked with a "Second Front." Using a robot bulldog and an electric razor (which cuts the three dots-and-a-dash Morse code for "V" symbol into the cat's fur), the mice chase the cat away — and the traitorous mouse gets a pie in the face. Although the plot is essentially a remake of *It's Got Me Again* (1932), this cartoon has almost more verbal, visual, and musical topical references than it can hold.

    I; *Japanese Caricature; "V"; Collaborator; Air Raid Warden; Fascist; Bonds; Armed Forces; World War I*

145   Figaro and Cleo (Walt Disney/RKO — 10/15/43)

Producer: Walt Disney; *Director:* Jack Kinney; *Script:* Ralph Wright; *Animators:* Les Clark, Ham Luske, Marvin Woodward, Don Lusk; *Music:* Paul Smith

    Figaro and Cleo, the cat and goldfish from *Pinocchio* (1940), appear in this more or less standard cat vs. mouse cartoon, with a black "Mammy" (à la the early Tom and Jerry shorts) as the referee. Mammy says: "That's the trouble with the world today — folks jes won't live and let live…. We gon' have peace for the duration in this house." Ironically, most scenes of the black maid have been cut for some Disney TV showings of this cartoon.

    II; *Blacks*

146   Flop Goes the Weasel (Warner Bros — 2/20/43)

Producer: Leon Schlesinger; *Director:* Charles M. Jones; *Music:* Carl W. Stalling

    A weasel steals an egg while Mammy Hen is away from her nest. He plans to cook an "Egg Delight Supreme" (while reading the recipe, he stumbles over the requirement of "an ounce of sugar," finally saying "Oh, well," and going on the next ingredient). But the egg hatches a little black chick (who acts like Tweety Bird but has a stereotyped black accent), and the weasel is on the receiving end of considerable violence. Chuck Jones's war-time shorts often had little or no topical references, and even the sugar shortage gag in this one is very oblique.

    II; *Shortages; Blacks*

147   Greetings Bait! (Warner Bros—(c) 5/22/43)

Producer: Leon Schlesinger; *Director:* I. Freleng; *Script:* Tedd Pierce; *Animator:* Manuel Perez; *Music:* Carl W. Stalling

The Wacky Worm, a green Jerry Colonna caricature, uses various ruses to lure fish onto a fisherman's hook, disguising himself as a sandwich, a mermaid, etc. However, he meets his match in a feisty crab, who steals a fish, then goes after the Worm. At one point, the crab's eyes on the ends of their stalks provide a "periscope" view of his prey. Finally, the Worm challenges the crab to take off his shell and fight, and warns the audience: "For the benefit of those with faint hearts, weak stomachs, and 4-F ratings, we will return you to the surface" during the battle. When the fisherman (another Colonna caricature) finally hauls up his line, the battered Worm is weakly hanging on. The main character had previously appeared in *The Wacky Worm* (1941). Jerry Colonna—whose catch-phrases included "Greetings, gate!" and "Ah, something new has been added!"—was a popular radio comedian whose voice, popping eyes, handlebar moustache, and gag lines were caricatured in numerous Warner Bros. cartoons of the late 1930s and 1940s (despite the fact that most of the feature films he appeared in were for Paramount!).

II; *Draft*

148   Happy Birthdaze (Paramount—7/16/43)

Director: Dan Gordon; *Script:* Carl Meyer; *Animators:* Graham Place, Abner Kneitel

Popeye and his shipmates (one of whom seems a little effeminate) are reading their "V Mail" (letters to servicemen which could be folded up to form their own envelopes, and which were sent at a special rate). Olive's letter to Popeye says she has saved "just enough sugar to bake a cake for your birthday party." Popeye invites Shorty along, since the diminutive sailor is depressed because he has no friends. Shorty's enthusiastic but inept actions nearly wreck Olive's apartment and he and Popeye wind up in the furnace of the building covered in birthday cake.

II; *Armed Forces—Navy; Shortages; "V"; Black*

149   He Can't Make It Stick (Columbia—6/11/43 or 7/23/43?)

Producer: Dave Fleischer; *Directors:* Paul Sommer, John Hubley; *Script:* Milt Gross, Stephen Longstreet; *Animators:* Volus Jones, Jim Armstrong; *Music:* Eddie Kilfeather

"Schicklegruber" (Hitler) is a wallpaper hanger whose paper (black swastikas on a red background) keeps falling down. He persists, hanging the paper in houses representing various occupied countries, but always fails to make it stick, and is laughed at by all. The OWI report on this short notes: "In dubious taste [and] beside the point in July 1943."

I; *Hitler; Nazis; France?; Netherlands?; Czech?; Poland?; Norway?; Greece?*

150   Her Honor, the Mare (Paramount—11/26/43)

Director: I. Sparber; *Script:* Jack Mercer, Jack Ward; *Animators:* Jim Tyer, Ben Solomon

Popeye's nephews befriend a horse — rejected by the glue factory as 4-F — but Popeye won't let them bring her in the house. The boys tell Popeye "the painter is coming up," hoisting the mare past the window, and the horse's rear end becomes a lugubrious Hitler-face caricature. Later, the nephews pretend to be asleep and snore the three dots-and-a-dash "V" theme from Beethoven's Fifth Symphony. The mare gives birth to four colts and is allowed to stay. The first Popeye short cartoon in Technicolor (several Fleischer Popeye "specials" of the 1930s were in color).

II; *Hitler; Draft; "V"*

151   Hiss and Make Up (Warner Bros— 9/11/43)

Producer: Leon Schlesinger; *Director:* I. Freleng; *Script:* Michael Maltese; *Animator:* Gerry Chiniquy; *Music:* Carl W. Stalling

Granny warns the constantly-fighting Wellington the cat and Roscoe the dog that she'll throw them out into the snow if she hears any more noise. The two pets try to get each other ejected: the dog releases mechanical mice, and the cat stamps muddy dog paw-prints all over one room. When Granny comes downstairs and turns on the light in that room, the dog (wearing an air raid warden's helmet) shouts "Hey, put out that light!" Finally, the canary frames them both, and Wellington and Roscoe are tossed into the snow, but the cat has the last laugh — he has the canary in his mouth. Very similar to *Hare Force* (1944), where the protagonists are Bugs Bunny and a stupid dog.

II; *Air Raid Warden*

152   Home Defense (Walt Disney/RKO —11/26/43)

Producer: Walt Disney; *Director:* Jack King; *Animators:* Paul Allen, Nick Nichols, Judge Whitaker, Hal King, Ray Patterson, Marvin Woodward; *Music:* Paul Smith

"Front Admiral" Donald Duck and his nephews, attired in comic-opera military uniforms, man a coastal listening post. When Donald falls asleep, his nephews fool him into thinking the enemy are attacking by manipulating a toy airplane and tiny gingerbread-men parachutists. When Donald learns the truth, he drums them out of the "service," but when an inquisitive bee enters the "ear" of his listening device, Donald thinks it is an enemy plane and welcomes his troops back. He orders them to halt the source of the buzzing noise and they do, with disastrous results. Home front themes such as air raid wardens and listening posts guarding against enemy aircraft were familiar to World War II audiences, and the concept of Donald earnestly listening through a strange machine for airplanes— and visualizing a Japanese carrier attack — was not unusual for the time. Some scenes of Huey, Dewey, and Louie shooting guns have been cut for Disney TV airings of this cartoon.

I; *Home Defense; Armed Forces — Japan*

153   Hop and Go (Warner Bros— 2/6/43)

Producer: Leon Schlesinger; *Director:* Norman McCabe; *Script:* Melvin Millar; *Animator:* Cal Dalton; *Music:* Carl W. Stalling

Two Scots rabbits and Claude Hopper the kangaroo (voiced by Pinto Colvig) have a jumping contest. Claude dumps the scrap metal he's been carrying in his pouch, and jumps high enough to freeze himself (and sees a sign reading "Price ceiling — meat prices frozen at this level," a reference to wartime price controls). Finally, he unloads a keg of TNT, which explodes on Tokyo.

II; *Home Defense; Rationing; Japan; Scrap Metal; Armed Forces — Air Corps; World War I; Australia?*

154   The Hungry Goat (Paramount — 6/25/43)

Director: Dan Gordon; *Script:* Carl Meyer; *Animators:* Joe Oriolo, John Walworth; *Music:* Winston Sharples

Depressed because all old tin cans are being collected for scrap metal drives, a goat ("Billy da Kid") plans to commit suicide by drowning. However, when he reaches the dock he spots a battleship and starts to devour the anchor. Sailor Popeye tries to stop him, but misses and hits the admiral! Popeye is sentenced to swab the deck as punishment, while the admiral goes ashore to see a movie. Billy da Kid continues to eat parts of the ship and Popeye struggles to prevent the destruction. The admiral sees this unfold on the screen (the theatre is showing a "Popeye" cartoon), and rushes back to the dock to try to save his vessel. As the film concludes, the goat — now in the theatre audience himself — has the last laugh. Unlike a similar goat in *Scrap Happy Daffy* (1943), q.v., this goat isn't an Axis agent — he's just hungry.

II; *Armed Forces — Navy; Scrap Metal*

155   An Itch in Time (Warner Bros — 11/20/43)

Producer: Leon Schlesinger; *Director:* Robert Clampett; *Script:* Warren Foster; *Animator:* Robert McKimson?; *Music:* Carl W. Stalling (using themes by Raymond Scott)

A hillbilly flea (singing "There's food around the corner") attacks Elmer Fudd's dog. Elmer warns the dog that a bath is imminent if he doesn't stop scratching. The dog tries to endure the flea's attacks, but finally succumbs and Elmer drags him towards the tub. As the cartoon concludes, the flea is carrying off Elmer and the dog on a platter labeled "Blue Plate Special — No Points," and singing "There'll be no more Meatless Tuesdays for me!" Memorable cartoon with many topical references, including a "Flea Administration Ration Book" and a "Hair Raid Shelter." When Elmer's cat sees the flea taking Elmer and the dog away, he says "Now I've seen everything!" and shoots himself! This gag was also used in *The Sour Puss* (1940), *Horton Hatches the Egg* (1942), and *The Stupid Cupid* (1944) (all but the latter directed by Clampett). The same flea character, singing the same song (with the words now changed to "There's a home around the corner") appears in *A Horsefly Fleas* (1948).

II; *Home Defense; Shortages*

156   Jack Wabbit and the Beanstalk (Warner Bros — 5/29/43)

Producer: Leon Schlesinger; *Director:* I. Freleng; *Script:* Michael Maltese; *Animators:* Jack Bradbury, Phil Monroe; *Music:* Carl W. Stalling

Bugs Bunny discovers giant carrots at the top of a beanstalk — part of a moronic giant's "Victory Garden." The giant (a spoof of "Lenny" from *Of Mice and Men*) doesn't want to share his vegetables with the furry intruder, and they tangle. At one point, Bugs hides in the giant's hair; when the giant puts on a hat, Bugs says "What is this, a blackout? I didn't hear no sireen!" When he lights a match to see what's up, a voice yells "Put out that light!" He later takes an elevator down the beanstalk to escape, while the giant falls to earth ("Look out for that first step — it's a lulu!"). Giant carrots also figured in *Lumber Jack Rabbit* (1954), with Paul Bunyan as the gardener plagued by Bugs; Popeye had a similar Jack-and-the-Beanstalk experience in *Ration Fer the Duration* (1943), q.v.

II; *Victory Garden; Home Defense*

157   *Jasper Goes Fishing (Paramount — (c) 7/28/43)
Director: George Pal

One Sunday morning, the ringing of the church bell arouses Professor Scarecrow and his pal the Crow, so the aggravated duo intercepts Jasper and convinces him to go fishing instead of attending Sunday school. The Scarecrow says: "Why boy, dere's so many fish dat they done drafted the ones without dependents." However, when Jasper, Professor Scarecrow, and the Crow drop their fishing line into the pond, this disrupts the fishes' prayer meeting. The fish deacon and his congregation (including flying fish "dive bombers") mobilize to punish the miscreants, blowing them all the way to the lawn of Jasper's church with a cannon shell ("Praise de Lord! We's got the ammunition."). This Puppetoon bears some resemblance to *Swing Social* (MGM, 1940), q.v.

I; *Armed Forces — Air Corps; Draft*

158   A Jolly Good Furlough (Paramount — 4/23/43)
Director: Dan Gordon; *Script:* Joseph Stultz; *Animators:* Joe Oriolo, John Walworth; *Music:* Winston Sharples

After Popeye sinks a Japanese island fortress (which disappears beneath the waves to the sound of a toilet flushing, courtesy stock footage from *You're a Sap, Mr. Jap*, 1942, q.v.), he is awarded a furlough. When he gets home, he's immediately run over by Olive's car (which has shoes instead of tires and a crooked "V" on the door). Settling down in his backyard hammock for a rest, Popeye sets off an alarm which his nephews believe indicates "a Nazi or a Jap" spy has invaded. Learning it is Uncle Popeye, they demonstrate their prowess at home defense — Popeye is "blown up" in a mock air raid, painted with camouflage paint, stung by bees (inside a gas mask), and given first aid. He's run over again by Olive on his way out. Returning to the "Theatre of War — Service Men Free" in a rowboat, Popeye shoots the messenger bird bringing news that his leave has been extended.

I; *Home Defense; "V"; Armed Forces — Navy; Shortages; Japanese Caricatures; Nazis*

159   Jungle Drums (Paramount — 3/26/43)
Director: Dan Gordon; *Script:* Robert Little, Jay Morton; *Animators:* Orestes Calpini, H.C. Ellison; *Music Arr:* Sammy Timberg

Nazis, based inside a stone temple deep in the African jungle, shoot down an Allied plane passing overhead. Lois Lane, the only survivor of the crash, hides information about a convoy; she is captured by the Nazis — led by a monocle-wearing, shaved-head stereotype — but won't talk. When the enemy agents find the data anyway, they hand her over to the natives to be burned at the stake. Clark Kent is a passenger in another plane passing overhead, and becomes Superman to rescue Lois. Superman mops up the Nazis and Lois warns the convoy via radio, so that the Nazi submarine wolfpack sent to sink it is destroyed instead. Hitler receives the bad news in his headquarters as a storm rages outside. Only 5 of the 17 Superman cartoons produced by Fleischer and Famous Studios during the war contained major topical references.

I; *Nazis; Hitler; Armed Forces — Air Corps, Merchant Marine, Germany; Blacks; Atrocities*

160   Keep 'Em Growing (20th Century–Fox — 7/28/43)

Producer: Paul Terry; *Director:* Mannie Davis; *Script:* John Foster; *Music:* Philip A. Scheib

Since the farmers' sons have gone to war, the farm animals pitch in to plant, tend, and harvest the crops. Each animal contributes in the manner to which he is best suited: a worm drills holes for seeds, a goat uses his horns to plow, and so on. As they work, the animals sing "Our army needs support to win that victory," and "We volunteered to do our bit, to keep our country strong and fit, and feed our sons of liberty, across the sea." Similar to *All Out for "V"* (1942), q.v., although more narrowly construed.

I; *Home Front; Production; "V"; Armed Forces — Army*

161   The Last Round-Up (20th Century–Fox — 5/14/43)

Producer: Paul Terry; *Director:* Mannie Davis; *Script:* John Foster; *Music:* Philip A. Scheib

Private Gandy Goose and Sgt. Cat are blown into the stratosphere by a munitions accident at the Army Proving Grounds. They land in a swastika-festooned Germany where even the bugs say "Heil." The two GIs climb up to Berchtesgarden ("Adolf Schicklegruber, Proprietor") to confront Hitler (a screaming pig) and Mussolini (a hyperactive, grunting monkey), who are making war plans. Gandy and Sgt. Cat have no mercy on the Axis leaders. This cartoon is somewhat similar to *Mopping Up* (1943), q.v., which also portrays Hitler and Mussolini as a pig and monkey, respectively.

I; *Hitler; Mussolini; Armed Forces — Army; Nazis*

162   Little Red Riding Rabbit (Warner Bros — 12/18/43)

Producer: Leon Schlesinger; *Director:* I. Freleng; *Script:* Michael Maltese; *Animator:* Manuel Perez; *Music:* Carl W. Stalling

An obnoxious bobby-soxer Red Riding Hood heads for Granny's house with a basket of goodies — including Bugs Bunny. A lurking wolf spots the basket and beats Red to the house, where he finds a note reading: "Working swing shift at Lockheed (signed) Granny." Going inside, the wolf has to chase three other wolves out of Granny's bed before he can set his trap. Bugs and the wolf tangle, but Red constantly interrupts them and they finally gang up on her. The popular war-oriented tune "They're Either Too Young or Too Old" is heard several times.

II; *Production; Women in Labor Force*

163   The Lonesome Mouse (MGM — 5/22/43)

Producer: Fred Quimby; *Directors:* William Hanna, Joseph Barbera; *Animators:* Irven Spence, Pete Burness, Kenneth Muse; *Music:* Scott Bradley

Tom and Jerry go at it again, with Jerry (the mouse) aggressively assaulting Tom this time. At one point he draws a Hitler moustache and forelock on a picture of Tom and spits on it! Mammy Two-Shoes, the black maid (seen only from the knees down), spots a smashed vase and says "That's sabotage!" The Tom and Jerry cartoons had little or no dialogue and few other opportunities for topical references; in fact, with several notable exceptions (like *Blitz Wolf*, 1942, q.v.), MGM's wartime cartoons were the least topical of all those from companies producing animated shorts.

II; *Hitler; Blacks*

164   Meatless Tuesday (Universal — 10/25/43)

Producer: Walter Lantz; *Director:* James Culhane; *Script:* Ben Hardaway, Milt Schaffer; *Animators:* Paul Smith, Pat Matthews; *Music:* Darrell Calker

Andy Panda's mailbox is crammed with ration books, cooking tips, and the like, but he can't find anything to his liking in the book *1001 Recipes for Meatless Tuesdays by Hedda Lettuce*. When he hears a nearby rooster crow, Andy is consumed by a desire for roast chicken, but the fowl is too slippery and Andy winds up in a Statue of Liberty pose, festooned with carrots and Liberty brand tomatoes.

I; *Rationing*

165   The Merry-Go-Round (Paramount — 12/31/43)

Director: Seymour Kneitel; *Script:* Joe Stultz; *Animators:* Graham Place, Abner Kneitel

Popeye is too shy to propose to Olive Oyl, so his sailor pal Shorty agrees to help. Olive is busy cleaning her apartment and doesn't pay any attention to the two men until Shorty does a Charles Boyer impression and kisses her, at which point she becomes enamored of *him*. This cartoon begins and ends on a battleship, where Popeye has pin-ups of Olive around his hammock and Shorty has photos of Dorothy Lamour (in the end, Popeye has appropriated Shorty's cheesecake shots and forces his pal to stare at Olive's pictures).

II; *Armed Forces — Navy*

166   Mopping Up (20th Century–Fox — 6/25/43)

Producer: Paul Terry; *Director:* Eddie Donnelly; *Script:* John Foster; *Music:* Philip A. Scheib

Incensed by Hitler's radio broadcast, Private Gandy Goose and Sgt. Cat call up the dictator and warn him they are on their way. They bomb Berlin and chase Hitler (a pig) and Mussolini (a monkey) all the way to Egypt. Gandy's plane transforms into a tank and pursues the two Axis leaders, until a Japanese plane appears, at which point Gandy's tank changes back into a plane! The goose drops a bomb full of termites on the Japanese plane — chewed into three pieces, the aircraft falls into the sea and is consumed by sharks.

I; *Hitler; Mussolini; Armed Forces — Army, Air Corps, Japan; Japanese Caricatures*

167 Nursery Crimes (Columbia —10/8/43)

Producer: Dave Fleischer; *Director:* Alec Geiss; *Script:* Alec Geiss; *Music:* Joe DeNat

A professor tells the "real story" behind Mother Goose's nursery rhymes. When he gets to Jack Spratt, who could eat no fat, Jack explains "My ration card ran out."

II; *Rationing*

168 The Old Army Game (Walt Disney/RKO —11/5/43)

Producer: Walt Disney; *Director:* Jack King; *Animators:* Nick Nichols, Paul Allen, Bob Carlson, Hal King; *Layout:* Bill Herwig; *Music:* Paul Smith

Sgt. Pete discovers his soldiers have all gone AWOL; he catches Private Donald Duck trying to sneak back into camp, but Donald hides under one of three boxes outside the barracks, and a variation on the old shell game ensues. At one point, Donald steps in a hole and he and the sergeant think his legs have been cut off! Donald prepares to commit suicide with a pistol (this has been cut on some Disney TV broadcasts of the cartoon) before realizing he isn't maimed after all. At the conclusion, as Pete is chasing Donald with a bayonet, they pass a sign reading "National Speed Limit — 35 miles per hour," so they continue the chase in slow motion.

I; *Shortages; Armed Forces — Army*

169 One Ham's Family (MGM — 8/14/43)

Producer: Fred Quimby; *Director:* Tex Avery; *Script:* Rich Hogan; *Animators:* Preston Blair, Ed Love, Ray Abrams; *Music:* Scott Bradley

The smart little pig who built his house of bricks is now married and has a son, Junior. The Wolf, meanwhile, is still lurking about. On Christmas Eve, Junior — trying to catch Santa Claus in the act — mistakes the Wolf for St. Nick. By the end of the cartoon, Junior has denuded the Wolf to make a fur coat for Mama Pig. Earlier, as Junior is peering up the chimney, "48 points" is superimposed on his hindquarters. The title of this cartoon is a spoof of the popular radio show "One Man's Family."

II; *Rationing*

170 Pass the Biscuits, Mirandy! (Universal — 8/23/43)

Producer: Walter Lantz; *Director:* James Culhane; *Script:* Ben Hardaway, Milt Schaffer; *Animator:* Paul Smith; *Music:* Darrell Calker

Hillbilly housewife Mirandy bakes the world's toughest biscuits, and eventually finds herself in uniform, firing biscuits at German tanks with her garter. The cartoon concludes with a shot of Hitler, Mussolini, and Hirohito (the latter two portrayed as monkeys) looking disgruntled. The title song was also the basis of a live-action musical short around this time.

I; *Hitler; Mussolini; Japanese Caricature; Hirohito; Armed Forces — Germany, Women*

171   Patriotic Pooches (20th Century–Fox — 4/9/43)
Producer: Paul Terry; *Director:* Connie Rasinski; *Script:* John Foster; *Music:* Philip A. Scheib

Inspired by an Uncle Sam recruiting poster and a radio commentator who asks, "Do you hate Hitler and the Axis?" dogs join the Army. Signs on their dog houses read "Closed for the Duration" and their fleas are placed in "Flea Internment Camps." A little dog is consistently rejected because he is too small, but he eventually rounds up three Nazi pigs (including one named Adolf) who come ashore from a submarine, and is rewarded for his heroism. This cartoon contains a rare allusion to the internment of Japanese-Americans.

I; *Nazis; Armed Forces — Army; Hitler; Bonds*

172   Plenty Below Zero (Columbia — 5/14/43)
Producer: Dave Fleischer; *Director:* Bob Wickersham; *Script:* Leo Salkin; *Animator:* Howard Swift; *Music:* Eddie Kilfeather

The Crow is stuck in the frozen North with nothing to eat but acorns and leaves, although he'd rather have a steak ("If I had my ration card"). He also keeps his sugar in a safe, a standard rationing gag. The Fox has a steak and coffee in his knapsack, and the Crow decides to appropriate them. After a long struggle, the food disappears down a canyon, and the Fox and Crow are reduced to eating leaves.

II; *Rationing*

173   *Point Rationing of Foods (Office of War Information/War Activities Committee — 2/25/43)
(no credits; produced by the Leon Schlesinger unit of the Screen Cartoonists Guild, Local 852; Warner Bros. contributed a special music score.)

This 6-minute black-and-white cartoon, made using a combination of "Leica-reel" and limited animation techniques, was made for the Office of Price Administration (OPA) by 40 members of the Screen Cartoonists Guild Local 852 over a three-week period, working evenings and weekends. It opens with shots of Allied soldiers at the front; a commentator explains that since one of the best ways to supply their food is in cans, there is a shortage of canned goods. Transportation demands of the war and the farm labor shortage are also illustrated. Rationing is a way to make sure all receive their fair share — people are shown filing into a grocery store, and the last man leaves, empty-handed and in tears. Since everyone does not like the same foods, a point rationing system — under which scarcer items require more points — has been introduced. A young housewife is seen shopping — first she uses her points lavishly, but later starts to substitute low-point items for scarcer high-point ones: "This is one way to insure that everyone gets his share of food. This is the American way to Victory." The OWI reviewer commended this cartoon's sense of humor, noting it could have been very dull if delivered as a lecture, and that *Point Rationing of Foods* demonstrates "how well animated cartoons can be used in theaters to explain national emergencies."

I; *Armed Forces — Army, Russian?, British; Shortages; Rationing*

174 Porky Pig's Feat (Warner Bros—7/17/43)

Producer: Leon Schlesinger; *Director:* Frank Tashlin; *Script:* Melvin Millar; *Animator:* Phil Monroe; *Music:* Carl W. Stalling

Porky Pig and Daffy Duck are guests at the Broken Arms Hotel, but the German-accented, monocle-wearing manager won't let them leave until they pay their bill. When Daffy presents him with a ration book, the manager clips it to shreds with a paper punch. Finally, Porky and Daffy call Bugs Bunny for advice, but the wily rabbit reveals he too is a prisoner of the Broken Arms.

II; *Rationing*

175 Private Pluto (Walt Disney/RKO — 4/2/43)

Producer: Walt Disney; *Director:* Gerry Geronimi; *Animators:* George Rowley, John Lounsbery, Al Bertino, Josh Meador, Philip Duncan, Les Clark, Nick Nichols; *Layout:* Bruce Bushman, Charles Philippi; *Music:* Oliver Wallace

Pluto is warned to beware of saboteurs while on guard duty. The dog patrols a turreted coastal gun (the detailed interior animation suggests the influence of the training films made at Disney), but runs afoul of two chipmunks who use the cannon's barrel to crack their nuts. Pluto is no match for the ingenious schemes of the rodents. The chipmunks in this cartoon are the prototypes for Chip 'n' Dale, who returned to bother Pluto in *Squatter's Rights* (1946). By the summer of 1942, thousands of dogs—nicknamed "coasties"—were actually being used to patrol America's shores.

I; *Armed Forces — Army; Spy-Saboteur*

176 Professor Small and Mister Tall (Columbia — 3/26/43)

Producer: Dave Fleischer; *Directors:* Paul Sommer, John Hubley; *Script:* John McLeish; *Animators:* Jim Armstrong, Volus Jones; *Music:* Eddie Kilfeather

The title characters are working as vendors on a train when Small (the tall one) tosses a horseshoe away and shatters a mirror. Tall (the short one) protests that this means bad luck, and their train promptly falls off a bridge. Small and Tall struggle across the desert to Spook, Nevada, and enter the Creeps Hotel, which has a ghost for a hotel clerk. The clerk appears in various forms, including a doctor, a detective, and a ranting Hitler (who commits suicide). Small and Tall repair the broken mirror and are rewarded with a shower of money, a limousine, and a beautiful pair of women. However, Small tosses the mirror away and their luck deserts them once more. This cartoon has very stylized animation and graphics, quite unusual for the period.

II; *Hitler*

177 Ration Bored (Universal — 7/26/43)

Producer: Walter Lantz; *Director:* Emery Hawkins, Milt Schaffer; *Script:* Ben Hardaway; *Animator:* Bob Bentley; *Music:* Darrell Calker

Out for a drive, Woody Woodpecker spots a sign reading "Is This Trip Really Necessary?" and replies, "I'm a necessary evil." However, when he runs out of gas, he can't persuade the gas station attendant to sell him any fuel without a ration book. Woody decides to siphon gas out of other cars, but foolishly chooses a police car (with "V" license tags) and wakes up the cop inside. They chase each other around a junkyard (full of spare tires, oddly enough), and finally crash into a gasoline storage tank. After an explosion, Woody and the cop are seen coming out of the "Wing Rationing Board" in Heaven, as angels. The gas-stealing plot was reused in *Well Oiled* (1947).

I; *Rationing; "V"*

178   Ration Fer the Duration (Paramount — 5/28/43)

Director: Seymour Kneitel; *Script:* Jack Mercer, Jack Ward; *Animators:* Dave Tendlar, Tom Golden

Popeye's nephews would rather go fishing than tend a Victory Garden, until their uncle reminds them of the story of Jack and the Beanstalk. Popeye takes a nap (his pipe toots the "V" theme from Beethoven's Fifth Symphony) and dreams he climbs a beanstalk to a giant's castle. The giant — whose shirt reads "N.Y. Giants" (he wipes this off and says "I didn't think it was funny, either") — turns out to be a hoarder of tires (laid by a chicken instead of golden eggs), sugar, gasoline, etc. Saying "Uncle Sam can use this stuff," Popeye grabs a load of the scarce loot and runs for it, then wakes up to find it was only a dream. However, his nephews' garden has yielded some unusual produce, including tires and tin cans (as "Praise the Lord and Pass the Ammunition" is heard on the soundtrack).

I; *Victory Garden; Shortages; "V"; Production*

179   Reason and Emotion (Walt Disney/RKO — 8/27/43)

Producer: Walt Disney; *Director:* Bill Roberts; *Animators:* Milt Kahl, Ollie Johnston, Norm Tate, Bill Tytla, Ward Kimball; *Layout:* Hugh Hennesy; *Music:* Paul J. Smith

The conflict in the human mind between Reason (an egghead type) and Emotion (a caveman, reportedly a caricature of animator Ward Kimball) is depicted in this cartoon. Emotion is irrational, primitive, and easily swayed by rumors and propaganda — Hitler's emotional appeals to the fear, pride, and prejudices of the German people are cited as examples. Emotion imprisons Reason in a concentration camp. Typical American John Doakes is warned against letting scare headlines and rumors affect his attitude about the war. At the end, Reason and Emotion are shown working together (flying a warplane) to win the war for the Allies. Footage from this short — purged of the war references — was recycled for later Disney TV shows and videos.

I; *Hitler; Japan; Draft; Nazis; Fifth Column; Armed Forces — Air Corps; Britain; Concentration Camp*

180   Red Hot Riding Hood (MGM — 5/8/43)

Producer: Fred Quimby; *Director:* Tex Avery; *Animators:* Preston Blair, Ed Love, Irven Spence; *Music:* Scott Bradley

Red Riding Hood and Grandma revolt against the traditional nature of this fairy tale, so an offscreen MGM spokesperson agrees to tell the story in a "new way." The Wolf stops off at a Sunset Strip nightclub to catch the show. When the sexy, red-haired Red performs, the lecherous Wolf goes wild. Red's song includes a request that her boyfriends give her a B-19. The Wolf—doing a Charles Boyer impersonation—sweeps Red off her feet and promises her (*sotto voce*) "a new set of whitewall tires." Rejected by Red, the Wolf becomes the object of her man-hungry Grandma's affections. Grandma, clad in a slinky evening gown, pursues the Wolf ceaselessly; finally, he returns to the nightclub, exhausted and battered, and blows his brains out! However, his ghost is equally electrified by Red's song-and-dance! An alternate ending in which the Wolf is forced into a shotgun marriage with Grandma—with three children as a result—was cut after complaints by the Production Code Administration. Tex Avery's "Wolf" character somewhat resembles Adolf Wolf of *Blitz Wolf* (1942), q.v.

    II; *Armed Forces—Air Corps; Shortages*

181 *Sammy Salvage (War Production Board/War Activities Committee—(c) 1943)

Producer/Director: Ted Eshbaugh; *Songs and Music:* Austen Croom-Johnson, Alan Kent

    A short cartoon in Technicolor, independently produced by Ted Eshbaugh for the Conservation Division of the War Production Board, and distributed by the War Activities Committee. Designed to encourage scrap collection, it was widely shown in theatres during 1943 and 1944. A cherubic little boy in an Uncle Sam outfit marches down a typical small town Main Street singing "Junk ain't junk no more, 'cause junk can win the war! Collect today for the U.S.A." Various objects, including a trash can and horseshoes, jump up and form a tin man and his "pet" teapot. They fall in behind Sammy Salvage: "From the attic to the cellar, starting looking if you please, All your trash will go to smash, the pricky Japanese." As an old flivver pulls an obsolete plow out of his garage, a farmer joins the procession. Sammy plays his fife and other animated junk creatures (including an old tire) come along, finally marching straight into a flaming blast furnace in a smoking factory. The molten scrap becomes war materials, including a tank, battleship, and B-17 bomber. An offscreen narrator intones: "Your junk has wings, America sings, Liberty for ever more." Sammy Salvage reappears, makes the "V" for Victory sign and exhorts the audience to "Throw your scrap into the fight, junk can win the war!" He salutes the audience and a shot of the waving American flag appears.

    I; *Armed Forces—Army, Air Corps, Navy; Home Front; Japanese; Production;* "V"

182 Scrap for Victory (20th Century–Fox—1/22/43)

Producer: Paul Terry; *Director:* Connie Rasinski; *Script:* John Foster; *Music:* Philip A. Scheib

    Private Gandy Goose and Sgt. Cat are fighting on a Pacific island when their ammunition begins to run low. A call is made to Washington, and dozens of funny animals begin to collect scrap—as "Have You Got Any Scrap?" is sung on the soundtrack—which is turned into tanks, planes, and ammunition. Gandy and Cat receive the assistance they need to prevail in battle. One of the few cartoons to show a battle in progress (although the enemy is never seen), *Scrap for Victory* uses it only as a framework for another "animals on the home front"-themed plot. The OWI reviewer lauded the inventiveness of this cartoon and further stated "Its moral is well put over." However, the sequence in which a horse destroys fire hydrants and street lamps for scrap metal seems hardly commendable. In another scene, a large portrait on a junk wagon of a smug Hitler is left battered and grimacing by a rain of scrap metal.

I; *Armed Forces— Army, Air Corps; Scrap Metal; Production; Hitler*

183   Scrap Happy Daffy (Warner Bros— 6/19/43)

Producer: Leon Schlesinger; *Director:* Frank Tashlin; *Script:* Don Christensen; *Animator:* Art Davis; *Music:* Carl W. Stalling

Daffy Duck, wearing a Civil Defense helmet, runs a scrap yard. His boast — "Mussolini in scrap heap — Now let's junk Hitler"— is picked up by a newspaper and eventually reaches Germany, where a (literally) rug-chewing Hitler orders his forces to "destroy that scrap pile!" A submarine delivers a swastika-tagged goat ("A Focke-Wulf in sheep's clothing") to eat all of the scrap. Daffy, frustrated in his attempts to foil the menace, is ready to give up when his duck ancestors— a Pilgrim, a Minute Man, even an Abe Lincoln duck — appear and remind him "Americans don't give up!" Daffy turns into Super-American and saves his scrapyard from the Nazi menace. He wakes up and thinks it was all a dream, until he spots the submarine on top of his scrap heap! This black-and-white cartoon was the first Tashlin-directed short released after his return from a stint at Columbia. Daffy's reference to Mussolini's fall came a month *before* the Italian dictator was forced to resign.

I; *Scrap Metal; "V"; Hitler; Mussolini; Nazis; Home Defense; Historical American Figures; Japanese; Armed Forces— Germany*

184   Secret Agent (Paramount — 7/30/43)

Director: Seymour Kneitel; *Script:* Carl Meyer; *Animators:* Otto Feuer, Steve Muffati; *Music Arr:* Sammy Timberg

The last of the Superman cartoon series, this episode does not feature Lois Lane. Instead, a blonde female intelligence agent is pursued by Nazi spies trying to recover incriminating documents she has obtained. The spies ambush the woman and her police escort on a drawbridge. Meanwhile, Clark Kent has been captured by the spies— whose leader wears a monocle and has a Hitler moustache — but changes into Superman and rescues the agent before she can be crushed by the gears of the drawbridge. He then flies the young woman and her valuable information to the steps of the Capitol in Washington. The cartoon concludes with Superman saluting the American flag.

I; *Spies; Nazis; Hitler*

185   Seein' Red, White 'n' Blue (Paramount — 2/19/43)

Director: Dan Gordon; *Script:* Joe Stultz; *Animators:* Jim Tyer, Ben Solomon; *Music:* Winston Sharples

Blacksmith Bluto receives his draft notice (the messenger's bicycle has shoes instead of tires) and tries to persuade the draft board to give him an exemption.

Popeye fools Bluto into exposing his physical fitness— by making him lift a 1000-pound weight disguised as a sexy secretary (as "I Don't Want to Walk Without You" plays on the soundtrack)— so Bluto leaps out the window in an attempt to injure himself. He later tries to get hit by a car and a falling safe, but remains unhurt. Bluto finally tosses Popeye into an orphanage, where Japanese spies are working on "Military Secrets" and "Sabotage Plans." Disguised as little orphans (with a Hitler-faced rocking horse), the spies assault the unwary Popeye, and Bluto is forced to come to his aid. Popeye's super punch travels to Japan and decks Hirohito, then travels to Germany and flattens Hitler (who is consoled by Göring). Bluto, his patriotism finally aroused, joins the Navy.

I; *Japanese Caricatures; Hitler; Draft; Armed Forces— Navy; Hirohito; Göring; Spies; Draft Avoidance*

186   Shipyard Symphony (20th Century–Fox — 3/19/43)

Producer: Paul Terry; *Director:* Eddie Donnelly; *Script:* John Foster; *Music:* Philip A. Scheib

Animal workers, using a variety of unusual and imaginative methods, construct a warship in time to music conducted by an American eagle. After its completion, the ship is launched and salutes the Statue of Liberty by firing its guns as it passes. Another "animals on the home front" Terrytoon, this one is reminiscent of *Rhapsody in Rivets* (Warner Bros., 1941), in which a dog "conducts" the construction of a skyscraper to music.

I; *Production; Armed Forces— Navy*

187   Slay It with Flowers (Columbia — 1/8/43)

Producer: Dave Fleischer; *Director:* Bob Wickersham; *Script:* Leo Salkin; *Animators:* Phil Duncan, Grant Simmons; *Music:* Eddie Kilfeather

The Fox buys seeds for his rooftop Victory Garden at the Victory Seed Store ("Artichoke Hitler ... Beet Mussolini ... Squash the Japs") but the Crow appears and eats the seeds as fast as the Fox can plant them. The Fox tries to discourage the pest in various ways— including the creation of a Hitler scarecrow— but the Crow only desists when he learns the garden is a Victory Garden. The OWI report was rather rough on this short: "In view of the present shortage of film, this cartoon is an irresponsible waste of footage."

II; *Mussolini; Hitler; Victory Garden; Japanese Caricatures*

188   Somewhere in Egypt (20th Century–Fox — 9/17/43)

Producer: Paul Terry; *Director:* Mannie Davis; *Script:* John Foster; *Music:* Philip A. Scheib

GIs Private Gandy Goose and Sgt. Cat are camped in the desert. Gandy's flute-playing makes the Cat dream they are inside the Sphinx with assorted mummies, dancing girls, and sword-swinging guards. At one point in the dream, Gandy and the Cat pass a sign stuck in the sand: "Rommel Slept Here." Sgt. Cat wakes up and immediately orders Gandy to start playing again. Other Gandy Goose cartoons used the "all-a-dream" motif, including *Aladdin's Lamp* (1943), q.v.

II; *Armed Forces— Army, Germany; Blacks*

189   Spinach fer Britain (Paramount — 1/22/43)

Director: I. Sparber; *Script:* Carl Meyer; *Animators:* Jim Tyer, Abner Kneitel; *Music:* Winston Sharples, Sammy Timberg

Popeye is taking a cargo of spinach to England in his little boat when he runs afoul of a Nazi submarine, commanded by a tall, skinny officer and a short, fat one (both wearing Hitler moustaches). The U-boat destroys his ship, but Popeye piles the crates of spinach into a lifeboat and continues his journey, muttering "If I didn't have this cargo, I'd croak those Nazis." The enemy sub pursues Popeye, who rows into a minefield. An explosion sends the spinach into the U-boat, but Popeye eats some of his private stock of the canned vegetable and transforms himself into a human "depth charge" to commandeer the craft. Paddling the wrecked U-boat with his hands, Popeye gets lost in the fog and winds up in London, in front of No. 10 Downing Street (the Prime Minister's residence). He delivers his cargo, cracks the heads of the surviving Nazi sailors, and blows the "V" theme from Beethoven's Fifth Symphony on his pipe.

I; *Nazis; Britain; Hitler; "V"; Armed Forces — Germany*

190   *The Spirit of '43 (Walt Disney/U.S. Treasury Department — 1943)

Producer: Walt Disney; *Director:* Jack King; *Animators:* Josh Meador, Paul Allen, Ward Kimball, John Sibley, Judge Whitaker, Charles Nichols, Hal King, Marvin Woodward; *Music:* Paul J. Smith

Factory worker Donald Duck is torn between his two alter-egos on payday — a miserly Scots duck who urges him to save, and a zoot-suited spendthrift. As they battle over Donald's money, the Scots duck crashes into a wall and the red bricks, white mortar, and stars on a blue field (the window) form an American flag. The spendthrift is tossed into the sleazy "Idle Hours Club" (smashing the swinging door into a swastika shape), blows swastika-shaped smoke rings, and eventually begins to resemble Hitler. The club itself collapses into a "V" shape, and Donald rushes to the Internal Revenue Service to make an advance payment on his taxes. From this point on, footage from the latter half of *The New Spirit* (1942), q.v., was re-used. *The Spirit of '43* was distributed theatrically by the Treasury Department instead of through commercial channels.

I; *Hitler; Japan; "V"; Germany; FDR; Nazis*

191   The Stork's Holiday (MGM — 10/23/43)

Producer: Fred Quimby; *Director:* George Gordon; *Script:* Otto Englander, Webb Smith; *Animators:* Michael Lah, Rudy Zamora, Carl Urbano, Don Williams, Al Grandmain; *Music:* Scott Bradley

Doc Stork announces his retirement because the war has made delivering babies too dangerous. However, visions of his ancestors—who continued to fly through the Revolutionary, Civil, and First World wars— inspire the stork to don armor (made from an old stove) and deliver his cargo (of kittens). He has to contend with searchlights, anti-aircraft fire, barrage balloons, and anthropomorphized enemy fighter planes (their cowlings look like German helmets), but manages to triumph in the end, blowing a "V" with cigar smoke. This was the only 1943 MGM

cartoon not directed by Rudolf Ising, Hanna-Barbera, or Tex Avery. *Scrap Happy Daffy* (1943), q.v., used a similar "American ancestors" motif to inspire its hero.
I; *Germany; Historical American Figures; "V"; World War I; Armed Forces — Germany*

192   Sufferin' Cats (MGM — 1/16/43)

Producer: Fred Quimby; *Directors:* Joseph Barbera & William Hanna; *Animators:* Peter Burness, George Gordon, Kenneth Muse, Jack Zander; *Music:* Scott Bradley
Tom teams up with another cat in his perennial pursuit of Jerry the mouse. Tom is about to ax Jerry as his pal holds the mouse, but a red devil cat whispers in Tom's ear: "You don't have to share that mouse with that guy. You're a citizen, ain't you? You got rights. That mouse was yours first. You had priorities on him."
II; *Shortages*

193   Super-Rabbit (Warner Bros — 4/3/43)

Producer: Leon Schlesinger; *Director:* Charles M. Jones; *Script:* Tedd Pierce; *Animator:* Ken Harris; *Music:* Carl W. Stalling
In a pre-credits sequence that spoofs the Superman cartoon series, a figure soars over a skyscraper and someone says "It's a bird!" "No, it ain't a bird," comes the reply, "it's a dive bomber!" No, it's Super Rabbit! Bugs Bunny turns into Super Rabbit after eating special carrots created in a laboratory. His first mission is to foil Cottontail Smith's plan to wipe out all the rabbits in Texas. When Smith and his horse eat some of the super-carrots and gain super powers as well, Bugs says "This looks like a job for a *real* superman," and emerges from a phone booth in United States Marine dress blues. He marches off to "Berlin, Tokyo, and points east," telling his opponents, "Sorry fellas, I can't play wit' ya any more. I got some important work to do."
II; *Armed Forces — Marines; Germany; Japan*

194   Swing Your Partner (Universal — 4/26/43)

Producer: Walter Lantz; *Director:* Alex Lovy; *Script:* Ben Hardaway, Milt Schaffer; *Animator:* Paul Smith; *Music:* Darrell Calker
Homer Pigeon wakes up his horse to take him and his girl to the square dance. The horse, who had been dreaming of a huge pile of sugar cubes, rebels. By the end of the cartoon, Homer is pulling the carriage while the horse rides! One of the musicians at the dance is a dead ringer for Disney's Goofy.
II; *Shortages*

195   There's Something About a Soldier (Columbia — 2/26/43)

Producer: Dave Fleischer; *Director:* Alec Geiss; *Script:* Ed Seward; *Animators:* Grant Simmons, Chic Otterstrom; *Music:* Paul Worth
This short shows people from all over the country joining the armed forces, including blacks, Eskimos, even dogs, elephants, pigs, and other animals! A little boy is depressed because he's too young to enlist, but in the end he gets to carry a "V" banner in a parade. The OWI remarked: "If it's supposed to promote enlisting, it is safe to say that it failed." The title comes from a popular song and was also used for a 1943 Columbia feature film.
I; *Armed Forces — Army, Navy, Air Corps, Marine Corps; "V"; Blacks*

196 Tin Pan Alley Cats (Warner Bros— 8/25/43)

Producer: Leon Schlesinger; *Director:* Robert Clampett; *Script:* Warren Foster; *Animator:* Rod Scribner; *Music:* Carl W. Stalling, Milt Franklyn (song)

"Cats Waller" (a cat caricature of jazz musician/composer Fats Waller) chooses the wild Kit Kat Club over the sedate Uncle Tomcat's Mission next door. Once inside the nightclub, surrealistic visions taunt the drum-playing cat, including bizarre Hitler and Hirohito caricatures dancing together. Stalin appears, kicks Hitler, and forces him to do a Russian dance. Cats Waller finally flees the Kit Kat Club and joins the mission band. Footage from *Porky in Wackyland* (1938) was reused in this cartoon, with color added. The jazz music on the soundtrack is performed by Eddie Beal and his band.

II; *Blacks; Hitler; Hirohito; Stalin*

197 To Duck ... Or Not to Duck (Warner Bros—1/9/43)

Producer: Leon Schlesinger; *Director:* Charles M. Jones; *Script:* Tedd Pierce; *Animator:* Robert Cannon; *Music:* Carl W. Stalling

Elmer Fudd and his hunting dog Larrimore are berated by Daffy Duck, who challenges Elmer to a "fair fight"—a boxing match with a duck referee and an all-duck (except for Larrimore) audience. As the referee is "demonstrating" foul punches on Elmer, "We Did It Before and We Can Do It Again" is heard on the soundtrack. Later, when Elmer is knocked out, "Captains of the Clouds" plays. Chuck Jones wasn't too fond of topical references, but music director Stalling slipped these two in.

II; *World War I; Armed Forces — Air Corps*

198 Tokio Jokio (Warner Bros— 5/15/43)

Producer: Leon Schlesinger; *Director:* Cpl. Norman McCabe; *Script:* Don Christensen; *Animator:* I. Ellis; *Music:* Carl W. Stalling

Purportedly a captured Japanese newsreel ("Nipponews of the Week"), this black-and-white short includes segments on "Civilian Defense" (an "air raid siren" consists of two men sticking pins in each other and howling in pain; an "aircraft spotter" is painting spots on an airplane; Fire Prevention Headquarters has burned down) and "Kitchen Hints" (in the Professor Tojo Cooking Class, one learns to make a sandwich by placing a meat ration card between two bread ration cards). In the "Nippon-Nifties Style Show," the Japanese Victory suit has "no cuffs, no pleats, no lapel" (there is no suit!). "Headline Personalities" highlights Admiral Yamamoto, who boasts he will visit the White House (an "editor's note" shows Yamamoto's reserved room, complete with electric chair); General Homma (commander of the Japanese troops occupying the Philippines) exhibits coolness under fire by hiding in a hollow log, and the log's previous occupant — a skunk — responds by donning a gas mask. "Flashes from the Axis" features Lord Hee-Haw (a reference to actual Nazi propaganda broadcaster "Lord Haw Haw"), who tells Hitler he got a "Wish You Were Here" postcard from Rudolf Hess (in a prison camp); Mussolini is exhibited as "Rome's Number One Ruin." In the final sequence, entitled "Japanese Navy All at Sea," various disasters and ridiculous aspects of the Japanese Navy are depicted. A one-man torpedo weapon is shown (the pilot screams "Let me outta here!")—curiously enough, such a weapon, called the "Kaiten," was actually introduced by Japan in 1944. Although this cartoon is an accurate spoof of the Hollywood newsreel format, its content is extremely outrageous and racist (in several scenes the Japanese have distinctly rat-like features).

I; *Japanese Caricatures; Hitler; Mussolini; Nazis; Armed Forces— Japan; Tojo*

199 Too Weak to Work (Paramount — 3/19/43)

Director: Seymour Kneitel; *Animator:* George Germanetti, Tom Johnson; *Script:* Jack Ward, Jack Mercer; *Music:* Winston Sharples

Popeye is hard at work painting the lifeboats on his battleship, but Bluto is goldbricking, and pretends to be sick so he won't have to work. Popeye visits Bluto in the hospital but discovers his pal is faking. Dressing up like a nurse, Popeye puts his shipmate through the wringer, shrinking him in a steam cabinet, then inflating him to blimp proportions with gas. Finally, he revives Bluto with spinach and the energetic sailor paints everything in sight, including Popeye. The popular song "I've Got Spurs That Jingle, Jangle, Jingle" is used extensively on the soundtrack.

II; *Armed Forces— Navy*

200 Tortoise Wins by a Hare (Warner Bros— 2/23/43)

Producer: Leon Schlesinger; *Director:* Robert Clampett; *Script:* Warren Foster; *Animator:* Robert McKimson; *Music:* Carl W. Stalling

In this sequel to *Tortoise Beats Hare* (1941), Bugs Bunny — believing his opponent won the previous race due to his "streamlined" shape — adopts a turtle-like costume for the rematch. However, this confuses some rabbit gangsters, who have bet on Bugs to win, and they inadvertently sabotage his efforts. Discovering their error, they commit suicide! Bugs displays "A" and "C" gas ration cards at one point, and later claims "I got a secret weapon." A newspaper headline mentions a "Jap cruiser," and a chorus of turtles sing "He Did It Before and He Can Do It Again."

II; *Rationing; Japan; Hitler*

201 *The Truck That Flew (Paramount —(c) 8/6/43)

Producer/Director: George Pal; *Orig. Book:* Dudley Morris

A little boy dreams his bed turns into a truck and flies through the air. He is attacked by three airplanes (with slanted "eyes"), flown by bespectacled, bucktoothed pilots. The boy shoots them down (with his finger), and they form a "V" as they crash; he proudly paints three Japanese flags on his bedpost. This was a Puppetoon (dimension animation rather than cartoon animation).

II; *Japanese Caricatures; "V"; Armed Forces— Japan*

202 The Uninvited Pest (MGM — 7/17/43)

Producer: Fred Quimby; *Director:* Rudolf Ising; *Music:* Scott Bradley

Barney Bear wants to get some sleep, but a little squirrel has eyes for the bear's bowl of walnuts. At the conclusion of this cartoon, the squirrel has made a shambles of Barney's house and runs into a closet to hide from the enraged bruin.

When Barney opens the closet door, a cascade of junk falls on him, including an air raid warden's helmet and a tire.

II; *Air Raid Warden; Shortages*

203   *Victory Through Air Power (Walt Disney/United Artists— 8/13/43)

Producer: Walt Disney; *Director:* H.C. Potter; *Director of Photography:* Ray Rennahan; *Art Director:* Richard Irvine; *Technicolor Color Director:* Natalie Kalmus; *Technicolor Associate:* Morgan Padelford; *Interior Decorations:* William Kiernan; *Narrator:* Art Baker; *Animation:* David Hand; *Story Director:* Perce Pearce; *Story Adaptors:* T. Hee, Erdman Penner, William Cottrell, James Bodrero, George Stallings, Jose Rodriguez; *Sequence Directors:* Clyde Geronimi, Jack Kinney, James Algar; *Art Directors:* Herbert Ryman, Donald DaGradi, Tom Codrick, Charles Philippi, Elmer Plummer, Don Griffith, Cliff Devirian, Glen Scott, Karl Karpe, Bill Herwig; *Animators:* Ward Kimball, John Lounsbery, Hugh Fraser, George Rowley, John Sibley, Norm Tate, Vladimir Tytla, Joshua Meador, Carleton Boyd, Bill Justice, Ed Aardal, John McManus, Oliver M. Johnston Jr., Marvin Woodward, Harvey Toombs; *Backgrounds:* Albert Dempster, Dick Anthony, Claude Coats, Ray Huffine, Robert Blanchard, Joe Stahley, Nino Carbe; *Music:* Edward H. Plumb, Paul J. Smith, Oliver Wallace; *Production Manager:* Dan Keefe; *Film Editor:* Jack Dennis; *Sound Recording:* C.O. Slyfield, Lodge Cunningham

This feature-length film is dedicated to Billy Mitchell, a proponent of air power as early as the 1920s, who was "ignored and ridiculed." The history of aviation is briefly chronicled, including sequences of air warfare during World War I (comical Hun pilots shoot their own propellers before the invention of synchronized machine guns). The career of Major Alexander de Seversky (who wrote the 1942 book which inspired this movie) is summarized, and Seversky himself appears in live-action footage and describes how Hitler used air power to gain the advantage in 1939. The Japanese attack on Pearl Harbor is also mentioned. Seversky proposes that the Allies develop a strategy of long-range bombing to disrupt Hitler's supply lines, and also break the Japanese grip on the Pacific. This last point is illustrated with scenes of an American eagle attacking a Japanese "octopus" (an animated version of the islands of Japan), until the octopus releases its grip on the "sword of war" and relinquishes the territory it has conquered. Walt Disney was so impressed with Seversky's book that he undertook the film as an independent contribution to the war effort, releasing it through United Artists after his usual distributor, RKO, turned it down (it was not successful at the box-office). *Victory Through Air Power* contains little humor after the "history of aviation" sequences and is primarily a straight documentary-style retelling of Seversky's theories.

I; *Armed Forces— Air Corps, Japan, Germany, RAF; World War I; Pearl Harbor; Russia; Nazis; Hitler*

204   Victory Vehicles (Walt Disney/RKO — 7/30/43)

Producer: Walt Disney; *Director:* Jack Kinney; *Assistant Director:* Lou Debney, Ted Sebern, Bea Selck; *Script:* Ralph Wright, Webb Smith; *Animators:* Ed Aardal,

Andy Engman, Hugh Fraser, Bill Tytla, Bill Justice, John Sibley, Les Clark, Frank Thomas, Ward Kimball; *Layout:* Don DaGradi; *Music:* Ned Washington, Oliver Wallace (song)

Since automobiles, gas, and tires are in short supply during the war, this cartoon illustrates some alternative means of transportation. Goofy and others demonstrate go-carts, rollerskates, cycles, a magnet-driven vehicle (which also collects scrap metal as it goes), and pogo sticks. There are also visual references to the war, including signs reading "Beat the Jap With Scrap," "Buy Defense Bonds," "Draft Board," "Rationing Board," and so on. Includes the song "Hop On Your Pogo Stick."

I; *Home Front; Japanese Caricatures; Draft; Scrap Metal; Bonds; Production; Home Defense; Air Raid Warden; Germany; Rationing*

205   The Vitamin G-Man (Columbia — 1/22/43)

Producer: Dave Fleischer; *Directors:* John Hubley, Paul Sommer; *Script:* Jack Cosgriff; *Animator:* Jim Armstrong; *Music:* Eddie Kilfeather

A student detective is given a bizarre course of instruction by an old professor. At one point he peers into the professor's beard with a magnifying glass and sees a flea safari marching through the "jungle." Later, the detective consults a textbook on footprints and sees illustrations of "crow's feet," "athlete's foot," "hot foot," and "a tire (obsolete)."

II; *Shortages; Blacks*

206   War Dogs (MGM — 10/9/43)

Producer: Fred Quimby; *Directors:* William Hanna, Joseph Barbera; *Animators:* Pete Burness, Kenneth Muse, Irven Spence, Jack Zander; *Music:* Scott Bradley

Another "dogs in the army" cartoon! At the beginning, one dog dreams of catching a buck-toothed Japanese soldier. Most of the short depicts the dogs in training: one attacks a Hitler poster, others learn first aid, how to pitch tents, etc. Incompetent Private Smiley of the WOOFs has a run-in with a 16-inch gun hidden in a haystack, winding up inside the cannon's barrel.

I; *Armed Forces — Army, Air Corps, Japan; Hitler; Japanese Caricatures; Bonds; Nazis*

207   What's Buzzin' Buzzard (MGM — 11/27/43)

Producer: Fred Quimby; *Director:* Tex Avery; *Animators:* Ed Love, Ray Abrams, Preston Blair; *Music:* Scott Bradley

Two starving buzzards (one is a Jimmy Durante caricature) spot a rabbit (labeled "No Points") hopping across the "Painted Desert, Local 852." The rabbit gives them the slip, and the buzzards (one of whom has a "Closed for the Duration" sign posted in his mouth!) begin considering each other as potential meals. They finally capture the hare, but he shows them on a calendar that it is Meatless Tuesday. The cartoon concludes with a live-action shot of a steak (repeated due to "requests from the audience").

II; *Rationing*

208   Willoughby's Magic Hat (Columbia — 4/30/43)
Producer: Dave Fleischer; *Director:* Bob Wickersham; *Animators:* Phil Duncan, Howard Swift; *Script:* Sam Cobean; *Music:* Paul Worth
Meek Mr. Willoughby Wren acquires super strength after donning a hat made from Samson's hair. He saves a gorgeous blonde from a mechanical monster that can turn itself into a tank. Willoughby smashes the monster and hangs a "Scrap for Victory" sign on it.
II; *Scrap Metal; "V"*

209   The Wise Quacking Duck (Warner Bros— 5/12/43)
Producer: Leon Schlesinger; *Director:* Robert Clampett; *Script:* Warren Foster; *Animator:* Phil Monroe; *Music:* Carl W. Stalling
Mr. Meek tries to obtain a duck dinner for his "Sweetiepuss," but the dinner — Daffy Duck — won't cooperate. At one point Daffy tucks his head inside his collar and flops around, spraying ketchup gruesomely. Going inside Meek's house, Daffy puts a serious dent in the man's sugar supply. Making airplane noises (as "Captains of the Clouds" plays on the soundtrack), Daffy soars into the air and drops an egg through his thumb and forefinger ("Look folks, a secret bombsight!") onto Meek's head. Finally forced into a roasting pan at gunpoint, Daffy does a striptease to the tune of "It Had to Be You."
II; *Armed Forces — Air Corps*

210   Wood Peckin' (Paramount — 8/6/43)
Director: I. Sparber; *Script:* Joe Stultz; *Animators:* Nick Tafuri, Tom Golden; *Music:* Winston Sharples, Sammy Timberg
Popeye selects a tree to make into a new mast for his sailboat, but a tough woodpecker who lives in the tree objects. Popeye wins out in the end and chops down the tree, but allows the bird to keep his home at the top. As "Praise the Lord and Pass the Ammunition" is heard in the background, the woodpecker (imitating Edward G. Robinson's voice) says: "Home, sweet home. And listen you mugs out there, it's well worth fighting for, see?"
II

211   The Yankee Doodle Mouse (MGM — 7/26/43)
Producer: Fred Quimby; *Directors:* William Hanna, Joseph Barbera; *Animators:* Irven Spence, Pete Burness, Kenneth Muse, George Gordon; *Music:* Scott Bradley
The action of this cartoon takes place in the basement of the house where Tom (cat) and Jerry (mouse) live. Jerry flees to his "Cat Raid Shelter" with Tom in pursuit; the little mouse retaliates with "hen grenades" (eggs) and uses a spatula to launch a brick that sinks Tom, floating on a pot in the washtub. "Lt. Jerry Mouse" sends a communiqué to "headquarters," reading "Sited Cat, Sank Same." Wearing a bottle-cap helmet, Jerry drives his cheese-grater "jeep" along Tom's backside, then uses a bag of flour to make a smokescreen to escape. When Jerry, flying a makeshift airplane (with the popular shark's-mouth paintjob), begins to bomb Tom with lightbulbs, Tom fights back with fireworks. Jerry is forced to bail out, using a brassiere as a parachute! The cat attempts to tie Jerry to a skyrocket,

but the tricky mouse turns the tables and it is Tom who is launched. The rocket explodes in the sky, creating an American flag that Jerry salutes. His final report reads "Send More Cats!" Jerry's communiqués in this cartoon were parodies of actual (or reputedly actual) messages, including "Sited Sub, Sank Same," and "Send More Japs!" A blackface caricature of Tom has been cut from some TV prints. Academy Award, Best Cartoon (1943).

I; *Armed Forces — Army, Air Corps; Blacks; World War I; "V"*

1944

212   The Anvil Chorus Girl (Paramount — 5/26/44)
Director: I. Sparber; *Script:* Bill Turner, Jack Ward; *Animators:* Dave Tendlar, Morey Reden; *Music:* Winston Sharples

Popeye and Bluto are sailors on shore leave who meet lady blacksmith Olive Oyl. She needs an assistant, so they try to outdo each other in proving their worth. A sign outside the blacksmith's shop reads "Sale on Horse Shoes— No Coupons Required" (human shoes were rationed during the war). Bluto wins the contest, so Olive leaves him to mind the shop while she and Popeye go out on a date! Very similar to *House Tricks* and *Service With a Guile* (both 1946), in which Popeye and Bluto fight to see who can help Olive build a house and run a gas station, respectively.

II; *Women in Labor Force; Armed Forces — Navy; Rationing*

213   The Barber of Seville (Universal — 4/10/44)
Producer: Walter Lantz; *Director:* James Culhane; *Script:* Ben Hardaway, Milt Schaffer; *Animators:* Verne Harding, Les Kline; *Music:* Darrell Calker

Woody Woodpecker visits Tony's barber shop, but the proprietor is out (according to a sign) getting his (pre-induction) physical. Woody victimizes two would-be customers while singing an aria from the eponymous opera by Rossini. One of the customers gets a "Victory" haircut (in the shape of a V). *Rabbit of Seville* (Warner Bros., 1950) utilized the same concept and music, replacing Woody with Bugs Bunny (with Elmer Fudd as the amateur barber's unfortunate customer).

II; *"V"; Draft*

214   Batty Baseball (MGM — 4/22/44)
Producer: Fred Quimby; *Director:* Tex Avery; *Animators:* Ray Abrams, Preston Blair, Ed Love; *Music:* Scott Bradley

The Yankee Doodlers are scheduled to play the Draft Dodgers at the W.C. Field, but the pitcher is the only player who shows up (his uniform reads "4-F")— signs on all of the other positions read "1-A." The announcer says "The players have taken their positions— oops! Forgot about the war." Later, an oversized batter comes to the plate, and his jersey reads "B-19." Otherwise, non-topical spot gags about baseball.

II; *Draft; Armed Forces — Air Corps*

215   Bear Raid Warden (MGM — 9/9/44)

Producer: Fred Quimby; *Director:* George Gordon; *Animators:* Arnold Gillespie, Michael Lah, Ed Barge, Jack Carr; *Music:* Scott Bradley

According to the signs on his house, Barney Bear has the "Fire Watcher ... Air Raid Warden ... Demolition Clearance" responsibilities for his neck of the woods. Enforcing a blackout requires considerable effort, especially when a firefly refuses to douse his lights. Finally subduing the recalcitrant bug, Barney spots his own home, lights blazing. Rushing inside to turn them off, Barney is hit on the head by a picture of himself in his air raid warden outfit.

I; *Air Raid Warden*

216   Big Heel-Watha (Buck of the Month) (MGM — 10/21/44)

Producer: Fred Quimby; *Director:* Tex Avery; *Script:* Heck Allen; *Animators:* Ray Abrams, Preston Blair, Ed Love; *Music:* Scott Bradley

Big Chief Rain-in-Face announces to his tribe that due to "heap big ration program muddle" and the meat shortage, he will award the hand of his daughter, Minnie Hot-Cha, to the first brave who brings back fresh meat. "4-F" Heel-Watha (who has a long nose and talks like Droopy) stalks the forest animals, which are helpfully marked with their ration status: rabbit (8 points), bird (1/2 point), deer (48 points, plus 6 more "points" for the antlers), and skunk ("No Ration Points Necessary"). However, the dopey brave's primary target is Screwy Squirrel (a self-advertised "Black Market Special"), who tears up Heel-Watha's ration book, throws eggs at him, hits him in the head with a mallet, and pulls a "Blackout Switch" that plunges the screen into darkness (of course, when Heel-Watha lights a match to see what's going on, Screwy shows up as an air raid warden and clubs him across the head). Finally, Screwy has mercy on his opponent and allows himself to be captured. Screwy (sometimes called Screwball) Squirrel was the star of a handful of cartoons but didn't catch on as a continuing character. His adenoidal voice was provided by Wally Maher, based on a teenage character Maher played on the radio show "Tommy Riggs and Betty Lou."

I; *Rationing; Armed Forces — Air Corps; Air Raid Warden; Draft; Black Market; Production*

217   Booby Hatched (Warner Bros — 10/14/44)

Producer: Leon Schlesinger; *Director:* Frank Tashlin; *Script:* Warren Foster; *Animator:* I. Ellis; *Music:* Carl W. Stalling

A mother duck hatches her brood (among them, ducklings named Franklin, Eleanor, Winston, and Leon — the first three named after famous people, and the latter after producer Schlesinger), but the last egg, "Robespierre," manages to poke only his legs out of his shell. He wanders around blindly, in search of warmth: when a kerosene lamp's flame dies, the unhatched duckling says "Darn this fuel oil shortage!" Robespierre (still in the shell) winds up in a wolf's soup kettle but is saved by his mom. Remade in 1948 as *The Shell-Shocked Egg*, but with turtles instead of ducks.

II; *Shortages, FDR; FDR-E; Churchill*

218 Brother Brat (Warner Bros—7/15/44)
Producer: Leon Schlesinger; *Director:* Frank Tashlin; *Script:* Melvin Millar; *Animators:* Art Davis, Isadore Ellis; *Music:* Carl W. Stalling

The cartoon opens with a narrator extolling the virtues of women in the labor force, accompanied by a montage of female workers in an aircraft plant. The narrator says "Superwoman" has "overcome all problems, obstacles, and difficulties except — where the heck to put the kids while she's working!" A muscular "Rosie the Riveter" type, who doesn't want to be an "absentee," browbeats Porky Pig into babysitting her little Butch while she builds planes at "Blockheed." Before she leaves, she gives Porky a copy of "Child Psychology by Pistol P. Momma" to help. Porky tries to follow the book's instructions and amuse the surly Butch, who prefers to ogle the pinups in *Esquire Jr.* and mistreat Porky's cat. When Butch bites him, Porky flings the infant into the kitchen; the child emerges from a pile of utensils with a pot on his head and transforms into a Winston Churchill caricature, who flashes the "V" sign and says "Of course you know, this means war! We will fight until Hitler and his Nazi gangsters suffer disastrous, overwhelming, complete defeat!" Butch then starts chasing Porky around the house with a knife, but the pig is saved by the arrival of the riveter. She tells Porky he didn't use the book correctly, and employs the tome to smack Butch's rear end!

I; *Women in Labor Force; "V"; Churchill; Production; Hitler; Tojo*

219 Buckaroo Bugs (Warner Bros—8/26/44)
Producer: Leon Schlesinger; *Director:* Robert Clampett; *Script:* Lou Lilly; *Animators:* Manny Gould, Robert McKimson; *Music:* Carl W. Stalling

A mysterious "Masked Marauder" has been stealing all the carrots from the Victory Gardens in the San Fernando Alley. "Brooklyn's famous fighting cowboy," Red Hot Ryder (a precursor to Yosemite Sam, only younger and dumber) arrives to investigate and meets Bugs Bunny. Bugs pretends to rob the 5:15 train of its valuable cargo: sugar, gasoline, shoes, tires, and butter (all items in short supply during the war). Red and his equally dim-witted horse make various futile attempts to capture the wily rabbit.

II; *Victory Garden; Rationing*

220 Bugs Bunny Nips the Nips (Warner Bros—4/22/44)
Producer: Leon Schlesinger; *Director:* I. Freleng; *Script:* Tedd Pierce; *Animators:* Gerry Chiniquy, Gil Turner; *Music:* Carl W. Stalling

"Somewhere in the Pacific," Bugs Bunny drifts along in a crate, watching for the "inevitable island" to turn up. It does, but it is occupied by Japanese soldiers. Bugs confronts one bare-foot, buck-toothed, sword-wielding enemy soldier, but temporarily fools him by dressing up like Hirohito. The soldier and Bugs both go aloft in Zeroes, but Bugs strips the man's plane away, and — as the man drifts to earth via parachute — hands him an anvil, remarking "Here's some scrap iron for Japan, Moto!" Back on the ground, Bugs is temporarily stymied by a giant sumo wrestler, but disguises himself as a geisha to get the upper hand. Finally, he drives up in a "Good Rumor" ice cream truck, handing out ice cream bars (with hand grenades inside) to the Japanese troops. After a series of explosions, Bugs thinks he has wiped out the enemy, but one battered soldier dashes up and presents his "lucky stick" that earns him a free ice cream bar (with another grenade inside!). Bugs, now bored, tries to hail a passing American ship, but changes his mind when a sexy, sarong-clad female bunny emerges from the jungle. *Bugs Bunny Nips the Nips* resembles *Herr Meets Hare* (1945), q.v., as well as the non-topical *Wackiki Wabbit* (1943). "Trade Winds" and "Someone's Rockin' My Dreamboat" are heard on the soundtrack.

I; *Japanese Caricatures; Armed Forces— Japan; Scrap Metal; Armed Forces— Navy; Hirohito*

221   The Butcher of Seville (20th Century–Fox —1/7/44)

Producer: Paul Terry; *Director:* Eddie Donnelly; *Script:* John Foster; *Animator:* Bill Tytla; *Music:* Philip A. Scheib

Like *Carmen's Veranda* (1944), q.v., an opera performance provides a framing story for this short. One tier of the opera house is devoted to patrons wearing zoot suits. As the story begins, a wolf butcher is sitting in his empty shop, surrounded by signs reading "No Meat To-day" and "Sold Out." The devil advises him that the milkmaid's cow will provide "300 pounds of beef, I vow," and the rest of the cartoon is devoted to the chase. The meat shortage is the inspiration for this cartoon although there are no overt wartime references.

II; *Shortages*

222   Carmen's Veranda (20th Century–Fox — 7/28/44)

Producer: Paul Terry; *Director:* Mannie Davis; *Script:* John Foster; *Music:* Philip A. Scheib

This short has the framing story of an opera performance. A pretty girl cat's mother — a Wagnerian hippo— wants her to marry the repulsive Count Dodo (a monocle-wearing dog). Dodo brings gifts of butter, gasoline, and nylons, but the cat sends for her lover Tyrone (Gandy Goose) to rescue her (some improvement!). In the end, Mama Hippo marries Dodo herself.

II; *Shortages*

223   Commando Duck (Walt Disney/RKO — 7/2/44)

Producer: Walt Disney; *Director:* Jack King; *Animators:* Judge Whitaker, Paul Allen, Hal King, Harvey Toombs, Dan Towsley, Ed Aardal; *Music:* Oliver Wallace

Donald Duck parachutes into the jungle to wipe out a Japanese airfield. As he travels down the river on a rubber raft, Japanese snipers (including one disguised as a rock and one posing as a slant-eyed, buck-toothed tree) try to stop him, but Donald thinks their bullets are merely mosquitoes and presses onward. His raft gets caught beneath a waterfall and fills up with water until it finally explodes— the air base is wiped out by the ensuing tidal wave. Donald observes the ruined installation and reports: "Contacted enemy, washed out same." The most blatantly anti–Japanese Disney cartoon of the war, this short nonetheless concentrates mostly on Donald Duck rather than the racial aspects of the enemy. Currently-available versions of this cartoon from Disney have most or all of the Japanese references removed.

I; *Japanese Caricatures; Armed Forces— Army, Japan; Hirohito*

224   The Disillusioned Bluebird (Columbia — 5/26/44)

Producer: Dave Fleischer; *Director:* Howard Swift; *Script:* Edward Seward; *Animators:* Jim Armstrong, Grant Simmons; *Music:* Eddie Kilfeather, Sir Lancelot (songs)

A bluebird on a night flight over Europe is caught in an air raid — he's blinded by spotlights, gets caught on a parachute, and finally catches a ride on a shell to a peaceful Caribbean island and meets laid-back crow "Calypso Joe." The bluebird finds true happiness on the island, especially after meeting a Carmen Miranda-like lady bird.

I; *Blacks; Armed Forces; South America*

225   The Dream Kids (Columbia — 2/5/44)

Producer: Dave Fleischer; *Director:* Bob Wickersham; *Script:* Sam Cobean; *Animators:* Phil Duncan, Chic Otterstrom; *Music:* Eddie Kilfeather

This short opens with a sign reading "Government request birds not to fly south this winter — conserve feathers!" The Crow is therefore stuck up north in the cold, and the Fox keeps throwing him out of *his* warm house. The Crow reads a "Dream Book" and learns how to induce dreams and nightmares; he uses this to trick the Fox into leaving the warmth of his bed. However, the Fox does the same thing to the Crow, and regains his berth.

II; *Shortages*

226   Duck Soup to Nuts (Warner Bros— 5/27/44)

Producer: Leon Schlesinger; *Director:* I. Freleng; *Script:* Tedd Pierce; *Animator:* Richard Bickenbach; *Music:* Carl W. Stalling

Porky Pig is hunting ducks (Elmer Fudd must be out of town)— Daffy Duck to be precise. After Daffy boasts "I got a contract with Warner Brothers," and tries to con Porky into doing a love scene, complete with blonde wig, Porky says, "Now I'll tell *your* future, gremlin — you're going to be a dead duck!" Daffy peers into the barrel of Porky's shotgun and sees a Vargas-style pinup (as "They're Either Too Young or Too Old" plays). When Daffy's bill gets caught in the gun, Porky shoots him into the air and the duck falls back to earth with a bomblike whistle. Finally, Daffy asks Porky, "Out of ammunition?" and when the pig replies in the affirmative, Daffy says "Praise the Lord!"

II; *Armed Forces*

227   The Egg-Yegg (Columbia —12/8/44)

Director: Bob Wickersham; *Script:* Sam Cobean; *Animators:* Ben Lloyd, Volus Jones; *Music:* Eddie Kilfeather

The Crow receives a package containing two eggs and a letter that reads: "Under separate cover am sending you two refugee eggs. Trusting that you will afford them protection and a good home until they hatch. [signed] an Egg-cited Mother." "Professor" Fox is on an egg-collecting expedition — he and the Crow tangle over the eggs until they finally hatch and resolve the problem. The idea of "refugee eggs" was inspired by the practice of sending British children to Canada and the United States to get them out of the war zone.

II; *Refugee*

228   First Aiders (Walt Disney/RKO — 9/22/44)

Producer: Walt Disney; *Director:* Charles Nichols; *Script:* Harry Reeves, Rex Cox;
   Animators: Norman Tate, Marvin Woodward, George Nicholas, Andy Engman,
   Charles Nichols, Ed Aardal, Bob Youngquist; *Layouts:* Bruce Bushman; *Backgrounds:* Lenard Kester; *Music:* Oliver Wallace
      Minnie Mouse is a nurse's aide practicing first aid at home. She utilizes Pluto
in her attempts at artificial respiration and bandaging, but the dog is tormented
by kitten Figaro, who takes advantage of his helplessness. Finally, both Pluto and
Figaro take a tumble down a flight of stairs, and Minnie has two patients to work
on. A shot of Pluto emerging from a trash can with the lid on his head, briefly
converted into a Chinese stereotype, has been cut from current versions of this
cartoon.
      II; *Home Front; China*

229   From Hand to Mouse (Warner Bros — 8/5/44)

Director: Charles M. Jones; *Script:* Michael Maltese; *Animator:* Robert Cannon;
   Music: Carl W. Stalling
      A mouse persuades a lion to release him by promising to save the larger ani-
mal's life some day. When the lion lets him go, the mouse runs away and yells
"Sucker!" The lion repeatedly recaptures the mouse but time and again is conned
into letting the rodent go free. At one point the mouse prevents the lion from eating him by holding up a sign reading "12 points," and asking "Got your ration
stamp, Bub?" When the lion says no, the mouse produces a rubber stamp and
brands his antagonist "SUCKER." This is a semi-remake of *The Lyin' Mouse* (1937).
      II; *Rationing; Blacks*

230   The Ghost Town (20th Century–Fox — 9/22/44)

Producer: Paul Terry; *Director:* Mannie Davis; *Script:* John Foster; *Music:* Philip
   A. Scheib
      Gandy Goose and Sourpuss Cat (now civilians) are in the desert, heading for
a ghost town. They are plagued by a phantom vulture, who eats their horse and
chases them into the town. Gandy and Sourpuss visit a saloon, whose only customers are ghosts. The spirits sing a song, one verse of which goes: "You can play
the host, serve butter on toast, and nice big ten-pound roast; and do it every day,
no ration points to pay." The goose and cat escape with a bag of gold, but when
they reach safety and open the sack, the vulture pops out!
      II; *Rationing*

231   Goldilocks and the Jivin' Bears (Warner Bros — 9/30/44)

Director: I. Freleng; *Script:* Tedd Pierce; *Animation:* Ken Champin; *Music:* Carl
   W. Stalling
      Black caricature jazz musicians Big Size Bear, Middle Size Bear, and Wee
Small Bear go for a walk to allow their red-hot instruments to cool down after a
jam session. The Big Bad Wolf (also a black caricature) is waiting next door for
their neighbor Red Riding Hood to come home, but a messenger brings a telegram
for Red's granny reading: "Sorry Grand Mater, can't be there till later, working at

Lockheed as a rivatater — Red." The Wolf switches his attention to Goldilocks (he has a paper which indicates Red Riding Hood is worth six ration points, and Goldilocks, none) when the little girl shows up at the Three Black Bears' home: "With this food shortage, what am I waiting for?" The Bears come home to find the Wolf chasing Goldilocks around the house; thinking the intruders are "jitterbugs," the furry musicians seize their instruments, and start playing hot swing music. The exhausted Wolf tries to escape, but is caught by Granny, who forces him to keep dancing with *her*, despite his burning feet.

II; *Women in Labor Force; Shortages; Blacks*

232   Happy Go Nutty (MGM — 6/24/44)

Producer: Fred Quimby; *Director:* Tex Avery; *Script:* Heck Allen; *Animators:* Ed Love, Ray Abrams, Preston Blair; *Music:* Scott Bradley

Screwy Squirrel relentlessly attacks Meathead the dog throughout this cartoon. In one scene he wears a camouflaged helmet and — referring to "commando stuff"— pounds on Meathead with a knife! Only afterwards does Screwy show the audience the knife was made of rubber.

II; *Armed Forces— Army*

233   *A Hatful of Dreams (Paramount, 1944)

Producer/Director: George Pal

Brooklyn youth Punchy loves the blonde Judy, but he is outclassed by rival suitors. When Punchy is given a magical straw hat, he is turned into Superman and is able to win Judy's love with gifts that include "nylon hose." Brought before a judge to explain his largess, Punchy passes the hat around — one juror dreams he is a jeep driving soldier.

II; *Shortages; Armed Forces — Army*

234   *Hell Bent for Election (Industrial Films and Poster Service/ United Auto Workers—1944)

Executive Producer: Stephen Bosustow; *Director:* Charles M. Jones; *Script:* Robert Lees; *Production Design:* Zack Schwartz; *Music:* Earl Robinson; *Lyrics:* E.Y. Harburg, assisted by Karen Morley

The streamlined "Win the War Special," a train bearing Franklin D. Roosevelt's visage, is racing the 1929 model "Defeatist Ltd.," running on a parallel set of tracks. Uncle Sam, the telegrapher at the next station, tells worker Joe he has to throw the switch and derail the Defeatist Ltd. But a sinister "Wrecker" (a caricature of a Southern politician), tries to lull Joe to sleep with "Campaign Champagne," a "Phillie Buster" cigar, and mallet made by "Smith Connally & Co." When Joe protests, "We're out to win the war," the Wrecker snarls, " I tell you this is Roosevelt's war!" and briefly transforms into a Hitler caricature. As Joe dreams, a billboard featuring Hitler, Mussolini, and a Japanese caricature comes to life. Joe wakes up and throws the switch, allowing the munitions-laden Special to race onward to victory. The "Post War Observation Car" displays veterans' benefits and full employment as it goes by. Made in 1943 for the 1944 presidential election campaign, *Hell Bent for Election* was financed by the United Auto Workers union and produced by the company that would later become UPA. During

1944 and 1945, the company made the "Flight Safety" series of cartoons for the Navy. The animation in *Hell Bent for Election* is not as stylized as later UPA films, but is certainly more "modern" than most commercial cartoons of 1944.

I; *Hitler; Mussolini; FDR; Japanese Caricatures; Production*

235   How to Be a Sailor (Walt Disney/RKO — 1/28/44)

Producer: Walt Disney; *Director:* Jack Kinney; *Animators:* Andy Engman, Hugh Fraser, Ed Aardal, John Sibley

The history of sailing is told through scenes featuring caveman Goofy, Viking Goofy, Columbus Goofy, and pirate Goofy. Finally, contemporary Navy sailor Goofy, asleep in a hammock on a battleship, is awakened by the battle stations alarm. He scrambles to load a torpedo tube, but accidentally trips and launches himself through the tube at the enemy — a fleet of Japanese ships with buck teeth, slant-eyed anchor holes and glasses. Goofy smashes through the ships and crashes into the Rising Sun, shattering it. The Japanese caricatures are cut in some (but not all) extant versions of this cartoon.

I; *Armed Forces — Navy, Japan; Japanese Caricatures*

236   I Got Plenty of Mutton (Warner Bros — 3/11/44)

Producer: Leon Schlesinger; *Director:* Frank Tashlin; *Script:* Melvin Millar; *Animator:* I. Ellis; *Music:* Carl W. Stalling

A hungry wolf spots a newspaper headline reading "O.P.A. Ruling! No Meat for Wolves — Hollywood or Otherwise!" (The Office of Price Administration was in charge of preventing price inflation during the war.) But a "dogs for defense" article informs the wolf that the local sheepdog has joined the "WAGS" (there is a blue star on his doghouse, indicating that a resident is in the armed forces). The sheep are now being guarded by Killer Diller, a muscular ram. The wolf disguises himself as a sexy ewe — wearing false eyelashes and a sarong — to fool Killer, but becomes the object of the ram's amorous attentions. Finally, the wolf tears off his disguise and shouts "I'm a wolf!" to which Killer Diller replies: "So what? So am I!" as he chases him off into the sunset.

II; *Armed Forces — Army; Rationing*

237   Innertube Antics alternate title: Strange Innertube (MGM — 1/22/44)

Producer: Fred Quimby; *Director:* George Gordon; *Animators:* Ed Barge, Arnold Gillespie, Michael Lah; *Music:* Scott Bradley

A donkey — wearing clothes and acting quite a bit like Disney's Goofy — wants to do his part for the scrap rubber drive, but his neighbors' piles of scrap are much more impressive (the donkey is reduced to collecting things like pencil erasers). He accidentally stumbles across a half-buried innertube in his backyard. The innertube, which behaves like a living thing, resists all of the donkey's efforts to dislodge it, until finally the tube explodes out of the ground, trailing a huge pile of tires, rubber boots, and so on. The donkey winds up atop the biggest scrap pile of all.

I; *Shortages*

238   Lulu Gets the Birdie (Paramount — 3/31/44)

Director: I. Sparber; *Script:* Carl Meyer; *Animators:* Dave Tendlar, Morey Reden, John Walworth, John Gentilella; *Music:* Fred Wise, Sidney Lippman, Buddy Kaye (song)

"Little Lulu," a cartoon character created by "Marge" (Marjorie Henderson Buell) in the 1930s for *The Saturday Evening Post* magazine, was Paramount's replacement for Superman as their second series (after Popeye) in late 1943; the last Lulu cartoon was released in early 1948. In this cartoon, family maid Mandy (a black caricature with an Aunt Jemima–like kerchief) says "a little birdie" told her Lulu messed up the kitchen, and Lulu sets out to find the stool pigeon. There are several verbal references to the war in Mandy's dialogue: "Somebody's been making sabotage in mah kitchen," and "Save mah soul, we've been blitzkrieged!" In the final scene, as Lulu is about to receive a spanking from her father, she is reading a book on first aid. It is possible some of the other Lulu cartoons may contain mild topical references, including *Eggs Don't Bounce* (1943) and *Lulu's Birthday Party* (1944), but both are unconfirmed.

II; *Blacks; Germany*

239   Meatless Flyday (Warner Bros—1/29/44)

Producer: Leon Schlesinger; *Director:* I. Freleng; *Script:* Michael Maltese; *Animator:* Jack Bradbury; *Music:* Carl W. Stalling

After the credits— scored to the war-relevant song "They're Either Too Young or Too Old"—a spider with a foolish laugh (the voice of Tex Avery) sets out to catch a fly for dinner, using a sugar cube as bait. The fly gives the spider a hot foot—falling to the floor in flames, the spider shouts "Look! I'm a Zero, I'm a Zero!" He tricks the fly into eating lead pellets painted to look like candy, then attempts to use a magnet to catch him. The fly enters the workings of a neon sign with the spider in pursuit, but an air raid warden spots the sign blinking to life and shouts "Put out that light!" The spider finally captures the fly, but is foiled when he spots a calendar reading "Sept. 27th — Meatless Tuesday." The infuriated spider runs to the Capitol to complain.

I; *Armed Forces — Japan; Rationing; Home Defense — Air Raid Warden*

240   Mouse Trouble (MGM —12/1/44)

Producer: Fred Quimby; *Directors:* William Hanna & Joseph Barbera; *Animators:* Irven Spence, Ed Barge, Kenneth Muse, Ray Patterson; *Music:* Scott Bradley

Tom the cat receives a mail-order book *How to Catch a Mouse*, but even the most scientific and logical schemes detailed inside fail to produce results. Finally, Tom piles up a huge stack of explosives— including a "Block Buster" bomb — to try to blow Jerry the mouse out of existence. However, he succeeds only in leveling his own house.

II; *Armed Forces — Air Corps*

241   Mutt 'n' Bones (Columbia — 8/25/44)

Director: Paul Sommer; *Script:* Eddie Seward; *Animators:* Chic Otterstrom, Grant Simmons; *Music:* Eddie Kilfeather

Mutt the dog dreams he has all the bones in the world, but when he awakes realizes he has just one. The "War Bones Drive" is on, and Mutt is finally persuaded by a patriotic bulldog and signs reading "Don't Be A Hoard Hound" to donate his treasured possession.

I; *Shortages; Bonds*

242 My Boy Johnny (20th Century–Fox — (c)5/12/44)

Producer: Paul Terry; *Director:* Eddie Donnelly; *Script:* John Foster; *Music:* Philip A. Scheib

This cartoon optimistically looks forward to the end of the war (which was more than a year away). Planes and ships come home, and the Statue of Liberty turns handsprings to welcome them. Soldier animals — including Gandy Goose — parachute down to greet their families. Soldiers parade down the street as a song on the soundtrack says "the Army we will re-employ, a job for every soldier boy." Factories produce consumer goods like washing machines and refrigerators. Gandy and his offspring visit a new home, a modernistic house with many automatic devices. The final scene shows demobilized (human) servicemen and their new brides in church. This cartoon is split between spot gags about futuristic inventions and images of returning servicemen. *When G.I. Johnny Comes Home* (1945), q.v., also uses "When Johnny Comes Marching Home" (with new lyrics) in the same context, and *Post War Inventions* (1945), q.v., contains more gags about modern life in the post-war era.

I; *Armed Forces — Army, Navy; Home Defense; Postwar*

243 The Pelican and the Snipe (Walt Disney/RKO — 1/7/44)

Producer: Walt Disney; *Director:* Ham Luske; *Animators:* Ollie Johnson, Ham Luske, Ward Kimball; *Layouts:* Ken Anderson; *Music:* Oliver Wallace

"A Walt Disney South American Production." Monte, a pelican, and his snipe friend Vidi live on a lighthouse in Montevideo, Uruguay. Monte is unaware that he flies in his sleep, and Vidi must constantly be on guard to keep his friend out of danger. However, when Vidi ties an anchor to his friend's leg, Monte thinks he is playing a joke on him and becomes angry. That night, Monte flies in his sleep and strays into the path of a flight of Flying Fortresses on night maneuvers. He wakes up just in time to save Vidi from being blasted by practice bombs. Narrated by Sterling Holloway, this short was originally intended to be part of the 1945 feature *The Three Caballeros*.

I; *Armed Forces — Air Corps; South America*

244 Pitchin' Woo at the Zoo (Paramount — 9/1/44)

Director: I. Sparber; *Script:* Bill Turner, Jack Ward; *Animators:* Nick Tafuri, Tom Golden

Popeye and Olive Oyl visit the zoo, where employee Bluto is hanging up a sign: "Don't Feed Meat to the Animals — Feed It to the Keeper." Bluto and Popeye have an argument over Olive, while she gets into mischief in the animal cages. At one point Bluto says, referring to Popeye: "You'd only see an ugly face like that in an animated cartoon." Later, Bluto promises Olive: "I'll give you ... a mansion *and* a pair of nylon stockings."

II; *Shortages*

245   Plane Daffy (Warner Bros— 9/16/44)

Director: Frank Tashlin; *Script:* Warren Foster; *Animator:* Cal Dalton; *Music:* Carl W. Stalling

Courier Homer Pigeon falls into the clutches of the sinister but sexy Nazi spy, Hatta Mari. After drinking a "Mickeyblitz Finnkreig," Homer spills his secrets to the "seducktress" (as "Would It Be Wrong" is heard on the soundtrack), then shoots himself in remorse. "Notorious woman-hater" Daffy Duck takes the next assignment, and soon lands in Hatta Mari's lair. Daffy manages to resist her charms long enough to swallow his secret document, but she forces him to stand inside an X-ray machine. As Hitler, Göring, and a green-faced Goebbels watch via TV, the document is revealed — "Hitler is a stinker." Göring and Goebbels say "that's no secret — everybody knows that!" and Hitler shoots them. This cartoon somewhat resembles the Private Snafu cartoon *Spies* (1943). Universal also had a character named "Homer Pigeon" (*Swing Your Partner*, 1943, q.v.), but apparently nobody seemed to care if Warners used the name, too. Another cartoon with "We Did It Before and We Can Do It Again" on the soundtrack.

I; *Hitler; Spies; Nazis; Armed Forces— Air Corps; Göring; Goebbels; World War I*

246   Porkuliar Piggy (Columbia —10/13/44)

Director: Bob Wickersham; *Script:* Alec Geiss; *Animators:* Chic Otterstrom, Ben Lloyd; *Music:* Eddie Kilfeather

Li'l Abner and his cohorts, stars of Al Capp's comic strip, first appeared on screen in *Li'l Abner* (1940), a live-action feature film produced by Vogue Productions and released by RKO Radio Pictures. In 1959, Paramount produced a live-action version of the Broadway musical based on Capp's work, but the 1944 Columbia cartoon series—consisting of only five shorts— is all but forgotten. In this episode, Li'l Abner's favorite pig is kidnapped by the sinister owner (who sports a Hitler-esque moustache) of "Black's Market." Before the porker can be reduced to ham, sausages, and other meat products for sale, Li'l Abner tries to save his pet, but botches the attempt. However, Mammy Yokum steps in to save the day.

II; *Shortages; Black Market; Hitler*

247   Puppet Love (Paramount — 8/11/44)

Director: Seymour Kneitel; *Script:* Joe Stultz; *Animators:* Joe Tyer, William Henning; *Music:* Winston Sharples, Sammy Timberg

Popeye and Bluto get shore leave from their battleship, but Bluto has constructed a life-size marionette of Popeye that he uses to annoy Olive Oyl. The real Popeye is of course dumbfounded when Olive blames him for the puppet's rudeness. With the aid of spinach, Popeye turns the tables on his rival.

II; *Armed Forces — Navy*

248   Russian Rhapsody (Warner Bros— 5/20/44)

Producer: Leon Schlesinger; *Director:* Robert Clampett; *Script:* Lou Lilly; *Animator:* Rod Scribner; *Music:* Carl W. Stalling

The second Warners "gremlin" cartoon, this was originally to be called *Gremlins from the Kremlin,* but the title was changed since Disney was planning a feature about gremlins. A map of 1941 Europe is shown — the Italian "boot" is showing considerable wear and tear (toes are sticking out!). Hitler makes a radio speech, mostly double-talk with references to "Friz Freleng" (Warner Bros. cartoon director), "What's cookin', Doc," and "der zoot suit mit der reet pleat!" Since none of his "New Odor" bombers has been able to bomb Moscow successfully and return, Der Fuehrer vows to pilot a plane himself to wipe out Stalin and "that Irish general, Tim O'Shenko" (a reference to Soviet military leader Marshal Timoshenko). However, as soon as Hitler is airborne, "gremlins from the Kremlin" begin their mischief, while singing their theme song (a combination of "The Volga Boatman" and "O Tchichornya," aka "Dark Eyes"). They hammer off rivets, saw through the interior of the craft, swap Hitler's "C" gas ration sticker for a lesser-value "A" sticker, smash the plane's controls, and stick Hitler in the rear end with a tack. The harassed dictator pursues his tormentors with a knife, but is frightened by a Stalin mask. Finally, "termite-skis" chew off the bomber's wings and Hitler falls out of the stricken plane. On the ground, he tries to hide, but his plane crashes on top of him, creating a gravesite complete with tombstone. As the gremlins dance on Hitler's grave, he pops up and does an imitation of comedian Lew Lehr: "Nutzis is the cwaziest people!" The gremlins are caricatures of the Warner Bros. cartoon staff, including producer Leon Schlesinger and voice artist Mel Blanc. One line of the gremlins' song makes an oblique reference to Disney's Academy Award-winning cartoon: "Napoleon and his armies never got to first base, now we'll push those Natzi Nazis right in Der Fuehrer's face!"

I; *Hitler; Stalin; Rationing; Nazis; Ally — Russia; Armed Forces — Germany; Italy*

249   *Say Ah, Jasper (Paramount —(c)3/20/44)

Director: George Pal

This Puppetoon begins with a howling Jasper running home to his mother, complaining about his aching tooth. The Scarecrow and the Black Crow (who seem to be imitating Amos 'n Andy's voices) watch him go by, and the Crow says "He came by here like a P-38." The Lockheed P-38 "Lightning" was a twin-engine Air Corps fighter-bomber, well-known at the time as the aircraft used to fatally ambush Japanese Admiral Yamamoto's plane on 18 April 1943. The rest of the short concerns Jasper's attempts to relieve his toothache. Note: TV prints of this short mistakenly carry the title *Say Ha Jasper.*

II; *Blacks; Armed Forces — Air Corps*

250   Slightly Daffy (Warner Bros— 6/17/44)

Producer: Leon Schlesinger; *Director:* I. Freleng; *Script:* Michael Maltese; *Animation:* Virgil Ross; *Music:* Carl W. Stalling

General Daffy Duck and cavalry trooper Porky Pig are defending a fort against hostile Indians. Daffy accidentally swallows a lot of bullets and becomes a living machine gun, routing the attackers. Early in this cartoon, Daffy has trouble rousing Porky from a sound sleep: over Porky's bunk hangs a sign reading "Buy Bonds." A remake of *Scalp Trouble* (1939), reusing much of the earlier film's animation footage. The bonds sign was a portrait of Petunia Pig in the original cartoon.

II; *Bonds*

251   Spinach-Packin' Popeye (Paramount — 7/21/44)

Director: I. Sparber; *Script:* Bill Turner; *Animators:* Joe Oriolo, Dave Tendlar

Popeye donates a gallon of blood at the Blood Bank (as "Praise the Lord and Pass the Ammunition" plays), then rushes off to an inter-service boxing match, which he loses to Army fighter Bluto. Olive Oyl rejects the sailor, turning his photo around to reveal a matching shot of Bluto in his Army uniform, and starts to walk out, wearing a WAAC uniform. To prove he's no weakling, Popeye shows her scenes from *Popeye the Sailor Meets Sindbad the Sailor* (1936) and *Popeye Meets Ali Baba and his Forty Thieves* (1937), but she refuses to listen. Popeye wakes up to discover it was all a dream; when he visits Olive, she is now dressed in a WAVE uniform. The Famous Studios-Paramount Popeye shorts frequently used footage from the Fleischer color Popeye specials of the 1930s.

I; *Armed Forces — Navy, Army, Women*

252   The Stupid Cupid (Warner Bros—11/25/44)

Producer: Leon Schlesinger; *Director:* Frank Tashlin; *Script:* Warren Foster; *Music:* Carl W. Stalling

Cupid (who looks suspiciously like Elmer Fudd) shoots his arrows at various animals, including birds, horses, a dog (who kisses the cat he was chasing), and Daffy Duck. Daffy falls in love with a hen, but runs afoul of her tough rooster husband. The topical reference is purely visual: Cupid shoots a bluebird, who zooms into the air, briefly changing into a P-38 "Lightning" fighter plane before turning back into a bird and snaring his mate. The cat who's been kissed by the dog says "Now I've seen everything!" and shoots himself nine times!

II; *Armed Forces — Air Corps*

253   The Swooner Crooner (Warner Bros— 5/6/44)

Director: Frank Tashlin; *Script:* Warren Foster; *Animator:* George Cannata; *Music:* Carl W. Stalling

Porky Pig manages the "Flockheed Eggcraft" factory (a spoof of Lockheed Aircraft), which — according to its sign, is engaged in "100% War Work" (the sign also has a "V" spelled out in eggs). The hens, sporting "War Worker" ID badges, check in at the gate, punch their time cards, and begin producing eggs in assembly-line fashion. In one shot, Porky is shown packing eggs into cartons labeled "To China," "To Britain," and "To Russia." However, the chickens are distracted by emaciated singing rooster "Frankie" (a Sinatra caricature), and "absentee" signs begin popping up on the nests. Porky advertises "Rooster Auditions" and interviews several potential candidates, including Al Jolson, Cab Calloway, and Jimmy Durante caricatures. He chooses "the Old Groaner," a Bing Crosby chicken, who lures the hens back to their nests to produce more eggs. Frankie and Bing compete to inspire the hens to lay, and even work their magic on Porky, who lays a pile of eggs himself. Academy Award nominee.

I; *Women in Labor Force; Production; Blacks; Ally — China, Britain, Russia; "V"*

254   Tick Tock Tuckered (Warner Bros— 4/8/44)

Producer: Leon Schlesinger; *Director:* Robert Clampett; *Script:* Warren Foster; *Animator:* Tom McKimson; *Music:* Carl W. Stalling

A remake of *Porky's Bad Time Story* (1937). Porky Pig and Daffy Duck are employees of the Fly By Nite Aircraft Company who are warned by their boss that they'll be fired if they are late to work one more time. Porky and Daffy go to bed at 8:00 so they can wake up on time, but howling cats, bright moonlight, a storm, and water dripping from the ceiling prevents them from falling asleep. The next morning they rush madly to work only to discover it's Sunday and the plant is closed. The topical reference occurs the first time Porky and Daffy leave for work: as they roar out of the garage in their car, they literally turn the building inside-out, revealing numerous tires and drums of gasoline they were hoarding inside.

II; *Shortages; Production*

255   Tom Turk and Daffy (Warner Bros— 2/12/44)

Producer: Leon Schlesinger; *Director:* Charles M. Jones; *Script:* "The Staff"; *Animator:* Ken Harris; *Music:* Carl W. Stalling

Pilgrim Porky Pig is pursuing a turkey, who turns to Daffy Duck for assistance. After several painful (for the turkey) attempts at camouflage, Daffy hides the fugitive bird inside a snowman. However, Porky's description of the sumptuous feast he had planned persuades Daffy to turn over the turkey ("the yams did it!"). The disgruntled turkey mutters "Quisling!" (a reference to the pro–Nazi Norwegian politician whose name became synonymous with traitor during World War II). Porky soon switches his attention to hunting Daffy, and the turkey gets his turn to "help" Daffy hide.

II; *Nazis; Collaborator*

256. The Weakly Reporter (Warner Bros— 3/25/44)

Producer: Leon Schlesinger; *Director:* Charles M. Jones; *Script:* Michael Maltese, Tedd Pierce; *Animator:* Ben Washam; *Music:* Carl W. Stalling

Spot gags in newsreel format which show the viewer "how daily life on the home front has been affected" by the war. The Statue of Liberty wears a civil defense armband and the stone heads on Mt. Rushmore are sporting civil defense helmets. Soldiers escort a pound of butter like a cargo of gold and a butcher charges a woman to sniff a steak ("While there is sufficient food for all, many items fall into the luxury class" says the narrator). An ambulance arrives at the scene of an accident and "rescues" a whitewall tire rather than the human victim; a man has to use a periscope to drive because his windshield is completely covered with gas ration and other war-oriented stickers. Women are shown working as welders, cabbies, etc.; WAACs learn commando tactics so they can fight their way through crowds at sales of nylon stockings. "We Did It Before and We Can Do It Again" is used once more on the soundtrack of this cartoon, which contains some limited-animation and stylized sequences.

I; *Women in Labor Force; Historical American Figures; World War I; "V"; USO; Air Raid Warden; Armed Forces — Women, Navy, Army, Air Corps; Bonds*

257   We're On Our Way to Rio (Paramount — 4/21/44)

Director: I. Sparber; *Script:* Jack Mercer, Jack Ward; *Animators:* Jim Tyer, Ben Solomon; *Music:* Winston Sharples

On shore leave in Rio, Navy sailors Popeye and Bluto both fall for Olive, a Carmen Miranda–type singer in a cafe. Bluto embarrasses Popeye by touting him as the champion samba dancer of the USA, but Popeye's spinach — labeled "17 Points," the actual ration points for a can that size — helps him defeat Bluto and win Olive. At one point, Popeye and a parrot greet each other, saying "Hi ya, neighbor" (an oblique reference to the Good Neighbor Policy). Very similar to *Kickin' the Conga Round* (1942), q.v., this cartoon contains two catchy songs and some nice background visuals.

II; *Rationing; South America; Armed Forces — Navy*

258   What's Cookin', Doc? (Warner Bros—1/1/44)

Producer: Leon Schlesinger; *Director:* Robert Clampett; *Script:* Michael Sasanoff; *Animator:* Bob McKimson; *Music:* Carl W. Stalling

Bugs Bunny attends the Academy Awards banquet expecting to win the Best Actor Oscar. When the prize goes to James Cagney, Bugs blurts out "That's sabotage!" Bugs — after a false start with a "Stag Reel" — shows footage from *Hiawatha's Rabbit Hunt* (1941 — here called *Little Hiawatha*) to prove that he should have won. He gets an Oscar after all — the Booby Prize, a rabbit-shaped statuette with effeminate mannerisms. The only topical reference is almost subliminal: a newspaper headline announcing the Academy Awards is shown, and a sub-headline on the same page reads "Jap Cruiser Blown Up."

II; *Armed Forces — Japan*

259   Yankee Doodle Donkey (Paramount —11/27/44)

Director: I. Sparber; *Script:* Jack Mercer, Jack Ward; *Animators:* Nick Tafuri, Tom Golden; *Music:* Sammy Timberg

This was a "Noveltoon," a Famous Studios series of cartoons with no continuing character that served as a sort of tryout spot for potential stars (like Casper the Friendly Ghost). In this short, Spunky the Donkey spots a billboard reading "Join the WAGS and Hound the Axis." He tries to join up, wearing a bowl as a helmet, but his clumsy marching, bray, and long ears expose him as a donkey, not a dog, and he is gruffly rejected. Later, due to his thick hide, Spunk rescues the WAGS when they are attacked by the Flea Army. The Army's K-9 corps were actually nicknamed the WAGS during World War II.

I; *Armed Forces — Army*

260   The Zoot Cat (MGM — 2-26/44)

Producer: Fred Quimby; *Director:* William Hanna & Joseph Barbera; *Animators:* Ray Patterson, Kenneth Muse, Irv Spence, Pete Burness; *Music:* Scott Bradley

After Tom's girl (cat) friend rejects him as a "square," he makes a zoot suit out of a hammock, inspired by a radio ad which describes the suit as having "pants that begin at the chin, zoom to a 54-inch knee, then fade softly to a 3-inch Victory cuff." Jerry and Tom chase each other and the zoot suit gets soaked, shrinking to Jerry's size at the finale. Zoot suits, originally popular among blacks in Harlem, later migrated to California and were adopted by Mexican-American youths. During the war, zoot suits were considered an unpatriotic waste of material with their wide pants legs, high waist, and broad shoulders, although a modified zoot suit with "Victory" accessories was later produced.

II; "*V*"; *Shortages*

1945

261   The Bashful Buzzard (Warner Bros— 9/5/45)

Producer: Edward Selzer; *Director:* Robert Clampett; *Script:* Michael Sasanoff; *Animators:* Robert McKimson, Rod Scribner; *Music:* Carl W. Stalling

In this sequel to *Bugs Bunny Gets the Boid* (1942), q.v., Mama Buzzard sends her offspring out in search of meat. They fly off in formation (to the tune of "Captains of the Clouds") and attack farmyards in dive-bomber style. Only the dopey "Killer" (aka Beaky Buzzard) has trouble bringing home his prey.

II; *Shortages*

262   Behind the Meatball (Warner Bros— 4/7/45)

Producer: Edward Selzer; *Director:* Frank Tashlin (uncredited); *Script:* Melvin Millar; *Animator:* I. Ellis; *Music:* Carl W. Stalling

A dog, disgusted by the meat shortage, rejects the vegetables he is given to eat ("Bugs Bunny food!"). After throwing a tantrum he turns to the audience and says: "I want meat! You've had this feeling before, haven't you, folks?" A steak falls off a delivery truck and the dog vies with a bulldog and a little terrier for it. The terrier finally eats the steak and the other two dogs have to be content just dreaming about "real" food.

II; *Shortages*

263   *Cap'n Cub (Film Classics— 3/45?)

Producer/Director: Ted Eshbaugh; *Supervisor:* Charles B. Hastings; *Special Effects:* Harry Hamsel; *Animators:* Ozzie Evans, Jack Tyrrell, A.C. Hutchinson, Bill Weaver, Winfield Hoskins; *Backgrounds:* Henri G. Courtais

This 10-minute Technicolor cartoon was apparently made in 1943 but not released until 1945. Produced by veteran New York animator Ted Eshbaugh, *Cap'n Cub* (also advertised under the title *Cap'n Cub Blasts the Japs*) was intended to be the first in a series featuring the bear cub aviator, but languished on the shelf for two years until it was picked up by indie clearinghouse Film Classics for distribution. The short opens with Cap'n Cub reviewing a military parade featuring turtle "tanks," skunks—followed by a hippo in a tutu with a perfume atomizer (possibly a reference to Disney's *Fantasia*)—and so on. Cap'n Cub declares "What we need is airplanes!" and a montage of scrap metal and rubber being converted into aircraft follows. The finished planes form a conga line and are matched up with their animal pilots. Once in the air, Cub's squadron runs into a flight of Japanese bombers (piloted by Japanese-caricature monkeys). A cowboy bear shoots down several enemy planes with his six-guns; a baby kangaroo pops out of his mother's pouch to destroy another bomber. Cap'n Cub blasts the last bomber into pieces. As it explodes, a Rising Sun is briefly formed, but quickly withers away. Cub gives the "V" sign as his comrades' planes fly in a "V" formation behind him.

I; *Armed Forces— Air Corps, Japan; Production; Scrap Metal; Japanese Caricatures; "V"; South America*

264   Dippy Diplomat (Universal — 8/27/45)

Producer: Walter Lantz; *Director:* James Culhane; *Script:* Ben Hardaway, Milt Schaffer; *Animators:* Pat Matthews, Grim Natwick; *Music:* Darrell Calker

Woody Woodpecker learns Wally Walrus is hosting a cookout for Russian ambassador Ivan Awfulitch. Woody disguises himself as the diplomat and crashes the barbecue, freeloading to his heart's content until the walrus gets wise.

II; *Ally— Russia*

265   Dog Watch (Walt Disney/RKO — 3/16/45)

Producer: Walt Disney; *Director:* Charles Nichols; *Script:* Eric Gurney; *Animators:* Norman Taté, Marvin Woodward, George Nicholas, Jerry Hathcock, Sandy Strother, Bob Youngquist, John McManus; *Layout:* Bruce Bushman; *Effects:* Andy Engman, Ed Aardal; *Music:* Oliver Wallace

The captain of a docked Navy freighter assigns Pluto to guard the ship while the crew takes shore leave. An obnoxious rat sneaks on board and a chase ensues. The rodent makes it to the Officers' Mess and prepares a huge sandwich for himself, bribing Pluto with cookies and leftovers. When a sailor appears, the rat flees, and Pluto is blamed for the disorder and missing food. Tossed in the brig, the disgraced dog looks out the porthole and spots the rat (with the sandwich), trying to escape via one of the mooring lines. Shaking the rope, Pluto causes the rat to fall into the water.

II; *Armed Forces— Navy*

266   Draftee Daffy (Warner Bros—1/27/45)

Producer: Edward Selzer; *Director:* Robert Clampett; *Script:* Lou Lilly; *Animator:* Rod Scribner; *Music:* Carl W. Stalling

Daffy Duck is patriotically reading war news in the paper, boasting of how he'd like to get in on the fight, singing "If I Could Be With You One Hour Tonight" to a painting of General Douglas MacArthur on his wall. But when he receives a phone call from the draft board, Daffy panics. The "little man from the draft board" shows up and the cowardly duck flees in terror. Each time he thinks he's lost him, the little man pops up and says "Oh now, I wouldn't say *that*." As Daffy tries to escape, the man asks "Is this trip really necessary?" Finally, leaping into a rocket marked "Use in Case of Induction," Daffy blasts off, but the missile plows straight into the ground and winds up in Hades. Even there, Daffy can't avoid the draft man. The voice and catch-phrase of the little man were based on the character of "Mr. Peavey" from "The Great Gildersleeve" radio show.

I; Draft; Armed Forces— Army, Marine Corps; MacArthur; Historical American Figures; Draft Avoidance

267   *The Flying Jeep (United Artists— 8/20/45)
Producer: John Sutherland (no other credits available)
The second in the "Daffy Ditties" series released by United Artists. Utilizing figures made of clay and other materials, former Disney staffers Larry Morey and John Sutherland produced The Cross-Eyed Bull (Plastic Cartoons Inc., 1944), and followed it with this short. A jeep on a Pacific island base wants to fly, so it contrives a pair of wings and goes aloft, eventually downing a Japanese Zero. The "Motion Picture Herald" review (8/25/45) called this short an "elegant color fable" and said "color and comedy are excellently blended with musical overtones."

I; Armed Forces— Air Corps, Japan

268   For Better or Nurse (Paramount — 6/8/45)
Director: I. Sparber; Script: Joe Stultz, Irving Dressler; Animators: Dave Tendlar, John Gentilella; Music: Winston Sharples
A remake of Hospitaliky (1937): Popeye and Bluto, enamored of nurse Olive Oyl, compete to be the first to get injured and thus be admitted to the hospital where she works. However, both men are amazingly lucky and come to no harm. Popeye finally forces Bluto eat spinach and beat him up. At the end of the 1945 version, a battered Popeye is denied admittance because Olive is working in a dog and cat hospital! The wartime cartoon begins with Popeye and Bluto on a battleship. Later, Popeye climbs onto a floating target marked "Danger: Naval Gunnery Practice In This Area." As "Columbia, the Gem of the Ocean" plays, shells destroy the target with the exception of the exact spot Popeye is standing on. Later, when Bluto eats the spinach, his chest tattoo of a boat turns into a roaring battleship.

II; Armed Forces— Navy

269   Fresh Airedale (Warner Bros— 9/24/45)
Director: Charles M. Jones; Script: Michael Maltese; Animators: Ben Washam, Lloyd Vaughn, Ken Harris; Music: Carl W. Stalling
This cartoon begins with a prologue: "In a world torn by war — a world in which treachery, avarice, and hatred are prevalent...." A sneaky, greedy dog named Shep repeatedly contrives to have a cat blamed for his misdeeds. In one scene, Shep lets a burglar break into his master's house after receiving a bone as a bribe. The burglar remarks: "Oh yeah, the payoff— here you are, Quisling" (a reference to the infamous pro–Nazi Norwegian by that name). When Shep sees a newspaper clipping about the "Nation's Number 1 Dog" (a terrier resembling Fala, President Roosevelt's dog), the jealous canine travels across country to get even. At one point he passes a sign reading "Philadelphia ½ mile, No Vacancies" (a reference to the wartime housing shortage in Washington, D.C.). The Scottie saves Shep from

drowning, but Shep takes credit for saving *him*. He is given a ticker-tape parade as the disgusted cat looks on.

II; *Collaborator*

270   Goofy News Views (Columbia — 4/27/45 or 6/21/45?)

Producer: Raymond Katz; *Director/Script:* Sid Marcus; *Music:* Darrell Calker

Another newsreel spoof. In one sequence, a football team in a huddle plants a Victory Garden.

II; *Victory Garden*

271   A Gruesome Twosome (Warner Bros— 6/9/45)

Director: Robert Clampett; *Script:* Warren Foster; *Animators:* Robert McKimson, Manny Gould, Basil Davidovitch, Rod Scribner, I. Ellis; *Effects Animation:* A. C. Gamer; *Backgrounds/Layout:* Tom McKimson, Michael Sasanoff; *Music:* Carl W. Stalling

Two cats—a dopey one and a Jimmy Durante caricature—try to capture Tweety Bird to impress a pretty girl cat. They even disguise themselves in a horse costume, but Tweety throws in an irritated bumble bee and, later, an angry bulldog. Earlier, the Durante cat sings to the girl cat: the lyrics include the line, "You'd like a pair of nylons, huh? Gimme a little kiss!" (as he waves a pair of stockings at her). When the two cats fall off the telephone pole where Tweety has his nest, they transform into bomb shapes and Tweety says "Bombs away!"

II; *Shortages*

272   Hare Conditioned (Warner Bros— 8/11/45)

Director: Charles M. Jones; *Script:* Tedd Pierce; *Animators:* Ken Harris, Basil Davidovitch, Ben Washam, Lloyd Vaughn; *Backgrounds/Layout:* Earl Klein, Robert Gribbroek; *Music:* Carl W. Stalling

Bugs Bunny loses his job as part of a department store window display, but the manager has another position in mind for him — as a stuffed rabbit! Bugs and the "Great Gildersneeze" (a reference to the Great Gildersleeve radio character, portrayed by Harold Peary) chase each other around the store. Bugs impersonates an elevator operator and announces: "Sixth floor—girdles, nylons, alarm clocks, bourbon, butter ... and other picture postcards!" (referring to items scare or unavailable during wartime). At the end of the cartoon, both Bugs and the manager leap off the building's roof.

II; *Shortages*

273   Herr Meets Hare (Warner Bros—1/13/45)

Director: I. Freleng; *Script:* Michael Maltese; *Animators:* Gerry Chiniquy, Manuel Perez; *Music:* Carl W. Stalling

Bugs Bunny makes a wrong turn on the way to Las Vegas and winds up in Germany's Black Forest, where he meets hunter "Fatso" Göring. Bugs points out that the Nazi's medals are ersatz, provoking an angry outburst against Hitler, but the Field Marshal is reduced to a blubbering toady when Bugs impersonates Der Fuehrer. Bugs then dresses up like the heroine in a Wagnerian opera, inspiring

Göring to revert to Aryan form himself. Finally getting wise, Göring catches Bugs in a sack and delivers him to Hitler himself; the dictator is seen morosely playing solitaire in his headquarters in front of a map showing the decline of "Festung Europa" (Fortress Europe). However, both Hitler and Göring run off screaming after peeking inside the bag. Bugs emerges, dressed like Stalin and puffing on the soviet dictator's trademark pipe. He says "Does your tobacco taste different lately?" (a catch-phrase from a cigarette commercial of the period). One of the last wartime shorts to contain a Hitler caricature.

I; *Hitler; Stalin; Göring; Armed Forces — Marine Corps, Germany*

274   *Jasper's Booby Traps (Paramount —?5/45)

Producer/Director: George Pal

Trying to trick his nemesis, Professor Scarecrow, Jasper creates booby-trapped food in his ramshackle "Booby Trap Foundry." The scheme is exposed after the Scarecrow's sidekick Crow eats some bullet-filled candy and has explosive hiccups. "Well what do you know, a block-bustin' smorgasbord," the Scarecrow comments. A juicy porterhouse steak offered up by Jasper is really "a landmine smothered in onions." Despite the warnings, the Scarecrow is unable to resist a ham spiked with rockets, but the Crow avenges his friend, giving Jasper a loaded cigar, with dire results for both of them. This short begins with a brief rendition of "Praise the Lord and Pass the Ammunition," before the title literally blows up on screen.

II; *Armed Forces — Air Corps, Army; Shortages; Black*

275   Jerky Turkey (MGM — 4/7/45)

Director: Tex Avery; *Script:* Heck Allen; *Animators:* Preston Blair, Ed Love, Ray Abrams; *Music:* Scott Bradley

A Pilgrim (with the same salami-nose and Droopy-like voice as the hero of *Big Heel-Watha*, 1944, q.v.) wants a turkey dinner for Thanksgiving, but is unable to catch a Jimmy Durante–caricature turkey. At the end they are both eaten by a bear. Wartime gags abound in this cartoon. The ship "Mayflower," on its way to the New World, sails in the middle of a naval convoy and sports an anti-aircraft gun. There is a sign on the ship referring to "Henryk J. Kaiser" (a reference to industrialist Henry J. Kaiser, who developed the Victory ship program during World War II). Long lines of people wait to buy cigarettes at a drugstore; the town crier cries because he has a 1-A draft classification (the Pilgrim hunter, on the other hand, has "4-F" license plates on his shabby house trailer). The turkey operates "Ye Black Market" (a store painted black); the Pilgrim's muzzle-loading rifle at times resembles a machine-gun, and he later uses "Ye Bazooka." Fleeing from the hunter, the turkey dives into a sand-bagged foxhole but is ejected by (what else) a fox.

I; *Production; Shortages; Draft; Armed Forces — Navy, Merchant Marine; Black Market*

276   Life with Feathers (Warner Bros— 3/24/45)

Director: I. Freleng; *Script:* Tedd Pierce; *Animator:* Virgil Ross; *Music:* Carl W. Stalling

A meek lovebird, rejected by his mate "Sweetiepuss," decides to commit suicide by jumping into the mouth of Sylvester the Cat (who isn't referred to by name, but it's obviously Sylvester, voice and all). The cat — introduced picking through garbage cans for his dinner while whistling the war-oriented song "They're Either Too Young or Too Old" — is convinced it is a trick, and keeps spitting out the bird.

II

277 Mess Production (Paramount — 8/24/45)

Director: Seymour Kneitel; *Script:* Bill Turner, Otto Messmer; *Music:* Winston Sharples

Olive Oyl is a welder in a defense plant. Fellow workers Popeye and Bluto compete to save her when she is accidentally knocked senseless and begins strolling through the heavy machinery area. Popeye, buried under a pile of scrap metal, eats his spinach and fashions a tank out of the junk, then saves Olive and beats up Bluto.

II; *Scrap Metal; Production; Women in Labor Force*

278 Mighty Mouse and the Kilkenny Cats (20th Century–Fox — 4/13/45)

Producer: Paul Terry; *Director:* Mannie Davis; *Script:* John Foster; *Music:* Philip A. Scheib

This cartoon is very reminiscent of *Fifth Column Mouse* (1943), q.v. The mice and cats are constantly fighting, with the mice usually on the losing side, so they hold a meeting to organize militarily. In a montage sequence, the mice are issued bottle-cap helmets, a mouse draft board stamps "1-A" on acceptable recruits, and then the mice resist the cats with toy tanks and planes. At first the cats are stunned by the offensive, but the tide turns against the rodents until Mighty Mouse arrives to save the day. A rare example of a Mighty Mouse cartoon (in the no-dialogue, all-narration period) with a war reference, albeit an allegorical one.

II; *Draft; War Allegory*

279 Pop-Pie a la Mode (Paramount —1/26/45)

Director: I. Sparber; *Script:* Dave Tendlar; *Animators:* Joe Oriolo, Morey Reden; *Music:* Winston Sharples

Popeye, adrift on a raft in the "Specific Ocean," lands on an island where "Joe's Always Inn" is located. Joe, a huge black native wearing a top hat, views the stranded sailor as a prospective meal, and has him fattened up. Meanwhile, Joe reads *How to Serve Your Fellow Man*, by Ima Cannibal. Popeye is lured into a stewpot under the pretense it is a bathtub, but figures out what's going on when he sees the natives all carrying "meat ration books" (one little cannibal has a single ration stamp and sign that says "I Get the Neck"). Popeye escapes and thrashes the natives, but Joe's Inn turns into a fortress bristling with cannon. Popeye catches the shells, molds them into a single huge "Block Buster," and tosses it back, with explosive results. Unusual Popeye cartoon in which neither Bluto nor Olive Oyl appears.

II; *Rationing; Blacks; Armed Forces — Navy*

280   Post War Inventions (20th Century–Fox — 3/23/45, or June?)
Producer: Paul Terry; *Director:* Connie Rasinski; *Script:* John Foster; *Music:* Philip A. Scheib

Gandy Goose and Sourpuss Cat fall asleep while reading a book entitled *Post War Inventions*. They dream about rocket planes, dehydrated food, modern kitchens, television, and other scientific wonders. Another "dream" cartoon and another cartoon looking ahead to the end of the war, which was still some months away at the time of this short's release. One of the few Terrytoons of the era to feature a real pop song (not an original tune written for the cartoon) on the sound-track — "Let's Take a Walk in the Moonlight" is sung by a beautiful blonde on a TV broadcast.

I; *Postwar; Blacks*

281   The Screwy Truant (MGM — 1/13/45)
Producer: Fred Quimby; *Director:* Tex Avery; *Script:* Heck Allen; *Animators:* Preston Blair, Ed Love, Ray Abrams; *Music:* Scott Bradley

Screwy Squirrel skips school and is pursued by a dopey truant officer dog. Wartime references abound: the "little red schoolhouse" is now blue, because "Technicolor Red has gone to war" (a parody of the cigarette slogan "Lucky Strike Red Has Gone to War"). Red Riding Hood and the Wolf wander into this cartoon, and when Screwy gets to Grandma's house he finds a sign reading "CLOSED — Gone to Lockheed" (see *Little Red Riding Rabbit*, 1943, q.v.). The dog puts on an air raid warden's helmet to avoid Screwy's assaults, but Screwy whacks him with the helmet instead. Finally, the dog collapses and his eyelids read "Closed for the Duration."

II; *Production; Air Raid Warden*

282   A Self-Made Mongrel (Paramount — 7/29/45)
Director: no credit; *Script:* Carl Meyer; *Animators:* Dave Tendlar, John Walworth; *Music Arr:* Winston Sharples

"Dog-Face" the dog is welcomed into the home of a rich man, but the dog rebels when his master insists on treating him like a baby. When the dog claims "I'm a manhunter," the owner decides to play cops-and-robbers with his pet, but is knocked out by a *real* burglar. The thief is wary of Dog Face — "You'll just howl and tear me to little pieces" — but the dog replies "Not me, I'm savin' me energy for the war effort." At the end, the burglar steals the whole house! A Noveltoons series entry.

II

283   The Shooting of Dan McGoo (MGM — 3/3/45)
Producer: Fred Quimby; *Director:* Tex Avery; *Script:* Heck Allen; *Animators:* Ed Love, Ray Abrams, Preston Blair; *Music:* Scott Bradley

In Coldernell, Alaska, the "lady known as Lou" entertains at the local saloon, where she has been awarded an "E" pennant by the local wolves (in real life, these pennants were given to defense plants for excellence in production). Lou loves Dan McGoo, played by Droopy the dog. When Lou sings "Put Your Arms Around Me," the lyrics include lines like "When you look at me, my heart begins to float; then it starts a-bouncin' like a PT boat." McGoo's rival, the Wolf, appears in Army, Navy, and Marine Corps uniforms as he watches Lou perform. Other topical gags include "Old Block Buster" whiskey ("400 lb. proof"), and McGoo's retort to the wolf's complaint that his drink has been cut — "What do you want for ten cents, gasoline?" Tex Avery had previously spoofed Robert W. Service's poem "The Shooting of Dan McGrew" at Warner Bros. in *Dangerous Dan McFoo* (1939), with a dog that talked like Elmer Fudd as its protagonist.

II; *Armed Forces— Army, Navy, Marine Corps; Shortages; Production*

284   Simple Siren (Columbia — 9/20/45)

Director: Paul Sommer; *Script:* Ed Seward; *Animators:* Volus Jones, Don Williams
A mermaid tries to lure a fisherman into her clutches by advertising free food. When he attempts to escape, she uses "Submarine Detector: Radar" and a depth charge to catch him. In the end, it is all exposed as a dream — or was it?

II; *Armed Forces— Navy*

285   Swing Shift Cinderella (MGM — 8/25/45)

Producer: Fred Quimby; *Director:* Tex Avery; *Script:* Heck Allen; *Animators:* Ray
  Abrams, Preston Blair, Ed Love; *Music:* Scott Bradley
Sexy Cinderella (who talks like Katherine Hepburn) is pursued by the lecherous Wolf. Cinderella calls her fairy godmother for help, and the man-hungry witch speeds to the rescue on her motor scooter (which sports an "A" gas ration sticker). While the Wolf tries to escape from the godmother's romantic overtures, Cinderella goes night-clubbing in her pumpkin-turned-station wagon, but has to dash off before midnight — to catch the bus for war workers (she's a welder) on the midnight shift at the "Lockweed Aircraft Plant." She's relieved to be free of the horny Wolf's attentions, but all of the other (male wolf) workers on the bus say "Wanna bet?" Other topical references in this short include the appearance of a female cabdriver (a frequent motif in wartime feature films), and the fairy godmother's use of a jeep as she chases the recalcitrant Wolf.

I; *Production; Women in Labor Force; Rationing*

286   Tops in the Big Top (Paramount — 3/16/45)

Director: I. Sparber; *Script:* Joe Stultz, Carl Meyer; *Animators:* Tom Golden, John
  Walworth; *Scenics:* Robert Little; *Music:* Winston Sharples
Popeye and Olive Oyl are circus performers, with Bluto as the ringmaster who wants to cut Popeye out of the act. When Popeye sticks his head into a lion's mouth, Bluto tosses in a steak as well. The lion clamps down and Popeye says, "Hey! What is this, a blackout?" Later, Popeye spots Bluto cutting the safety net for the high-wire act and exclaims "That sabotagin' skunk!" In the end, spinach saves Popeye from a cage full of angry apes.

II; *Spy-Saboteur*

287   The Unruly Hare (Warner Bros— 2/10/45)

Director: Frank Tashlin; *Script:* Melvin Millar; *Animators:* Cal Dalton, Art Davis;
  Music: Carl W. Stalling

Elmer Fudd is surveying the path of a new railroad, which just happens to go directly over Bugs Bunny's home. Bugs causes Elmer a great deal of grief, but undoes his own efforts when he causes an explosion that lays all the track and rails in an instant. Bugs is speeding away on a train when he suddenly hops off and says "None of us civilians should be doing any unnecessary traveling these days," as "My Country 'Tis of Thee" plays on the soundtrack.

II; *Shortages*

288   Wagon Heels (Warner Bros — 7/28/45)

Director: Robert Clampett; *Script:* Warren Foster; *Animators:* Rod Scribner, Manny Gould, I. Ellis, J.C. Melendez; *Backgrounds/Layout:* Tom McKimson, Michael Sasanoff; *Music:* Carl W. Stalling

A close remake of *Injun Trouble* (1938). Porky Pig leads a wagon train into the West, home of Injun Joe, the Super Chief ("Woo! Woo!"). As the wagon train leaves civilization, it passes a billboard reading "Is This Trip Really Necessary?" With the help of Sloppy Moe, the pioneers succeed in defeating the hostile Indians.

II; *Shortages*

289   When G.I. Johnny Comes Home (Paramount — 2/2/45)

Director: Seymour Kneitel; *Script:* Jack Ward, Bill Turner; *Animators:* Al Eugster, Otto Feuer; *Scenics:* Robert Little

"PEACE" appears over the world's battlefields. Immediately afterwards, America's armies literally pour off troop transports and melt back into civilian life. Apparently fearing the wrath of the returning servicemen, "Draft Board No. 13" is hastily fortified. An ex-general salutes his former driver, now his boss. The "Wah Wah Baby Carriage" factory is reactivated. The latter half of this Nooveltoon is a bouncing ball singalong cartoon, with new lyrics to "When Johnny Comes Marching Home," accompanied by appropriate visuals. The lyrics include "Johnny Black left the college green, saw red flak in a B-19; Skies are blue now, and for his part, Johnny Black got the Purple Heart." One verse salutes (in a back-handed fashion) contributions of women in the armed forces like "Jenny"—"In a uniform she may look so cute, but we like her in a bathing suit." The cartoon concludes with a stylized farmer, factory worker, and businessman marching side-by-side into the future.

I; *Armed Forces — Air Corps, Women; Postwar; Draft; "V"*

290   Woody Dines Out (Universal — 4/23/45)

Producer: Walter Lantz; *Director:* James Culhane; *Script:* Ben Hardaway, Milt Schaffer; *Animator:* Don Williams; *Backgrounds:* Philip De Guard; *Music:* Darrell Calker

Woody Woodpecker's in the mood for food, but can't find an open restaurant. Wandering into a taxidermist's shop by mistake (its sign reads "We Specialize in Stuffing Birds"), Woody confuses the proprietor (a cat) by asking for a menu. The "ceiling prices" (price controls instituted by the government to prevent inflation) are marked—where else?—on the ceiling. When the taxidermist discovers a museum will pay handsomely for a stuffed Woody, he feeds the bird some "Blackout Borscht" to knock him out. The cat and bird chase each other around; in one scene, the cat is trapped beneath Woody's rapidly descending elevator (the meter on the elevator reads "Is This Trip Really Necessary?") so he dons a G.I. helmet, to no avail. Another throwaway gag can be seen on two stuffed bears: a "Cinnamon Bear" costs $100, but "Without Cinnamon" the other bear is only $20 — cinnamon and many other spices were hard-to-find luxuries during the war.

II; *Home Front; Shortages*

Private Snafu Cartoons

S1   Coming Snafu (June 1943)
Director: Chuck Jones

The character of Private Snafu is introduced in a spoof of a "coming attractions" movie trailer. An offscreen narrator says "SNAFU" stands for "Situation Normal, All ... *Fouled* Up.... He's the goofiest soldier in the Army." Snafu, who is rather thin and nerdy in this cartoon, is marching and carrying a rifle. The narrator claims Snafu is "a patriotic, conscientious ... kind of guy ... who thinks the Army's swell.... That is, with a few minor changes...." Snafu is distracted by a large cheesecake poster of a woman on a wall and marches right into a trap door. "Snafu represents all branches of the Army ... the Artillery ... the Tank Corps ... the Paratroops ... the Air Corps," the narrator says. "He's a real deep thinker." Snafu, with a stupid grin on his face, is driving a tractor with an airplane in tow, but is actually daydreaming about a burlesque queen stripping (probably animated by Robert McKimson). She's singing "Queen of the Burlesque" but just as she removes the last pieces of her clothing, "Restricted" is stamped strategically across her anatomy. Snafu has been so absorbed in this that he has progressively wrecked the aircraft he is towing. MPs arrest Snafu, who next appears behind bars shouting "Get me a lawyer!" The five musical notes signifying "You're a Horse's Ass" are heard as Snafu's visage transforms into the backside of a horse. The narrator concludes: "This *is* Snafu."

S2   Gripes (*Army-Navy Screen Magazine* no. 5, July 1943)
Director: I. Freleng

Pvt. Snafu complains about doing KP (Kitchen Patrol) as he cleans a mountain of dirty pots and pans while simultaneously peeling potatoes with his feet. He is later seen frenetically policing the camp grounds. Next, he stands in line as a battery of doctors with large hypodermic needles inoculate the soldiers. In a scene typical of the Snafu's cartoons mildly risqué content, one soldier's tattoo of a sexy woman screams as the needle plunges into her buttocks (the GI's arm). Snafu snorts, "If you're asking me, it's a pain in the prat." Snafu is issued his first three-day pass, but has to spend it in bed with a fever (a reaction to the shots), and grumbles that he would "make a few changes" to the Army if he had the power. Technical

Fairy 1st Class—a recurring character in the series, this diminutive, unshaven, cigar-smoking fairy wears GI shorts, a fatigue cap, and socks, carries a magic wand, and has a large pair of wings—materializes and tells Snafu: "I have a notion, to give you a promotion." With a wave of the fairy's wand, Snafu is placed in charge of the base. With a sleeve full of sergeant's stripes and smoking a "GI Perfecto" cigar, Snafu issues orders over the public address system: "Each GI gets two dames." In the next shot, Snafu and his pals pile into a jeep with a horde of squealing, busty women. The jeep is towing an outhouse—a soldier sticks his head out and says "And no more cleaning latrines." While a GI gets his uniform altered into a zoot suit, Snafu and a group of young women enact a harem scene. "Boy, am I good!" thinks Snafu. However, the Technical Fairy reappears: "Hear all that hummin'? I got a suspicion, the Germans are comin'." Snafu is confident: "I'll murder those poops. Where are my troops? Ah, nuts!" The soldiers aren't there, as the Technical Fairy explains: "They're a wash-up ... [with] no morale." A flight of Nazi planes passes overhead, and one drops a swastika-marked bomb on Snafu, as he frantically tries to dig a foxhole. The bomb halts in mid-air, a mechanical arm emerges and paints a target on Snafu's butt, then ... boom! However, it was all a fever-induced dream of Snafu's. When he awakes he happily returns to KP. The Technical Fairy says the moral of the story is "the harder you work, the sooner we'll beat Hitler—that jerk!" He lights up his cigar, which promptly explodes in his face.

S3   **Spies** (August 1943)
Director: Chuck Jones

The title of this episode appears over the drawing of an ear, a reference to the well-known series of propaganda posters which warned people the enemy might be listening. A significant part of the dialogue of this cartoon is delivered in rhyme. As he strolls along, Pvt. Snafu boastfully tells the audience he knows a military secret, but won't ever tell, literally zippering his mouth shut (he also has a padlock on the hotdog that serves as his brain). However, enemy spies are everywhere, including a bucktoothed cat in a drainpipe, a man hiding inside a mailbox, and a Japanese caricature in a baby stroller, who says "Oh, I bet we find it out." Snafu calls his mother to tell her he's going on a trip (as a Japanese spy, squeezed inside the phone box, listens); stopping off at a newsstand (which features girlie magazines), he mentions he will be going on a ship. Three men standing nearby reading magazines—*Lyfe* (whose cover features a picture of an unshaven Mussolini), *Golliers* (fat Göring on the cover), and *Fiberty* (a Japanese officer on the front)—are listening, and as they lower the magazines they are exposed as (who else) Mussolini, Göring, and a Japanese officer. Snafu steps into a nearby bar; as he gets drunk, two German-accented mooseheads on the wall turn to each other conspiratorially, their antlers forming a swastika. The booze melts Snafu's "pad-a-lock" and he approaches a pretty blonde, revealing he's going to Africa on a troopship leaving at 4:30. The blonde's feathered hat conceals a carrier pigeon, she has a miniature typewriter on her garter, and twin radio microphones (emblazoned with swastikas) in her bra, so Hitler personally gets wind of Snafu's "secret." He broadcasts a message to his U-boat wolfpacks. On board a troop transport,

Snafu spots the subs and shouts "Full speed ahead!" and is dumped in the ocean when the ship accelerates. The U-boats blast Snafu to hell with their torpedoes. A smiling Hitler devil (with a swastika on his chest) hands Snafu a mirror when the GI indignantly asks "Who the hell do you suppose it was who let my secret out?" The mirror identifies the culprit — Snafu's face, converted into a horse's rear end.

S4 The Goldbrick (*Army-Navy Screen Magazine* no. 9, September 1943)

Director: Frank Tashlin

On a rainy day, Pvt. Snafu is awakened from a sound sleep by a bugle blowing Reveille — directly into his face. "If I could only get out of drill, he grouses," and suddenly Goldy the Goldbrick appears (he is an overweight version of Technical Fairy 1st Class, with enlarged, lead-loaded buttocks). Goldy tells Snafu (to the tune of "Hi Lily, Hi Lily, Hi Lo"): "When there's cold and there's rain, and you don't want to train, just goldbrick, just goldbrick, just goldbrick...." Soon afterwards, Snafu is in bed at the infirmary, attended by a beautiful nurse. With Goldy's musical encouragement, Snafu continues to shirk his duties, including slit trench digging practice. The scene shifts to a Pacific island, and the peaceful ambiance is almost immediately interrupted by the sounds of battle. A sweating, panting Snafu can't keep up with his platoon buddies — Goldy recommends that he take a break, so Snafu enters the ramshackle "Honorable Booby Trap Hospital." After a huge mallet smashes Snafu's helmet down over his entire body, a Japanese tank — whose front end resembles a stereotypical Asian face, incorporating a Rising Sun motif — chases the hapless G.I. outside. As he unsuccessfully attempts to dig a trench, Snafu — his backside exposed — is crushed by the pursuing tank. Viewing the grave marker labeled "Pvt. Snafu, 14K Honorable Goldbrick," Goldy removes the mask that has concealed his true identity: a buck-toothed (*and* fanged) Japanese caricature, wearing a little derby hat! "Banzai! If find enough goldbricks, Japan could win war...."

S5 The Infantry Blues (*Army-Navy Screen Magazine* no. 11, September 1943)

Director: Chuck Jones

The cartoon opens with a closeup of marching boots, and then a disgruntled Pvt. Snafu bitches: "The Air Force gets the glory, and the Navy gets the cheers, but all the dogface ever gets — is mud behind the ears. I got the Infantry Blues." A montage shows Snafu lugging his load of gear through a swamp, desert, and other terrain, only to spot a sign reading "Rest Room 18000 mi." Technical Fairy 1st Class materializes and — with a wave of his magic wand — transports Snafu to the Tank Corps. But after bouncing around in an out-of-control tank and winding up dangling over the edge of a cliff, Snafu wishes he was somewhere else. TFIC grants this desire, putting Snafu at the controls of PT-13, but the former army private gets seasick. Snafu is next magically "transferred" to a P-38 fighter-bomber, and promptly crashes into the side of a mountain. Snafu crawls out of the wreck and spots the same road sign, "Rest Room 18000 mi.," as a smiling Technical Fairy says "I see you're back, sir. Here's your pack, sir." The two march off together.

S6   Fighting Tools (October 1943)
Director: Robert Clampett

After a montage of headlines proclaiming "Our Fighting Tools Prove Unbeatable," and shots of assorted American weapons, Pvt. Snafu — standing in his tent next to an artillery piece — sings "I'll be the world's greatest hero, with these guns I have nothing to fear-o, them Nazis will know what I mean-o, [when] I bury them in the latrine-o." A fat German soldier crawls up to Snafu's position and prepares to toss a "potato masher" stick grenade. Snafu spots the intruder and, jerking his M-1 carbine out of the ground, pokes the German in the butt with the gun. The obese Nazi gets up, shaking in terror, and shouts "Kamerad!" However, when he spots mud dripping out of the barrel of Snafu's carbine, he smiles and sings "That rifle looks just a bit gooey, if you think I'm scared you're plum screwy." He chases Snafu, who leaps behind a heavy machine-gun to defend himself, but the improperly-serviced weapon begins to overheat and melt, and the German whips out a knife to attack. Snafu's cannon briefly saves him, until once again his careless maintenance is exposed — the barrel is revealed to be the home of various animals, as well as the receptacle for dirty eating utensils. A last ditch attempt to escape in a jeep is foiled by the vehicle's dead battery. Blown out of his clothes by the German's grenade, Snafu lands behind the barbed wire of a Nazi prisoner-of-war camp and cowers there, naked as the German soldier sings about the so-called American "hero" being the "world's greatest zero." A close-up of Snafu becomes a shot of a horse's behind as the familiar "You're a Horse's Ass" theme plays.

S7   The Home Front (*Army-Navy Screen Magazine* no. 15, November 1943)
Director: Frank Tashlin

A snow-covered landscape appears on the screen (probably meant to represent the Aleutians), and the off-screen narrator intones: "It's so cold, it would freeze the nuts off a jeep!" (and as he says so, several lug nuts pop off a nearby jeep's wheels). Inside a Quonset hut, Pvt. Snafu — shivering despite his heavy clothing and the fact he's *sitting* on a wood stove — listens to a record of "There's No Place Like Home." Banging on the phonograph, Snafu grumbles, "They got it soft back there, they don't even know there's a war going on." He imagines his "old man" playing pool, his "ma" gossiping with her bridge club, "grandpa" ogling girls at a burlesque show, and his "gal" — the dark-haired Sally Lou — in a nightclub with a suave, middle-aged man (who briefly turns into a Tex Avery-style wolf). The freezing Snafu is visited by Technical Fairy 1st Class, whose magic wand produces a "televisor" (a TV set) to show the G.I. what the folks back home are *really* doing. As "My Old Man" is heard on the soundtrack, Snafu's father is shown in a factory, single-handedly creating tanks out of piles of parts ("V" for Victory is heard as rows of tanks exit the plant). Snafu's mother, assisted by her cat and horse (who enthusiastically spreads his own manure), surrounds her house with a towering Victory Garden ("V" for Victory heard once more). Snafu's grandfather, suspended over the side in a rocking chair sling, rivets and launches a row of Victory ships (more "V" on the soundtrack). Sally Lou has joined the WACs—"Every WAC Releases a Soldier" reads a poster. They all join together to sing "We're Working Like Hell in the Ol' Home Town." Snafu tries to kiss Sally Lou via the televisor, only to plant one on Technical Fairy 1st Class, who says "Gosh, I didn't know you cared."

S8   Rumors (December 1943)
Director: Friz Freleng

While sitting in the barracks latrine (so-called "latrine rumors" were a real concern of the U.S. military), a soldier reading a newspaper responds to Snafu's "It's a nice day" by sarcastically noting, "A nice day for a bombing." The off-screen narrator comments, "The hot air is blowing, a rumor is growing." Snafu starts thinking (the inside of his head is depicted as a pressure cooker); he warns another soldier that a bombing raid is imminent. The narrator: "Balloon juice — it's phony, but it makes nice baloney." A montage of baloney being processed through Rube Goldberg–like devices concludes with a soldier literally "shooting off his mouth," spewing a swarm of flying baloneys over the camp. Soldiers are overheard repeating rumors to their comrades: "the Brooklyn Bridge was blasted ... Coney Island was wiped out ... parachutists landed on the White House lawn...." In the mess hall, Snafu tries to eat a sausage, but it flies out of the bun and tells him that his "weapons are useless!" When he cracks open an egg, a bird-like creature with a trumpet-like mouth emerges to claim "the Japs are in California!" Snafu takes refuge in a trash can, only to be ejected by a gremlin who warns him about the enemy's "new secret weapon." Hiding under the sheets, Snafu discovers a fanged, horse-like monster next to him, who smugly notes "they" are attacking the camp. Pursued by various shadowy, howling demons, Snafu clambers up a telephone pole to escape the wild rumors: "The Russians are surrendering, the British are quitting, the Chinese gave up ... it's all over, we lost the war!" Finally, Snafu is shown in "Quarantine," wrapped in a strait-jacket and locked in padded Cell #13, muttering "nice weather for a rumor" as a loony sausage wearing a Napoleon hat bounces around muttering gibberish. The cartoon concludes with a parody of a newsreel logo: instead of cranking a camera, a man is grinding out baloney and the words "Sees ... Hears ... Knows ... Nothing" are shown.

S9   Booby Traps (*Army-Navy Screen Magazine* no. 19, January 1944)
Director: Robert Clampett

As shots of the smoldering remains of a battlefield are displayed, the off-screen narrator notes: "The enemy has fled, abandoning the area. As our forces move up, they must exercise great care.... Every object is a possible booby trap.... If you are a boob, you *will* be trapped." Pvt. Snafu skips around the battlefield (as "You're in the Army Now" plays), narrowly avoiding a booby-trapped shower. He tells the narrator: "I wish the hell you'd shut up! I ain't no boob and I won't be trapped!" (then sticks out his tongue). After barely escaping the consequences of milking a camel (whose udders are actually the detonators of a naval mine strapped to the animal), Snafu cannot resist going into a "harem," although the "harem girls" look suspiciously like dummies. However, Snafu only has eyes for an upright piano; flipping open some sheet music, he awkwardly tries to pick out "Those Endearing Young Charms" with a single digit. But his ineptitude saves his life, since he repeatedly hits a wrong note (the key for the "right" note is attached to a stick of dynamite). Giving up in frustration, he turns his attention to a hookah (water pipe); as he strikes a match on the breast of one of the "harem girl" mannequins, Snafu gets lustful thoughts about the "women," but discovers their spherical breasts and firm buttocks are actually bombs. Trying to flee, he narrowly avoids further booby traps, including a giant mouse trap and numerous trap doors. Just as he is almost home free, a little Hitler character appears and plays the correct sequence of notes of "Those Endearing Young Charms" on a triangle. Dashing back to the piano, Snafu plays the "right" note at last and blows himself up. Up in the clouds, an angelic Snafu sheepishly grins and says "At least up here I don't have to worry about no booby traps," but when he plays "Those Endearing Young Charms" on his harp, he is blown up again!

S10   Snafuperman (March 1944)

Director: I. Freleng

The obnoxious Pvt. Snafu is listening to loud swing music on his radio, and banging pots and pans in rhythm to the music. His barracks mates—attempting to study their maps, field manuals, and air recognition charts—try to get him to stop and engage in some constructive activity. Snafu responds: "Study? Nuts! When I get at them Nazis, I ain't going to clunk them over the head with no books.... What you've got to give them dopes is a bellyful of lead." Technical Fairy 1st Class materializes and (as the theme music from Paramount's "Superman" cartoon series is briefly heard on the soundtrack) waves his magic wand to convert the dumb soldier into "Snafuperman." In a pseudo-Superman outfit (complete with cape)— but still wearing oversized socks and his fatigue cap — Snafu declares "Oh boy, enemies of democracy, beware!" Taking a bomb (with "Adolf" written on it) about to be loaded onto a bomber, Snafu slips it into his pants and flies off toward Berlin. He drops his bomb, but Technical Fairy 1st Class recovers it, pointing out the U.S. Capitol building below: "The Americans are on our side, you know." A sheepish Snafu, searching for another target, spots a "lumbering Japanese tank." He pries it open with a can opener and — shouting "Come out, you bandy-legged disturber of world peace!"— uses a toilet plunger to extract the tank commander, a very angry Army general who indicates the U.S. flag painted on the side of the vehicle! Nervously saluting the officer, Snafu looks up and observes a "mess of Messerschmitts" (a joke used in *Daffy — the Commando*, 1943, q.v.) heading for an American port. Successfully intercepting their bombs, he stacks them up on a pier and sits proudly atop the pile, failing to notice those with delayed action fuses. After the predictable result of his ignorance, a battered Snafu is visited in the base hospital by Technical Fairy 1st Class, who asks if there is anything he can do. "Get me a field manual!" Snafu responds as "Blues in the Night" plays on the soundtrack.

S11 Private Snafu vs. Malaria Mike (*Army-Navy Screen Magazine* no. 23, March 1944)

Director: Chuck Jones

Mosquito Malaria Mike admires his image on a wanted poster he sees tacked up on a tree in a swamp, although "it don't do justice to my nose," he says in a gangster-ish voice, brandishing his harpoon-like snout. Just then, he's splashed with some water, and turns to notice the naked backside of Pvt. Snafu, bathing in a nearby stream. "Just my meat!" Malaria Mike examines a chart detailing the "Choice Cuts" of American soldiers, including the "filet mignon" (buttocks). Mike's assault on Snafu is initially foiled by the soldier's towel, preventing the mosquito from biting Snafu's rear end—a "face" the insect could "never forget." He's even more enthusiastic when he reads the soldier's dog-tags: blood type A, "just my type!" However, Snafu dons his pants and Mike stops to fill up on "Old Malaria, 999 Proof" before attacking again. Snafu, oblivious to his danger, bends over and the diving mosquito misses the target (he hits a tree instead, which shrivels up and dies). Finally, Snafu makes a mistake: he gets up from his cot to kiss a photo of his girlfriend, and his naked backside is bereft of the protective netting around his bed. Malaria Mike opens up a violin case and attaches a special tool to his snout, then successfully hits the mark. Some time later, Mike and his son are seated together in the insect's easy chair; the young bug asks Mike what *he* did during the "big war," and the adult mosquito directs his attention to the wall above the fireplace, where Snafu's head is mounted as a trophy. In a postscript, Snafu interrupts the cartoon's conclusion to thank his U.S. Army sponsors, the distributors of "G.I. repellent, mosquito nets, atabrine tablets, and good 'ol horse sense—gee, I wish the hell I'd used them."

S12 Diarrhea and Dysentery (*Army-Navy Screen Magazine* no. 24, March-April 1944)

Pvt. Snafu, having repeatedly ignored admonitions to keep his mess kit clean, comes down with a gastrointestinal disease. The climax depicts Snafu in distress, bent over and clutching his helmet, as he races for the latrine. This was not a full Snafu episode, only a brief insert in the *ANSM*.

S13 A Lecture on Camouflage (April 1944)

Director: Chuck Jones

Technical Fairy 1st Class greets the audience and, using a flip chart and his magic wand as a pointer, delivers a lecture. "Modern camouflage is an art and a science, if used intelligently." A little *boat* is shown chugging along a road, and is immediately targeted in a swastika gunsight. A direct hit reveals the "boat" to be Snafu and his jeep; with TF1C's encouragement, Snafu takes cover in some woods, but has to be reminded to cover his tracks. Safe and relaxing in the shade of a tree while smoking a cigarette, Snafu is not alarmed when the "tree" (in a German accent) asks for a light. However, the swastika-shaped smoke rings that emerge from the "tree" afterwards alert Snafu to his danger. TF1C: "Of course, the enemy sometimes uses camouflage too." As Snafu tries to sneak away, he's followed by the tree, a stump, and a boulder, all with boots sticking out from the bottom.

After a run-in with a German cannon, Snafu tries to hide in the shadow of another tree, but the effect of the shifting sun confuses him and he winds up under the shadow of a German observation balloon, which promptly drops a bomb on the hapless G.I. Technical Fairy 1st Class concludes his lecture: "If you want to fool 'em, just make yourself part of the natural surroundings." To illustrate, he jumps into his chart and joins two alluring, bare-breasted mermaids. The gag about an enemy soldier disguised as a tree was used as early as *Shoulder Arms* (1918) by Charlie Chaplin; in *Commando Duck* (1944), q.v., Donald Duck was menaced by a Japanese sniper in arboreal masquerade.

S14   Gas (May 1944)
Director: Chuck Jones

An Army camp — located "3642½ Miles [from] Brooklyn" — schedules a "gas drill." When the gas alarm sounds, the soldiers rush out of their tents wearing their gas masks and assemble on the parade ground. With the exception, of course, of Private Snafu. When he belatedly appears, Snafu opens his gas mask case, first extracting a sheer bra, then a bemused Bugs Bunny! This earns him extra drill under the supervision of a tough sergeant. Finally, an exhausted Snafu returns to his tent and tosses his gas mask into a trash can. Later, relaxing under a tree in a flower-strewn meadow (as "In the Good Old Summertime" plays), Snafu fails to notice an airplane which passes overheard, spraying gas. An anthropomorphic gas cloud (animated by Bob Cannon) parachutes to earth and, after spotting Snafu with binoculars, declares he will "surround" the lazy G.I. Barely escaping the noxious gas cloud, Snafu frantically chases the trash truck hauling away his gas mask. The gas engulfs the truck, but Snafu emerges triumphant, his gas mask securely in place. The cartoon concludes as Snafu sleeps, his gas mask clasped in a lover's embrace. The mask bats its eyelashes and says "I didn't know you cared." Note: because of the extensive use of poisonous gas on the battlefield in World War One, there was a great fear it might be used during World War II, possibly even against civilian populations. And in fact by the end of the war, all of the major belligerents had extensive stockpiles of the weapons yet — out of mutual horror at the consequences — poison gas was never employed in combat during World War II. Nevertheless, troops of both sides were trained in gas warfare (training which was considered by the troops to be particularly useless, especially as the war progressed) and were required to carry gas masks into combat. The ultimate pragmatists, combat soldiers considered the masks excess weight to be jettisoned in battle zones.

S15   Going Home (mid–1944, but unreleased)
Director: Chuck Jones

Soon after his ship passes the Statue of Liberty, Private Snafu is welcomed back from the "global grind" to his hometown of Podunk. The off-screen narrator notes that "our returning hero ... has ... a million things to talk about.... Safe at home, away from battle, restricted stuff makes harmless prattle." Sitting at the dinner table with his family and blonde sweetheart, Snafu describes the operations of his outfit, the 999th, who fought alongside "the Brits" — his head transforming into a record player, as "We Did It Before and We Can Do It Again" is heard in the background. The narrator: "Now that you got that off your chest, why not go out and blab the rest?" Which is precisely what Snafu proceeds to do. Wandering around town, he tells a cop (and a crowd that soon gathers) about a secret base with a special concrete runway; as a female service station attendant puts gas in his car (with an eye-dropper), Snafu talks about "new Jap tanks." Seated next to a buxom brunette in a movie theatre, Snafu watches a newsreel about an American secret weapon that obliterated a "Jap island." The newsreel commentator concludes: "What hit you, Tojo? Wouldn't you like to know?" Grabbing the brunette, Snafu brags that it was a "flying bazooka," as his head becomes a movie projector and displays a schematic drawing of the "secret" weapon on the screen.

"Our next move" against the enemy is revealed by Snafu — a mimeograph machine this time — in a bar. Even behind a bush in the park, making out with a girl, Snafu can't shut up, describing a future operation against Bola Bola in the Pacific (which appears on an electric billboard). As he gets a haircut and manicure at the barber shop, the inept soldier puffs on a cigar and "confidentially" divulges the "latest dope." As the smoke from his stogie floats into the sky and merges with a skywriter's message, the narrator sarcastically comments "You might just as well write it all over the sky." Finally, Snafu is home, wildly jitterbugging with his girlfriend, when a news bulletin interrupts the dance music on the radio: "The War Department regrets to announce that due to recent leaks in restricted military information, our entire 999th division has been annihilated by the enemy." An angry Snafu erupts: "My own outfit! Some guy shot his mouth off. Any jerk that would do that ought to be run over by a streetcar!" Of course, a streetcar immediately plows through the living room and mows down Pvt. Snafu. (The rationale for not releasing this episode was probably related to its somewhat unflattering portrayal of the home front, including the implication that civilians — as opposed to spies (cf. *Spies,* above) — had been the conduit of the leaked information. It could also be construed that this cartoon makes light of an entire military unit being destroyed (it is also remotely possible that the reference to a "secret weapon" that destroyed a Japanese island could have struck a sensitive chord among those working on the atomic bomb).

S16 The Chow Hound (*Army-Navy Screen Magazine* no. 29, June 1944)

Director: Frank Tashlin

This cartoon is narrated by a bull from a ranch "down on the panhandle." Just as he was preparing for his honeymoon, "the Nazis and Japs declared war." Inspired by an "Uncle Sam Wants You" poster, the bull salutes and signs up, waving farewell to his cow-bride from the back of a train (as in *Cow Cow Boogie,* 1943, q.v.). "If Snafu could make it, brother, so could I. Boy, was I processed" — into canned meat! The cans (bearing his smiling visage) roll off a conveyor belt; crates of them are transported by truck and ship to reach Snafu and his fellow soldiers overseas. The crates are unloaded in an arctic setting, are carried on a camel into the desert, and are trucked into a Pacific combat zone, because Snafu "must eat, in spite of bomb and shrapnel blast." Naturally, Snafu is first into the chowline and nastily demands that food be piled high on his tray. He sits under a palm tree

and stuffs himself until his belly expands, then thoughtlessly tosses away the leftovers. The ghost of the bull busts the clueless Snafu in the butt, then looks into a
garbage can: "I joined up as food for Snafu, but all I became is just waste."

S17   Censored (*Army-Navy Screen Magazine* no. 31, July 1944)
Director: Frank Tashlin

At night in his barracks, Pvt. Snafu surreptitiously writes a letter to his girlfriend Sally Lou, informing her that — based on the equipment that has been
issued — his unit is headed for the South Pacific. However, as he attempts to crawl
past the censor's office to drop the letter in the mailbox, his protruding butt triggers an electric eye and his missive is censored. While riding on a troop train, Snafu
tries again, folding his letter into a paper airplane and sailing it out the window
(hoping a farmer seated in a buggy at a railroad crossing will get it). But the censor is ever vigilant: a mechanical arm emerges from the caboose, intercepts the
letter, and returns it to Snafu (the offending passages have been scissored out,
turning the letter into a paper doll). On a troop ship, Snafu turns his letter over
to a carrier pigeon, but an "assistant censor" hawk intervenes. Finally, as Snafu
sits in his tent (festooned with pinups) on a tropical island, Technical Fairy 1st
Class appears and agrees to help, since Snafu assures him that he and his sweetheart use a private code to communicate (many people actually did do this during World War II). Sally Lou — shown topless and wearing black stockings —
receives the letter and tells her mother about it over the phone: "My Snafu [is] in
a big surprise ... operation against the island of Bingo Bango." A telephone montage follows, showing the spread of the information via gossip, all the way to a
Japanese soldier (buck-toothed and bespectacled, very similar to the racial stereotype utilized in *Bugs Bunny Nips the Nips,* 1944, q.v.), who receives the news on a
pay phone on Bingo Bango! When he notifies Tokyo, the island receives immediate, massive reinforcements and camouflaged fortifications (underground bunkers,
fake palm trees that are really cannons, etc.). Snafu is in the first wave of American soldiers who assault the island in amphibious vehicles: "Boy, we caught them
with their pants down!" But the whole invasion force is trapped within the island's
lagoon, as the Rising Sun flag pops up from a volcano. Snafu awakens from his
nightmare, and Technical Fairy 1st Class hands him back the uncensored letter,
which Snafu cheerfully trims up with a pair of scissors: "Like I said, every man
his own censor." (Although the Iwo Jima campaign did not take place until Feb-
ruary-March 1945, the diagram in this cartoon of the underground bunkers and
the depiction of Bingo Bango as a volcanic island are eerily suggestive of the actual
Japanese stronghold.)

S18   Outpost (August, 1944)
Director: Chuck Jones

The narrator informs the audience that America's "far-flung outposts" are
manned by our diligent "sentinels." One of these outposts is a tiny Pacific island
(one palm tree), inhabited by Pvt. Snafu and his assistant, a gooney bird. While
the bird keeps watch from his perch in the tree, Snafu sits in a tent by a radio and
bitches about his "249 days in this godforsaken hole" (as he grouses, he receives

a message from headquarters informing him that his 249th request for a transfer has been denied). Snafu and the gooney bird go to sleep, each dreaming of a sarong-clad beauty (in the latter's case, a sarong-clad female gooney bird), but their dreams get mixed up and an irate Snafu wakes up and berates his feathered associate for "insubordination." (This may have been an oblique reference to the numerous Gandy Goose cartoons during the war in which Gandy and Sgt. Cat's dreams over-lapped.) Told to "scram!" the dejected bird goes out and spots a floating can, labeled "Pickled Fish Eyes with Rice." After initially reacting with disgust, the bird becomes excited (a Rising Sun halo appears above his head) when he sees writing on the bottom of the can: "Hon. K Ration Imperial Japanese Navy." Snafu, however, isn't interested in the odorous can, and orders the gooney bird to bury it. However, back at headquarters, a group of American officers becomes disturbed when it loses track of a "Jap task force," and sends out an urgent message to the outposts for information. Snafu's casual mention of the ration can brings an immediate response, and the gooney bird has to go dig up the can to provide a more detailed report. Afterwards, a flight of American bombers takes off and annihilates the Japanese fleet; the Rising Sun swirls around amid the debris and finally sinks, to the sound of a flushing toilet (as in *You're a Sap, Mr. Jap*, 1942, q.v.). At sunset, Snafu and the gooney bird are seated on the beach; Snafu still doesn't understand the role the ration can played in the Japanese defeat, and he tosses it into the ocean as his "theme" ("You're a Horse's Ass") plays on the soundtrack.

S19   Payday (*Army-Navy Screen Magazine* no. 36, September 1944)
Director: I. Freleng

"Somewhere in the Middle East," Pvt. Snafu is spending his payday wandering through the local bazaar, passing up stalls operated by the "Sheik" and "Son of the Sheik" (references to silent film hits for Rudolph Valentino). Technical Fairy 1st Class appears and opens up his own stand — "Invest in Your Future." A poster shows a brand new suburban home, a streamlined car in the driveway, a gorgeous wife, Snafu Jr. in a stroller, and a doghouse on the well-manicured lawn, as "My Blue Heaven" plays on the soundtrack. However, before Snafu can hand over his cash, a fat, ugly devil appears and lures him into a souvenir shop. The slick car on the poster progressively changes to an old Model T, a horse and wagon, bicycle, and finally, a pair of rollerskates. In the Caribbean, a pith-helmeted Snafu strolls down the road, fondling his wad of cash. There is a shot of a bank-book reading "no dollars, no sense." TF1C opens his booth once more, but this time a cloud of smoke exits a nearby bar, turns into a cocktail shaker and — with the help of the little devil — lures Snafu away once more. The house on the poster disintegrates into a flophouse, then vanishes. In an arctic setting, a smiling Eskimo counts the money he received from Snafu for a totem pole, which Snafu is struggling to take with him, strapped to his back (the devil hitching a ride on top). The "Last Chance" booth operated by TF1C is bypassed by Snafu, who prefers to risk his savings in a crap game in a Quonset hut. After he rolls "boxcars" and "snake-eyes," his postwar dream is further eroded: the stork repossesses Snafu Jr., the gorgeous wife departs with her suitcase, the dog leaves with his doghouse. Completely tapped out, a naked Snafu (wearing a cardboard box for modesty) exits the hut, finds a dime in the snow and — loses it in the crap game! Even the foundation of his dream house vanishes; in a rubble-strewn pit, a rat answers the phone and says "Snafu doesn't live here anymore." (Unlike the "Hook" cartoons made for Navy audiences, neither *Payday* nor any of the other Snafu cartoons urges G.I.s to purchase war bonds.)

S20   Target Snafu (*Army-Navy Screen Magazine* no. 38, September 1944)

Director: I. Freleng

As a flight of mosquitoes passes overhead in military formation, an offscreen narrator intones: "Another smashing blow against the enemy is underway. To understand what goes into such a raid...." A montage follows, showing mosquitoes called up by the Selective Service being processed at the Induction Center (one tough-looking insect is enraged when he is rejected because he isn't carrying enough germs). During basic training, new recruits must survive an obstacle course that includes G.I. Repellent, DDT spray, and mechanical fly swatters before they earn their coveted "wings." Later, a crippled "recon" mosquito makes a crash landing at his base; the photos inside the enemy barracks reveal one soldier whose mosquito netting is full of holes. An enlargement reveals the backside of the sleeping Pvt. Snafu. The photo is stamped "Target for Tonight," and an aerial assault is launched. Snafu is successfully dive-bombed, and as a result is incapacitated with malaria. Back at their base, the "13th Malaria Marauders" add another stenciled GI to their scoreboard and the mosquito who led the raid is awarded the "Order of the Rising Temperature." Significant portions of this cartoon were recycled by Warner Bros. for *Of Thee I Sting* (1946), substituting a fat farmer for Snafu. *Target Snafu* was a parody of one of the most famous wartime documentaries, the British *Target for Tonight* (Crown Film, 1941), which chronicled an RAF bomber raid over Germany.

S21   A Few Quick Facts (1944)

Director: Osmand Evans

This Snafu episode, only one minute long, was produced by United Productions of America and features limited (rather than full) animation. After a brief montage of Broadway neon signs advertising nightclubs, Snafu appears, counting his pay. The offscreen narrator addresses the target audience (GIs stationed overseas): "The pay you received may not have seemed like much [when you were stationed in the USA, but] over here" spending recklessly buys up limited resources and drives up prices, creating an inflationary situation with "little left for the locals." The narrator adds that even for the American soldier this eventually results in one having "money without buying power." He suggests they "salt some of it away ... it will help your future." The cartoon concludes with a shot of Snafu in civilian clothes, seated beside a pretty girl in his new (postwar) car.

S22   Three Brothers (*Army-Navy Screen Magazine* no. 42, October 1944)

Director: I. Freleng

Pvt. Snafu is frustrated at his current assignment, sorting endless piles of shoes. Technical Fairy 1st Class materializes and sympathizes with the soldier's self-described "morale problem." Snafu says his brother Tarfu (Things Are Really Fucked Up) has a "swell spot," working with codes, so TF1C decides to show him how things really are. Tarfu is actually the caretaker of a batch of spoiled carrier pigeons—while one takes a shower, he is even ordered to sit on her eggs! He covers the eggs with a cheesecake pin-up picture, and they immediately hatch! (Over 3000 soldiers were actually assigned to pigeon service in World War II.) Snafu then says his *other* brother Fubar (Fucked Up Beyond All Repair) has got it "great," but TF1C shows him Fubar is the live attack "dummy" for a group of K-9 trainees. To get the pack of unruly mutts to chase him, Fubar has to put on a buck-toothed Japanese mask. The sergeant tells the dogs they must be "tougher than the enemy. Tear him to bits!" Fleeing from the vicious hounds, Fubar briefly hides out with Bugs Bunny in the latter's hole. Snafu decides his current job really is important.

S23   In the Aleutians — Isles of Enchantment ("Oh, brother!") (February 1945)

Director: Chuck Jones

According to the narrator, "the Aleutians are a string of island bases extending over a thousand miles westward from the Alaskan peninsula … that the Japs once considered a backdoor to the United States." A little, bare-footed Japanese soldier (the stereotypical caricature) emerges from the ocean and skips eastward over the topographical map of the Aleutian Islands, toward a large door frame near the Alaskan mainland; but when he opens the door, a giant G.I. confronts him and stomps on his foot! The Japanese soldier quickly hobbles back across the islands, into the ocean, swimming toward Japan, seen as a distant spot on the horizon sporting a Rising Sun flag and a pagoda. "Now, the back of the U.S. is the front door to Tokyo." However, the weather is something else — the soldiers stationed there must deal with rapidly changing conditions. Snafu leaves a building on a sunny day — sweating in light clothing — but in rapid succession is forced to don a parka (snow) and a raincoat with windshield wipers (heavy rain). The "only vegetation on the islands is tall grass … no trees," adds the narrator, and a frustrated dog peevishly remarks "You're telling me?" Earthquakes are not uncommon, either, which can have "unexpected consequences"— participating in a crap game in a Quonset hut on the base, Snafu rolls seven but an earth tremor changes the dice to snake-eyes and he loses. Sudden winds called "williwaws" and icing on airplanes' wings are other dangerous problems (an Eskimo is shown ice-fishing on the wing of a C-3 transport plane). GIs have adapted to these conditions in various ways; one invention is the "snowgoes," jeeps fitted with skis. Moisture on airstrips is another annoying and hazardous condition: Snafu changes into a diving suit and enters a pond. Moments later, a bomber emerges and takes off, with Snafu sharing the ball turret with a fish (the fish parachutes out and lands in the mouth of a smiling, Jimmy Durante caricature walrus). (In June 1942, the Japanese invaded and occupied two islands in the Aleutians, Attu and Kiska. Over a year later, the Americans reconquered Attu, and the Japanese subsequently abandoned Kiska. The weather conditions in this region were extremely bad: many more U.S. Air Corps personnel were killed or injured in accidents than in combat.)

S24   A Few Quick Facts About Fear (1945)
Director: Zack Schwartz

The second limited-animation UPA Snafu entry has a "storybook" opening, featuring a mounted knight in armor and a castle. The narrator says if one believes the stories, the past was the day of the "fearless warrior" (Snafu's face pokes out of the helmet's visor) who was "afraid of practically nothing." But when a menacing griffin materializes, Snafu-knight experiences the same fear, "hands clammy … pounding heart … stomach flop" that today's soldier may experience during combat. As an x-ray shows what's going on inside Snafu, the narrator explains that when a man is scared, this "triggers the fear machine [which actually] prepares him to recognize danger. [Then] the nerves go into action … the glands produce … a shot of adrenaline … and all hell breaks loose … you see more clearly … hear more keenly … the body is ready to act fast…. [Thus] you can make [fear] work for you, instead of against you." This cartoon is about two minutes long. Like *A Few Quick Facts*, this UPA Snafu is distinguished from those made by Warner Bros. by its total lack of humor.

S25   It's MURDER She Says… (*Army-Navy Screen Magazine* no. 52, May 1945)
Director: Chuck Jones

The off-screen narrator says this is the "story of an outcast, now a hunted wanderer over the face of the globe [who left] in her wake … a trail of broken men." South America, the Pacific, and the rest of the globe are marked "Off Limits" for this malarial mosquito madam clutching a liquor bottle —"She spends her numbered days in a miserable hideout. Her name, Anopheles Annie." Annie joins two younger working "girls" at their table. "I used to be the toast of the hot spots," she says. "All over the world, I knocked them on their heels." Her comments are accompanied by a flashback montage of a young, slim, and alluring Annie serving up the "Guadalcanal Zombie," "Bizerte Bombshell," "Salerno Sling," etc. "I took my drinks straight, but the boys got theirs mixed — with a Mickey Finn." Annie dive-bombs a sleeping GI (who looks a lot like Snafu); soon there is a hospital ward full of her victims. "My percentages were going up. But then the same old vice squad that killed me off in Panama — parasitologists, entomologists— every damned 'ologist' in the country got on my trail." A montage depicts Annie on a "Wanted" poster, GIs reading pamphlets about malaria, etc. Relentlessly pursued by DDT, GI repellent, oil sprays, and bulldozers that fill in swamps, Annie cries and complains that "they busted in all the joints from Burma to Bizerte." Back in the present, Annie says "Thanks to Snafu, a smart operator can still sneak in for a one-night stand." She fishes out some photos from her cleavage, showing Snafu with his shirt off, refusing to take his Atabrine tablets, and so on. As a topless Snafu meanders down the road, the younger mosquitoes whistle and head straight for his torso. Tossing back one last drink, a smiling Annie concludes: "As long as that guy's around, a little gal can still make an honest living." This cartoon is largely presented in limited-animation format.

S26 Hot Spot (July 1945)
Director: I. Freleng

The Devil (who talks like radio character "The Great Gildersleeve") receives a phone call in Hell. He's told it is so hot in Iran that the place may be of interest to him; before visiting, he reads a guide book that claims the temperature reaches 180 degrees there, but dismisses this as "propaganda." Human activity there is restricted by the heat, and even a camel complains to the Devil that *he* is hot. The Americans arrive in Iran, constructing docks, and unloading and storing supplies. Even Pvt. Snafu is doing his bit, although griping as usual as he unloads crates marked "Lend Lease for Russia." The Devil admits "they work like the devil," but even he is being affected by the heat, taking salt tablets and doffing his clothes! Snafu and his buddies drive trucks through the mountains of Iran, transporting the supplies to Russia over narrow roads "unlike the highways you are used to back home." Meanwhile, an increasingly discomfited Devil is swallowing salt directly from the shaker and has hooked up an electric fan. As the narrator discusses the "picturesque" Trans-Iranian railway, Snafu has to jump off the train and manhandle the top crate of the load over a mountain every time the locomotive enters a tunnel. The Devil, stripped to his underwear, decides it is time to return to Hell, but when he arrives discovers the Iranian camel sitting at his desk: "I don't care what you say, I'm cool." This cartoon is mostly limited-animation. In late 1941, the British and Russians jointly occupied strategic parts of Iran to help guarantee the free flow of Lend Lease supplies to the Soviet Union. In 1942, the Americans were invited to participate and by late 1943 U.S. involvement was quite extensive in Iran.

S27 Operation SNAFU (October 1945)
Director: I. Freleng

At Japanese military headquarters in Tokyo, a diminutive general (a toothy stereotype whose samurai sword drags on the ground) is escorted into a heavily guarded vault. Opening the armored door, the general places a document folder inside a safe deposit box and departs. Afterwards, Pvt. Snafu emerges from another box and steals the folder, but trips an alarm as he exits the vault. He manages to elude the general, who pursues him, wildly swinging his sword. A newspaper headline proclaims: "Secret War Plans Stolen." Snafu ducks into a geisha house and disguises himself in a kimono, but attracts the lustful attentions of the general, who arrives to search the establishment. The general carries Snafu to another building, locks the door, and swallows the key. But instead of a romantic tryst, the general has brought Snafu before a tribunal of Japanese judges in traditional robes (possibly a reference to the Black Dragon society or the trial scene in *The Purple Heart*, 1944). Snafu smashes all three judges in the head with a hammer, their buck teeth protruding from their crushed skulls! He then escapes and steals a rowboat to flee; when the general leaps into the boat and swallows the plans, Snafu merely seizes the Japanese officer by his neck, tosses him into a sack, and keeps rowing. This is a rare Snafu cartoon which does not attempt to teach a lesson to the audience.

S28   No Buddy Atoll (October 1945)
Director: Chuck Jones

This cartoon is largely presented in limited-animation format. Pvt. Snafu is floating along in his roomy life raft—complete with a portable phone—singing "I'm All Alone." He periodically pauses to receive "test" phone calls on the communications apparatus, although he never discusses his predicament. Nearby on the ocean, a stocky Japanese admiral (in full dress uniform), is squeezed into a patched inner-tube raft with "Honorable Navy" crudely lettered on its side. As Snafu continues to sing, the admiral joins him in a duet; they simultaneously spot a deserted tropical island and separately land there, only later discovering each other's presence. The admiral grabs his samurai sword, while Snafu frantically searches through his gear—including pin-ups and a guitar—for a weapon. He finally pulls out a pocketknife, whose attachments include a can of K-rations and a hairbrush. He temporarily holds off the admiral with the knife's umbrella attachment, but this is sliced to pieces by the Japanese officer's sword. Snafu flees, and his floral-patterned pajamas allow him to blend in with the foliage. Back in uniform, the GI climbs a palm tree, loads up on cocoanuts, swings through the trees like Tarzan, and "bombs" the unsuspecting admiral. Back on the ground, Snafu gets another call—he hands the phone to the admiral, then ducks behind a tree and pushes down a plunger, which explodes a bomb attached to the telephone. The final shot of this cartoon shows Snafu operating a souvenir shop out of a bamboo hut—the items on sale include the admiral's hat, samurai sword, and life raft. Interestingly enough, the Japanese admiral is not portrayed in stereotypical bucktoothed fashion in this postwar release.

S29   Secrets of the Caribbean (1945, not released)
Director: Chuck Jones

This episode was made in 1945 at a cost of $9,000, but for reasons unknown it was shelved and never released. Pvt. Snafu is stationed in the Caribbean, guarding the Panama Canal. In his pursuit of a beautiful native girl he is roughed up by gigantic insects, attacked by howler monkeys, and nearly eaten by a carnivorous plant.

S30   Mopping Up (1945, not completed)
Director: Tex Avery

Plot information is unavailable on this cartoon, budgeted at $16,000. The animation drawings were completed, but the project was aborted before they were filmed.

S31   Seaman Tarfu (*Army-Navy Screen Magazine* no. 69, early 1946)
Director: George Gordon

This limited-animation episode was produced by Rudolf Ising and Hugh Harman. The off-screen narrator introduces "Seaman Tarfu in the Navy, as made by the Army." After a short history of the evolution of the American sailor's uniform, today's sailor is presented in a "scientifically streamlined uniform," assigned to an aircraft carrier in port. (The sailor turns into a Tex Avery-style wolf when an attractive young woman strolls by.) After another, nerdy sailor (who strongly resembles "Dan Backslide" from the 1942 Warner Bros. cartoon *The Dover Boys*) passes by in pursuit of a female (a running gag throughout the cartoon), Tarfu appears, rolling down the deck on a scooter. When the decks need to be swabbed, he merely pushes a button and accomplishes the task with a mechanical device (which also puts a diaper on a seagull to prevent further damage!). Some other vignettes follow, including one in which Tarfu enjoys lookout duty in the crow's nest, since he has his cigar, portable radio, and — most importantly — binoculars so powerful that they can peek over the horizon and spy on a woman in her lingerie. The narrator concludes: "For an appraisal of the American sailor as a fighting man, let's hear it from a recognized expert" — a little, buck-toothed Japanese sailor emerges from beneath the waves, astride the broken hulk of his warship. The girl-chasing sailor reappears as the cartoon concludes, only to find Pvt. Snafu is her escort — "What did you expect, sailor, the Army made this picture."

Mr. Hook Cartoons

These cartoons were produced for the U.S. Navy by Warner Bros. in black and white except for the first episode. The voice of Hook sounds like actor Arthur Lake ("Dagwood" in the *Blondie* series), although this cannot be confirmed (if it isn't Lake, it is someone imitating his voice and mannerisms).

H1   Take Heed, Mr. Tojo (c. 12 July 1944)

Director: Walter Lantz

Anytown, USA in 1953: J.M. Hook, Seaman 1/c (retired) resides in a pleasant house on Easy Street. The middle-aged Hook is snoring on the couch when his son, playing "commando," disturbs his slumber. Pointing out the tail section of a Japanese plane mounted on the wall, Hook tells his son how he "shot down a Zero without a gun.

In a flashback to 1943, baby-faced sailor Hook is stationed on an aircraft carrier, carrying out "an important assignment for the skipper" (swabbing the deck). News comes that a "Jap plane" has been sighted, but when the Americans launch aircraft to intercept the intruder, the sneaky, buck-toothed Japanese pilot hides his Zero in a cloud and watches them fly by. Afterwards, the enemy pilot, despite a misfiring engine (suggesting the inferiority of Japanese equipment), attacks the carrier in his *yellow* airplane with red "meatballs" on the wings. Hook is chased across the deck by bullets, winding up in the War Bonds cabin. Its safe has been shot open; inspired by a poster reading "Be a Hero, Down a Zero with War Bonds," Hook collects several bundles of bonds and a "How to Fly" manual, then leaps into an airplane and takes off.

The Zero is once more hiding inside a cloud; spotting Hook, the pilot smirks and tosses a dagger at the sailor, then twists Hook's *white* plane into knots during a dogfight (aided by a book on ju-jitsu). The American craft manages to pull out of its dive and rejoins the battle. Just when all seems lost — in one shot, the Zero's landing gear pummels Hook just as Popeye was attacked in *Fleets of Stren'th* (1942), q.v. — Hook tosses a bundle of war bonds at the Zero, immobilizing the enemy pilot; a second bundle destroys the Zero, sending the pilot (a tire around his neck) plunging to earth on a small island below. All that remains of him are his buck teeth, chattering gibberish.

In 1953, Hook tells his son that bonds not only helped win the war, they also made it possible for him to have a son. The boy responds: "That's not the way *I* heard it." This Technicolor cartoon was completed by Lantz and his crew in 1943 and copyrighted in 1944. Specifically commissioned by the U.S. Navy to promote War Bond purchases, it was apparently shown widely to naval personnel.

H2   The Return of Mr. Hook (1944-45)

Produced by Warner Bros., this cartoon opens with shots of battleships cruising at night. A flash of lightning illuminates the U.S.S. *California*. Seaman Hook appears, a war bond in hand, singing "Any Bonds Today" as he emerges from the ship's War Bond office, which sports a sign reading "Get Your War Bond Allotment Today." Farther down the deck, some other sailors — tall and handsome, compared to the squat Hook — are playing cards and gambling. They mock Hook for spending his money on bonds, but he tells them he has "postwar plans." A flash-forward begins: "Peace" occurs, and a fleet of ships returns to the USA from the Pacific, disgorging the demobilized military personnel. Hook runs past a burlesque house festooned with nude photos, instead going into a haberdashery and replacing his sailor's uniform with a civilian suit. He is reunited with his sweetheart Cookie: they buy a cottage, test the bedsprings of a new double bed, get married (hanging a "Man at Work" sign on the door after he carries her over the threshold), and start raising a large family. Back in the present, the other sailors line up to buy bonds, saying "We have postwar plans, too," and break into a chorus of "Any Bonds Today?" The cartoon concludes with the printed message: "Register To-Day, See Your War Bond Officer."

H3   The Good Egg (1944-45)

Although his warship is plowing through rough seas, Seaman Hook is sleeping soundly in his hammock. A little devil–Hook appears and uses his pitchfork to spear a War Bond the sailor has tucked in his pants. "How come you're throwing away your dough on them lousy War Bonds? Cash them in and blow them on a good time!" However, a white angel-Hook shows up; after the devil knocks off his halo, they fight for Hook's "soul" and the devil is ejected out the porthole. "When the time comes for you to climb back into civvies," the angel says, "you'll have a postwar nest egg waiting for you." He cracks open an egg to illustrate, extracting new clothes, some cash, and (with some embarrassment) a stork. The cartoon concludes with a second "War Bond Allotment Egg" cracking open, and a stork emerging with a baby and saying "Call for your War Bond Officer" (a parody of the "Call for Philip Morris cigarette commercial catchphrase).

H4 Tokyo Woes (1945?)

Director: Chuck Jones?

The first half of this episode is probably the most outrageous animated work produced by Warner Bros. for the U.S. military. The title parodies "Tokyo Rose," the name given to various women who made English-language propaganda broadcasts for the Japanese during World War II. The cartoon begins with shots of a radio tower (topped by the Rising Sun flag) on the main island of Japan, as an horrendous cacophony of gibberish is heard. Inside the radio studio, a fat, buck-toothed Japanese man (standing on a crate) winds up his unintelligible speech and presents, with a flourish, "Tokyo Rose!" A series of doors (including one marked "Honorable Asbestos") slide open, finally revealing an embarrassed Rose sitting on the toilet, reading the newspaper! Clad in a striped kimono, she demurely glides up to the microphone, then suddenly bursts into a frenetic explosion of jive (caricaturing comedian-singer Martha Raye at her wildest), revealing ragged black underwear, spindly legs, and huge platform shoes (clogs) as she gyrates. "Hi, you gates! How are all you jive artists out there on the jungle network? I've got a mess of hot platters for you today. Woody Herman, Gene Krupa, and ah — L, L, [Leopold] Stokowski! But first, I want you to hear from a really happy, contented captured American war prisoner from Brooklyn, N.Y." (Some American prisoners of war in Japan actually broadcast from Japan on the notorious "Zero Hour.") Rose waves an American flag, salutes, and leaps into the air.

The camera pans to a fat Japanese man with huge buck-teeth and wearing a derby, who speaks with a stutter and a heavy Japanese accent (Mel Blanc, doing his Porky Pig voice) as he reads from his script into another microphone: "Hello fellas, this is the Sad Sack [a reference to the comic book G.I.], and believe me, after the war I'm bringing my family to live here in To-, To-, To-, Ky ... in Japan! It's lovely, all they feed me is peaches and cream, pie à la mode, and I'm drinking nothing but re-, re-, rum and Coca Cola." He starts dancing as the popular tune by that title begins to play, but Rose roughly pushes him away from the microphone. "Thank you, thank you. And now, all you jive bugs [as her buck-teeth threaten to engulf the mike], before I slap on that first hot platter for you, just a few words about those War Bonds they're asking you to buy. To help the war effort? Phooey! I ask you, what good will bonds do?"

On an American battleship, Seaman Hook is stuffing bonds into his piggy bank, but pauses as he hears Tokyo Rose's question. Enraged, he rams a mop into the radio's speaker and says "What good will bonds do? I'll show her." He places a bond into a 16-inch shell and fires it at Japan. Just as Tokyo Rose finishes singing "Any Bonds Today?"—commenting "Oh boy, what corn!"—the shell crashes into the radio studio. It pauses above her head and opens up; a little War Bond (wearing a sailor's cap) emerges, lifts up Rose's wig, and hits her on her (shaved) head. Afterwards, he delivers a singing telegram: "Greetings from Uncle Sam's Navy, whose intentions are really quite plain, they're sending you more of these presents, again, and again, and again." He hands Rose an armful of bombs with burning fuses, asks her to sign for them, and departs in the shell. The Japanese broadcasters gleefully gather around their "presents," which promptly explode, leaving only their huge teeth, eyeglasses, and Rose's wig remaining. The first announcer says "Does your face feel different lately?"

A smiling Hook leans against his seabag (now labeled a "Bond Bag"), and an offscreen narrator says: "Yessirree, sailor, today your War Bonds are fighting with you on all battle fronts. But tomorrow, when the war is over, that shell will be returned to you." Hook is depicted leaning against a tree in a park back home, and desperately digs a hole and dives into it when the 16-inch shell makes its appearance. The little Bond sailor emerges (spying Hook's backside, he remarks "I never forget a face") and produces a magic wand that converts Hook to a civilian, providing him with "civvies ... some spending massoula and a real postwar job. Is there anything else you'll be wanting?" Hook nods, but indicates he'll take care of that himself: seated in a swanky convertible, the ex-sailor becomes a howling wolf as a buxom brunette strolls by. In the next shot, the car is parked in Lover's Lane, and a lipstick-smudged Hook emerges from the beauty's chest. Noticing the audience, he pulls down a shade, which allows the audience to see the silhouettes of the lovers kissing (as "Happy Days Are Here Again" plays). The cartoon concludes with the printed exhortation: "For a Happy Future—see your War Bond Officer Today!"

Appendix A. War-Related American Cartoons

This chart includes only short cartoons made for commercial theatrical distribution: no features or special productions (War Activities Committee, Coordinator for Inter-American Affairs, etc.), although these are included in the filmography and the subject coding and war-relevancy appendices. Additionally, *Invasion of Norway* (Cartoon Films, 1940) and *Cap'n Cub* (Film Classics, 1945) are not in the chart below, and shorts produced in dimensional animation (Puppetoons and *The Flying Jeep*) are also excluded. Releases in 1945 are for January–September only.

The numbers listed are war-relevant films and total films released (percentage of total releases with war relevance).

Distributor	1939	1940	1941	1942	1943	1944	1945	Totals
Columbia	1/23	0/24	4/24	10/20	11/22	5/19	2/11	33/143
	(4%)	(0%)	(17%)	(50%)	(50%)	(26%)	(18%)	(23%)
MGM	1/14	1/13	2/13	4/15	10/14	7/13	4/9	29/91
	(7%)	(8%)	(15%)	(27%)	(71%)	(54%)	(44%)	(32%)
Paramount	0/18	2/38	1/28	14/23	13/17	7/21	6/13	43/158
	(0%)	(5%)	(4%)	(61%)	(76%)	(33%)	(46%)	(27%)
RKO (Disney)	0/13	0/14	1/18	4/19	11/13	4/12	1/10	21/99
	(0%)	(0%)	(6%)	(21%)	(85%)	(33%)	(10%)	(21%)
20th Century–Fox	0/26	0/26	3/26	11/26	10/17	4/20	2/16	30/157
	(0%)	(0%)	(12%)	(42%)	(59%)	(20%)	(13%)	(18%)
Universal	0/20	1/18	4/13	6/14	7/10	1/8	2/6	21/89
	(0%)	(13%)	(30%)	(36%)	(70%)	(13%)	(33%)	(24%)
Warner Bros.	2/44	6/40	11/41	22/41	19/27	18/26	10/15	80/234
	(5%)	(15%)	(27%)	(54%)	(70%)	(69%)	(67%)	(34%)
Totals	4/158	10/173	26/163	71/158	81/120	46/119	27/80	257/971
	(2.5%)	(6%)	(16%)	(45%)	(68%)	(39%)	(34%)	(26%)
1939–1941:	40/494	(8%)						
1942–1945:	225/477	(47%)						

Appendix B. Frequency of Selected Topical References (All Cartoons)

Films with two or more references

Topical Reference	1939	1940	1941	1942	1943	1944	1945	Total
Armed Forces unspecified	3	0	1	1	0	1	0	6
AF-Army	0	2	17	25	19	9	2	74
AF-Air Corps	0	1	2	10	16	7	3	39
AF-Marine Corps	0	0	0	0	2	0	1	3
AF-Merchant Marine	0	0	1	0	1	0	1	3
AF-Navy	0	0	6	19	7	8	6	46
AF-British	0	0	0	1	2	0	0	3
AF-Royal Air Force	0	0	2	1	1	0	0	4
AF-German	0	2	1	4	9	1	1	18
AF-Japan	0	0	0	8	8	5	2	23
AF-Women	0	0	0	1	1	2	1	5
Bonds	0	0	1	18	5	4	0	28
Blacks	0	3	8	9	12	6	2	40
Draft	0	2	10	5	8	3	4	32
Draft Avoidance	0	0	0	0	1	0	1	2
Japan	0	0	1	14	22	4	1	42
Germany	0	0	1	2	5	1	0	9
Italy	0	0	0	1	0	1	0	2
Nazi/Fascist	0	2	4	4	19	4	1	34
Mussolini	0	0	2	3	7	1	0	13
Hitler	0	0	3	10	26	5	1	45
Tojo/Hirohito/Yamamoto	0	0	0	1	6	3	0	10
Shortages	0	0	0	16	28	20	12	76

Topical Reference	1939	1940	1941	1942	1943	1944	1945	Total
Production	0	0	0	8	10	4	6	29
AF-Russia	0	0	0	0	1	0	0	1
Czech	0	0	1	0	1	0	0	2
Women in Labor Force	0	0	0	2	1	5	2	10
Home Front	0	0	0	17	13	5	4	39
Pearl Harbor	0	0	0	1	1	0	0	2
Göring	0	0	0	0	3	1	1	5
Jews	0	0	0	0	2	0	0	2
Goebbels	0	0	0	0	1	1	0	2
Black Market	0	0	0	0	1	2	1	4
MacArthur	0	0	0	1	1	0	1	3
Home Defense/Nat'l. Defense/Air Raid Warden	0	0	3	13	11	5	1	33
Franklin D. Roosevelt/ Eleanor Roosevelt	0	1	2	2	2	2	0	9
Stalin	0	0	1	0	1	1	1	4
Churchill	0	0	0	1	1	2	0	4
Spy-Saboteur	1	1	2	5	7	1	1	18
"V"	0	0	4	23	17	5	2	51
War Allegory	4	2	1	2	1	0	1	11
World War I	0	0	0	9	6	2	0	17
World War II (thru 1941)	0	5	5	-	-	-	-	10
Historical American Figures	1	0	1	2	2	1	1	8
Postwar	0	0	0	0	0	1	2	3
South America	0	0	1	7	0	3	1	12
Pacifist	3	0	0	0	0	0	0	3
Terror Weapons	1	0	0	0	0	0	0	1
Atrocities/Concentration Camp	0	0	1	3	1	0	0	5
Neutrality/ Isolationist	0	2	0	1	0	0	0	2
Norway	0	1	0	0	1	0	0	2
Greece	0	0	1	0	1	0	0	2
Poland	0	0	1	0	1	0	0	2
Austria	0	0	1	0	1	0	0	2
Spanish Civil War	0	1	2	0	0	0	0	3
Russia	0	0	1	0	1	2	1	5
League of Nations	0	0	1	0	0	0	0	1
Britain/Commonwealth	0	0	3	3	2	1	0	9
Refugees	0	0	1	0	0	1	0	2
Netherlands	0	0	1	1	1	0	0	3
Collaborators/Fifth Col.	0	0	0	0	2	0	1	3
China	0	0	0	1	1	1	0	3
France	0	0	1	0	1	0	0	2

Appendix C.
War Relevancy

	I	II
1942:	42	33
1943:	44	45
1944:	19	30
1945:	8	22
Totals:	113	130

I. Cartoons directly dealing with World War II — without the topical aspects, these cartoons would either not have been made, the focus would have been considerably altered, or a number of the topical gags would not have been present.

II. Cartoons containing topical references but which are not dependent on the war for their theme.

Appendix D.
Featured Characters

Andy Panda (Universal)
Air Raid Warden (1942)
Andy Panda's Victory Garden
(1942)
Canine Commandos (1943)
Goodbye Mr. Moth (1942)
Meatless Tuesday (1943)
$21 a Day (Once a Month) (1941)

Barney Bear (MGM)
Barney Bear's Victory Garden
(1942)
Bear Raid Warden (1944)
The Flying Bear (1941)
The Rookie Bear (1941)
The Uninvited Pest (1943)
Wild Honey (1942)

Bugs Bunny (Warner Bros.)
All This and Rabbit Stew (1941)
Any Bonds Today? (1941)
Buckaroo Bugs (1944)
Bugs Bunny Gets the Boid (1942)
Bugs Bunny Nips the Nips (1944)
Case of the Missing Hare (1942)
Corny Concerto (1943)
Crazy Cruise (1942)
Falling Hare (1943)
Fresh Hare (1942)
Gas/Snafu (1944)

Hare Conditioned (1945)
Herr Meets Hare (1945)
Jack Wabbit and the Beanstalk
(1943)
Little Red Riding Rabbit (1943)
Porky Pig's Feat (1943)
Super Rabbit (1943)
Three Brothers/Snafu (1944)
Tortoise Wins by a Hare (1943)
The Unruly Hare (1945)
The Wabbit Who Came to Supper
(1942)
The Wacky Wabbit (1942)
What's Cookin', Doc? (1944)

Daffy Duck (Warner Bros.)
A Coy Decoy (1941)
Conrad the Sailor (1942)
Daffy — the Commando (1943)
Daffy's Southern Exposure (1942)
Draftee Daffy (1945)
Plane Daffy (1944)
Porky Pig's Feat (1943)
Scrap Happy Daffy (1943)
Slightly Daffy (1944)
The Stupid Cupid (1944)
Tick Tock Tuckered (1944)
To Duck — Or Not to Duck (1943)
Tom Turk and Daffy (1944)
The Wise Quacking Duck (1943)

Donald Duck (Disney)
  All Together/Canadian-US Bonds
    (1942)
  Commando Duck (1944)
  Der Fuehrer's Face (1943)
  Donald Gets Drafted (1942)
  Donald's Decision/Canadian-US
    Bonds (1942)
  Donald's Tire Trouble (1943)
  Fall Out, Fall In (1943)
  Home Defense (1943)
  The New Spirit (1942)
  The Old Army Game (1943)
  The Reluctant Dragon (1941)
  Sky Trooper (1942)
  The Spirit of '43 (1943)
  Timber (1941)
  The Vanishing Private (1942)

Droopy (MGM)
  Dumb-Hounded (1943)
  The Shooting of Dan McGoo (1945)

Elmer Fudd (Warner Bros.)
  Any Bonds Today? (1941)
  A Corny Concerto (1943)
  Fresh Hare (1942)
  The Hare-Brained Hypnotist (1942)
  An Itch in Time (1943)
  Rookie Revue (1941)
  To Duck or Not to Duck (1943)
  The Unruly Hare (1945)
  The Wabbit Who Came to Supper
    (1942)
  Wacky Wabbit (1942)

Fox and Crow (Columbia)
  The Dream Kids (1942)
  The Egg-Yegg (1944)
  Plenty Below Zero (1943)
  Slay It With Flowers (1943)
  Toll Bridge Troubles (1942)
  Woodsman, Spare That Tree (1942)

Gandy Goose (Terrytoons/
  20th Century–Fox)
  Aladdin's Lamp (1943)

Barnyard Blackout (1943)
Camouflage (1943)
Carmen's Veranda (1944)
Flying Fever (1941)
The Ghost Town (1944)
The Home Guard (1941)
The Last Round Up (1943)
Lights Out (1942)
Mopping Up (1943)
My Boy Johnny (1944)
Night Life in the Army (1942)
The One Man Navy (1941)
The Outpost (1942)
Post War Inventions (1945)
Scrap for Victory (1943)
Sham Battle Shenanigans (1942)
Somewhere in Egypt (1943)
Somewhere in the Pacific (1942)
Tire Trouble (1942

Goofy (Walt Disney)
  How to Be a Sailor (1944)
  The Reluctant Dragon (1941)
  Victory Vehicles (1943)

Jasper (George Pal/Paramount)
  Jasper Goes Fishing (1943)
  Jasper in the Haunted House (1942)
  Jasper's Booby Traps (1945)
  Say Ah, Jasper (1944)

Nancy (Terrytoons/20th Century–
  Fox)
  Doing Their Bit (1942)
  School Daze (1942)

Pluto (Walt Disney)
  The Army Mascot (1943)
  Dog Watch (1945)
  First Aiders (1944)
  Out of the Frying Pan, Into the Fir-
    ing Line (1942)
  Private Pluto (1943)
  Victory Vehicles (1943)

Popeye (Fleischer/Paramount)
  Alona on the Sarong Seas (1942)

Anvil Chorus Girl (1944)
Baby Wants a Bottleship (1942)
Blunder Below (1942)
Cartoons Ain't Human (1943)
Fightin' Pals (1940)
Fleets of Stren'th (1942)
For Better or Nurse (1945)
Happy Birthdaze (1943)
Her Honor the Mare (1943)
A Hull of a Mess (1942)
The Hungry Goat (1943)
A Jolly Good Furlough (1943)
Kickin' the Conga Round (1943)
Many Tanks (1942)
The Marry-Go-Round (1943)
Mess Production (1945)
The Mighty NaVy (1941)
Olive Oyl and Water Don't Mix
  (1942)
Pitchin' Woo at the Zoo (1944)
Pop-Pie Ala Mode (1945)
Puppet Love (1944)
Ration fer the Duration (1943)
Scrap the Japs (1942)
Seein' Red, White 'n' Blue (1943)
Spinach fer Britain (1943)
Spinach-Packin' Popeye (1944)
Too Weak to Work (1943)
Tops in the Big Top (1945)
We're on Our Way to Rio (1944)
Wood-Peckin' (1943)
You're a Sap Mr. Sap (1942)

Porky Pig (Warner Bros.)
Africa Squeaks (1940)
Ali Baba Bound (1940)
Any Bonds Today? (1941)
Brother Brat (1944)
Confusions of a Nutzy Spy (1942)
Corny Concerto (1943)
Meet John Doughboy (1941)

Naughty Neighbors (1939)
Old Glory (1939)
Porky Pig's Feat (1943)
Porky's Pooch (1941)
Porky's Poor Fish (1940)
Porky's Snooze Reel (1941)
Robinson Crusoe Jr. (1941)
The Swooner Crooner (1944)
Tick Tock Tuckered (1944)
Tom Turk and Daffy (1944)
Wagon Heels (1945)
We the Animals Squeak (1941)
Who's Who in the Zoo (1942)

Screwy Squirrel (MGM)
Big Heel-Watha (1944)
Happy Go Nutty (1944)
The Screwy Truant (1945)

Superman (Fleischer/Paramount)
Bulleteers (1942)
Destruction Inc. (1942)
The Eleventh Hour (1942)
Japoteurs (1942)
Jungle Drums (1943)
Secret Agent 91943)

Tom and Jerry (MGM)
The Lonesome Mouse (1943)
Mouse Trouble (1944)
Sufferin' Cats (1943)
The Yankee Doodle Mouse (1943)
The Zoot Cat (1944)

Woody Woodpecker (Universal)
Ace in the Hole (1942)
Barber of Seville (1944)
The Dippy Diplomat (1945)
Ration Bored (1943)
$21 a Day (Once a Month) (1941)
Woody Dines Out (1945)

Appendix E.
"Ambiguous" List

This list contains cartoons which could not be definitely included in the main filmography either because they were not available for screening to confirm war relevance, or because the references were not overt.

Disney/RKO

The Plastics Inventor (1944): Donald Duck constructs his own airplane out of plastic, following instructions given on a radio show. The plane actually flies, but it has one flaw — the plastic dissolves in the rain! Oblique references to wartime production and shortages of strategic materials.

Tugboat Mickey (1940): Mickey puts on a gas mask at one point in this short.

20th Century–Fox

The Mouse of Tomorrow (1944): the screen debut of "Super Mouse" (later changed to Mighty Mouse). While most of the Mighty Mouse cartoons from 1942–45 have been screened, only one overt reference has been discovered (*Mighty Mouse and the Kilkenny Cats*, 1945). *The Mouse of Tomorrow* has some peripheral topical references and several other cartoons—*The Sultan's Birthday* (1944 —cats wearing burnooses and riding flying carpets make a bombing and strafing attack on a mouse Baghdad) and *The Green Line* (1944 — militarized mouse vs. cat battles)— may be allegorical references to the war situation.

Paramount

Me Musical Nephews (1942): Popeye's nephews drive him wild with their musical "talents." Popeye, awakened from a nap, says "Clear the decks, man the guns, fire when ready!" And — implying that he's been away (at war?)— he tells the boys "You practice swell since your Uncle Popeye's been away." Remade in 1950 as *Riot in Rhythm*.

214

Universal

The Screwdriver (1941): Woody Woodpecker drives a motorcycle cop crazy; at one point the policeman flies up in the air, saying "I'm a dive bomber!"

The Beach Nut (1944): Wally Walrus relates (in flashback) to a crowd on the pier at a seaside resort why he is about to murder a certain notorious woodpecker. Among the many harassments he endured was being buzzed by a turbaned Woody Woodpecker on a flying carpet. The wacky bird does a "pilot to bombardier" routine while in flight.

Columbia

The House That Jack Built (1939): this cartoon concerns a bear who continually interrupts a beaver's work. Eventually, the bear sends termites to destroy the beaver's house. When the beaver gets mad, he forces the bear to rebuild his house. Released in the spring of the year, this could be construed as an allegory on the growing world crisis.

The Way of All Pests (1941): members of the insect world hold a mass meeting to decide upon a course of action to defend themselves against a human with a flyswatter. United, they attack the man.

Mr. Moocher (1944): the *Motion Picture Herald* review says the Crow "is much impressed by the advice given on a radio program, that the only way to live is at peace with one's neighbors, with kindness and understanding replacing fear and suspicion." (not screened)

Ku-Ku Nuts (1945): the *Motion Picture Herald* hints at a war reference. The Fox is a castaway on a desert island and "when the Crow makes his appearance, friend Fox decides he is in for a meat dinner — and no points required." (not screened)

Warner Bros.

Aviation Vacation (1941): spot gags about an airplane trip around the world, beginning in California. As the plane passes Mt. Rushmore, the carved heads include Franklin D. Roosevelt and Wendell Wilkie (Wilkie, a noted interventionist, had lost the 1940 election to FDR). After crossing the Atlantic, the aircraft flies over Ireland, but England and continental Europe are avoided.

Farm Frolics (1941): spot gags on a farm. One running joke concerns hungry piglets who anxiously watch the clock for feeding time, which is finally signaled by the Army's "mess call" played on a bugle.

Goofy Groceries (1941): after hours in a closed grocery store. A wild gorilla escapes from a box of "Animal Crackers" and runs amok. "Navy Beans" mobilize to fight him, as does some "Turtle Soup" which provides ersatz tanks.

The Trial of Mr. Wolf (1941): on the witness stand in court, the Wolf claims he was framed by Red Riding Hood and her Granny, a furrier. "What do you think's goin' on behind me own back? Sabotagie!" Later, in a sequence imitated in *Plane Daffy* (1944), q.v., the Wolf tries to escape, but every time he opens a door, Granny is waiting for him — once wearing a doughboy-style helmet and firing a machine gun, another time with a huge howitzer.

Aloha Hooey (1942): a seagull and a nerdy black crow jump ship to make time with Leilani, a sexy Polynesian bird on a tropical island. Their ship is named S.S. *Sabotage*.

Case of the Missing Hare (1942): Bugs Bunny clashes with obnoxious magician Ali Bama, who plasters a poster over the rabbit's home and later pushes a pie in Bugs' face. Bugs replies, "Of course you realize, this means war" in a voice which may be intended to evoke Winston Churchill.

Yankee Doodle Daffy (1943): performers' agent Daffy Duck tries to persuade disinterested producer Porky Pig to sign Sleepy LaGoon (a little duck) to a contract. Porky hops into a plane at one point to escape the persistent Daffy, but the agent dons an aviator's helmet and goggles, singing "We watch the skyways, over the land and sea, ready to fly wherever duty calls, ready to fly to be free."

Hare Ribbon (1944): Bugs Bunny and a dopey, red-haired dog square off. The last two-thirds of the cartoon take place underwater. Bugs dresses up like a mermaid to fool the dog, who briefly metamorphoses into a torpedo to pursue "her."

Stage Door Cartoon (1944): the title is a takeoff on the feature film *Stage Door Canteen* (1943), based on the actual establishment in New York that entertained servicemen. A similar club in Hollywood inspired *Hollywood Canteen* (1944), which was also spoofed in a cartoon (*Hollywood Canine Canteen*, 1946).

Appendix F. Selected War-Related Commercial Animated Shorts, 1915–1918

1915

"Canimated Nooz Pictorial No. 2" (Essanay) Wallace A. Carlson, November
Col. Heeza Liar and the Torpedo (Pathé)
Col. Heeza Liar and the Zeppelin (Pathé News #23) John Randolph Bray, April
Col. Heeza Liar at the Front (Pathé News #33) J.R. Bray, April
Col. Heeza Liar Fools the Enemy (Pathé) August
Col. Heeza Liar in the Trenches (Pathé News #31) J.R. Bray, April
Col. Heeza Liar Invents a New Kind of Shell (Pathé)
Col. Heeza Liar Runs the Blockade (Pathé)
Col. Heeza Liar, War Aviator (Pathé News #37) J.R. Bray, May
Col. Heeza Liar, War Dog (Pathé) J.R. Bray, August
The Dove of Peace (Mina) Harry Palmer, February
Pa Dreams He Wins the War (Pathé) W.C. Morris, August
Pa Lectures on the War (Pathé) W.C. Morris, August
Pa McGinnis Gets the Boys Out of the Trenches ("Keeping Up with the Joneses")
  (Mutual-Gaumont) H.S. Palmer, December
The Pilot of Peace (Pathé News #61) W.G. Morris, July
The Troubles of a Pacifist (Pathé News #102) December
Uncle Sam Gets Wise at Last (Pathé News #59) August

1916

"Canimated Nooz Pictorial" Numbers 6–10, 15 (Essanay) W.A. Carlson, March–
  September
Col. Heeza Liar Wins the Pennant (Paramount-Bray Pictographs #13) J.R. Bray,
  April
Dreamy Dud in the African War Zone (Essanay) W.A. Carlson, October
Mutt and Jeff in the Movies (Mutt and Jeff Film Company) Charles Bowers, June

Mutt and Jeff in the Outposts (M&JF) Charles Bowers
Mutt and Jeff in the Submarine (M&JF) Charles Bowers
Mutt and Jeff in the Trenches (M&JF) Charles Bowers
Scrambled Events (Gaumont-"Kartoon Komics") Harry Palmer, July
Signs of Peace (Essanay) W.A. Carlson, October

1917

The Awakening of America (Paramount-Bray Pictographs #68) May
Bobby Bumps' Submarine Chaser (Paramount-Bray Pictographs #72) Earl Hurd, June
Bobby Bumps' Tank (Paramount-Bray Pictographs #100) E. Hurd, December
Bobby Bumps Volunteers (Paramount-Bray Pictographs #66) E. Hurd, May
Bullets and Bull (International) "Happy Hooligan," December
"Canimated Nooz Pictorial" No. 28 (Essanay), W. A. Carlson, April
Col. Heeza Liar, Spy Dodger (Paramount-Bray Pictographs #59) J.R. Bray, March
Colonel Pepper's Mobilized Farm (Universal-"Powers Comic Cartoons") Pat Powers, August
The Eagle's Blood (Universal) Hy Mayer
The Evolution of the Dachshund (Paramount-Bray Pictographs #71) June
Freedom of the Seas (Hearst-Pathé News #21) T.E. and Will Powers, March
Goodrich Dirt at the Training Camp (Paramount-Bray Pictographs #92) W.A. Carlson, August
Goodrich Dirt and the Beach Nuts (Paramount-Bray Pictographs #83) W.A. Carlson, September
Heroes of the Past (Hearst-Pathé News #33) May
The International Ice Pond (Hearst-Pathé News #11) February
The New Recruit (International-Pathé) "Happy Hooligan," April
Peace Insurance (Hearst-Pathé News #27) April
The Rise of a Nation (Educational) Harry Palmer, June
Sic' Em Cat (Paramount-Bray Pictographs #77) July
Soldiering for Fair (Paramount-Bray Pictographs #64) F.M. Follett, "Quacky Doodles," April
Stung (Paramount-Bray Pictographs #65) April
The Submarine Chaser (Bud Fisher-Film Co.) C. Bowers & Raoul Barre, "Mutt and Jeff," July
The Tank (International) "Happy Hooligan," September
Uncle Sam's Dinner Party (Paramount-Bray Pictographs #81) August
Your Flag and My Flag (Kleine, Edison, Selig and Essanay) Paul Terry, July

1918

At the Front (Fox) "Mutt and Jeff," September
Bobby Bumps and the Speckled Death (Paramount-Bray) E. Hurd
Bobby Bumps Becomes an Ace (Paramount-Bray) E. Hurd, July
Bulling the Bolsheviki (Fox) "Mutt and Jeff," October
Doing His Bit (Educational-International) Frank Moser, "Happy Hooligan," May
The Dough Boy (Fox) "Mutt and Jeff," November

The Draft Board (Fox) "Mutt and Jeff," December
Efficiency (Fox) "Mutt and Jeff," August
The Freight Investigation (Fox) "Mutt and Jeff," April
Helping McAdoo (Fox) "Mutt and Jeff," April
How Charlie Captured the Kaiser (Universal) Pat Sullivan, September
Hunting for U-Boats (Fox) "Mutt and Jeff," July
Joining the Tanks (Fox) "Mutt and Jeff," July
The Kaiser's New Dentist (Fox) "Mutt and Jeff," September
Landing a Spy (Fox) "Mutt and Jeff," August
Liberty Bonds (Paramount-Bray Pictographs #18) C.T. Anderson, April
Our Four Days in Germany (Fox) "Mutt and Jeff," October
Over the Rhine with Charlie (Universal) Pat Sullivan, December
Pot Luck in the Army (Fox) "Mutt and Jeff," December
Putting Fritz on the Water Wagon (Paramount-Bray Pictographs #103) February
The 75-Mile Gun (Fox) "Mutt and Jeff," June
The Sinking of the Lusitania (Jewel) Winsor McCay, July
The Tale of a Pig (Fox) "Mutt and Jeff," June
A Total Eclipse (Fourth Liberty Loan cartoon) October

Notes

Chapter 1. Not for Kids Only

1. The George Pal "Puppetoons" and *The Flying Jeep* listed in the Filmography are dimensional or stop-motion animation shorts utilizing clay, plastic, or wooden figures which were manipulated and filmed, as opposed to cartoon drawings. These shorts are not counted in most industry statistics as animated cartoons.

2. Leslie Cabarga, *The Fleischer Story* (New York: Nostalgia Press, 1976): 157, 169.

3. In addition to numerous training films, Disney produced the animated sequences for Frank Capra's "Why We Fight" and "Know Your Allies/Enemies" series. Although most of the animation for these documentaries consists of maps or diagrams, there are a few imaginative moments, such as the swastika "termites" shown gnawing at the foundation of "fortress France" in *Divide and Conquer* (1942), or the depiction of the Japanese home islands as a dragon in *Prelude to War* (1943) and *Know Your Enemy — Japan* (1945).

4. Ten of first 11 Oscars for cartoons had gone to Disney, but the tide turned in the 1940s, not because Disney's shorts were not as good, but because the competition had improved so significantly. Richard Shale, *Academy Awards* (New York: Frederick Ungar, 1978): 206, 208–213.

5. Roy M. Prendergast, *A Neglected Art* (New York: New York University Press, 1977): 174.

6. The British produced a modest number of cartoons during the war. The Axis powers also produced some animated works, including *Il Dottor Churchill* (Italy, 1939), which portrays the British leader as a gorilla. There were a significant number of Japanese World War II cartoons. Ironically — given the pejorative depiction of the Japanese as monkeys in some Hollywood productions — one series character in Japan was an heroic monkey, seen in shorts such as *Osaru Sankichi Tatakau Sensukian* (Monkey Sankichi's Fighting Submarine, 1943). The Nazis also produced a color cartoon in the Netherlands, *Van den vos Reynaerde* (Reynaert the Fox, 1943), which featured a heroic fox pitted against a Jewish-featured rhinoceros. See Egbert Barten and Gerald Groeneveld, "Van den vos Reynaerde (1943): How a Medieval Fable Became a Dutch anti–Semitic Animation Film," *Historical Journal of Film, Radio and Television* 14:2 (1994): 199–214. The Russians apparently

made only one war-oriented cartoon, *Cinema Circus* (1942). Directed by Leonid Amalrich, this short depicts an unflattering caricature of Hitler who at one point tosses a bone to his three dogs, representing Mussolini, Horthy, and Antonescu.

7. Jacque Ellul, *Propaganda: The Formation of Men's Attitudes* (New York: Vintage, 1965): 9.

Chapter 2. Moving Lines Behind the Lines: Cartoons of World War I

1. An excellent history of newspaper political cartoons is Charles Press, *The Political Cartoon* (Rutherford, NJ: Fairleigh Dickinson University Press, 1981).

2. *Moving Picture World* (hereafter, *MPW*) 15 May 1915: 1166.

3. *MPW*, 21 August 1915: 1396.

4. *Library of Congress Copyright file* (hereafter, *Lib Cong*) MP592; *MPW* 22 April 1916: 633. Donald Crafton, in *Before Mickey: The American Animated Film, 1898–1928* (Cambridge, MA: MIT Press, 1982), mis-identifies this as *Col. Heeza Liar at Bat*. A brief clip from that cartoon (held in the collection of the Library of Congress) appears in *Wins the Pennant*. The Colonel was apparently a regular newshound — after reading about the Mexican Revolution, he takes a hazardous trip south of the border in *Shipwrecked* (1914).

5. *MPW* 22 April 1916: 652.

6. Emilio Aguinaldo (1868–1964) led a prolonged insurrection against American forces after the U.S. took possession of the Philippines following the Spanish-American War. See Stuart C. Miller, *Benevolent Assimilation: The American Conquest of the Philippines 1899–1903* (New Haven, CT: Yale University Press, 1982).

7. Crafton, (Cambridge, MA: MIT Press, 1982): 158.

8. Crafton 167.

9. *Lib Cong* MP539.

10. *Lib Cong* MP577.

11. *Lib Cong* MP622. William Jennings Bryan resigned as secretary of state in June 1915 to protest what he perceived as a growing belligerency on the part of the Woodrow Wilson administration. He became a vocal opponent of the Preparedness movement, whose best-known advocate was former president Theodore Roosevelt. See John Patrick Finnegan, *Against the Specter of a Dragon: The Campaign for American Military Preparedness, 1914–1917* (Westport, CT: Greenwood, 1974).

12. *Lib Cong* MP714.

13. *Lib Cong* MP831.

14. *Lib Cong* MP903.

15. *Lib Cong* MP734.

16. *MPW* 15 July 1916: 355. As early as the winter of 1915, Palmer had made a "timely" cartoon, *The Dove of Peace*. *MPW* 6 March 1915: 1504.

17. *MPW* 15 July 1916: 487.

18. *MPW* 22 July 1916: 638. Palmer's *The Rise of a Nation* (Educational, 1917) has been described as amusingly depicting the people of the United States answering the president's call to war. *MPW* 30 June 1917: 2118.

19. *Lib Cong* LU10652.

20. *Lib Cong* LU10657. Happy's December adventure, *Bullets and Bull*, involves a similar scenario. *Lib Cong* LU11791.

21. *Lib Cong* LU11377.

22. Women eager to practice their "First Aid" skills would be a source of humor in World War II as well. See *Barnyard Blackout* (1943) and *First Aiders* (1944).

23. *Motion Picture News* (hereafter *MPN*) 26 January 1918: 583. Bobby Bumps tackled the U-boat menace in Pictographs No. 72 in *Bobby Bumps' Submarine Chase*. *MPW* 30 June 1917: 2118.

24. *MPN* 9 February 1918: 871. This cartoon, which also makes references to the Prohibition movement, was part of Bray's "Historical Cartoons" series. Other relevant titles include *Uncle Sam's Dinner Party, Kaiser's Surprise Party, Von Loon's Non-Capturable Gun, A German Trick That Failed, Private Bass, Hiss Pass*. See Jeff Lenburg, *The Encyclopedia of Animated Cartoon Series* (Westport, CT: Arlington House, 1981): 16.

25. *Motography* 21 July 1917: 163, and *Lib Cong* MP973.

26. *Motion Picture Herald* (hereafter *MPH*) 18 August 1917: 2, 16. Also *Motography* 25 August 1917: 434. During 1918, Essanay issued a series featuring animated marionettes, including one entitled *Drafted*. *MPH* 8 June 1918: 30.

27. *MPN* 19 January 1918: 428.

28. American troops would not arrive in significant numbers in France until the spring of 1918.

29. *MPN* 18 May 1918: 2998.

30. *MPN* 24 August 1918: 1248, and *MPW* 18 May 1918: 1034. Publicity stated this film was made up of 25,000 drawings. It was over 8 minutes long, compared to an average of 3–5 minutes for animated cartoons of the period, which were usually part of a "split reel."

31. *Lib Cong* MP 1249, and *MPN* 5 October 1918: 2207. Chaplin's live-action short feature, *Shoulder Arms*, was released less than two weeks later.

32. *Lib Cong* MP 1005, and *Motography* 25 August 1917: 430. Mobilized farm animals were a frequent theme in World War II cartoons as well. See *The Home Guard* (1941), *Keep 'Em Growing* (1943), and *Swooner Crooner* (1944).

33. "Current Events" probably included British-distributed propaganda. Dutch cartoonist Louis Raemakers drew over 2,000 works for *De Telegraaf* up to 1917, many virulently anti–German. The British actively distributed these drawings overseas. By November 1917 they had appeared in 2,255 American newspapers. See Michael Saunders and Philip M. Taylor, *British Propaganda During the First World War, 1914–1918* (London: Macmillan, 1984): 176–177, 264. In fact, in September 1917 the British produced 12 sets of Raemaker's cartoons for theatrical release in England. See Rachel Low, *The History of the British Film, 1914–1918* (London: George Allen and Unwin, 1950): 172–173, and *MPW* 13 April 1918: 203.

34. *Motography* 28 April 1917: 909.

35. *Motography* 26 May 1917: 1124.

36. *MPW* 10 November 1917: 913.

37 *Motography* 12 January 1918: 75. Henry "Hy" Mayer, renowned caricaturist for *Puck* magazine, had been the "Current Events" cartoonist for several years.

38. *MPN* 18 Mary 1918: 2998. This was probably one of a popular series of

cartoons on food conservation produced by Paramount-Bray studios for the U.S. government. *Motography* 27 April 1918: 809.

39. Frederick L. Paxson, *America at War, 1917–1918* (Boston: Houghton Mifflin, 1938): 141.

40. *Lib Cong* FLA 2824.

41. *Motography* 18 August 1917: 346.

42. *Motography* 13 April 1918: 724.

43. *MPW* 1 June 1918: 1311. Under the Food Administration — headed by future president Herbert Hoover — hog prices had been pegged so high that farmers doubled production.

44. *MPW* 6 July 1918: 111 and *MPW* 17 August 1918: 1018.

45. *MPW* 7 September 1918: 1435.

46. *MPW* 26 October 1918: 529.

47. *MPW* 12 October 1918: 254. The film's title was a take-off on *My Four Years in Germany*, a feature film (based on a non-fiction book) released in March 1918.

48. *MPW* 19 April 1919: 433.

49. Crafton 196–199.

50. *Lib Cong* FEA 3506. It is possible this cartoon was only shown to the armed forces, not the general public.

51. *MPW* 3 May 1919: 705.

Chapter 3. Animated Talkies During the 1930s: A Political Overview

1. Only three cartoons from the late 1920s are known to have made direct reference to World War I–style trench warfare. All appear to be pacifistic: *Great Guns* (Oswald the Rabbit, Disney 1927), *Koko's War Dogs* (Out of the Inkwell #28, Paramount 1928), and *A War Bride* (Aesop's Fables, Paul Terry 1928). See *Lib Cong* MP 5219, MP 4954. Also Michael S. Shull, *Radicalism in American Silent Films, 1909–1929* (Jefferson, NC: McFarland, 2000): Appendix 2.

2. *Lib Cong* MP 2504.

3. Other cartoons caricaturing Gandhi, the proponent of Indian independence and non-violent resistance, include *Goopy Gear* (WB, 1931–32), *I Yam What I Yam* (Paramount, 1933), *I Like Mountain Music* (WB, 1933), *I Love a Parade* (WB, 1933), *Bosko's Nightmare* (WB, 1933), and *Peace Conference* (Columbia, 1935).

4. Roosevelt is depicted as a relatively youthful man wearing a casual cardigan sweater. He is definitely *not* wheelchair-bound in this cartoon.

5. A number of cartoons in this period promoted the new Roosevelt administration. Two which made specific reference to the NRA (National Recovery Administration) were *Christmas Night* (Van Beuren, 1933) and *Vulcan Entertains* (Iwerks, 1934).

6. Mussolini was also mentioned in a number of feature films of the 1930s. See Michael Shull and David Wilt, *Hollywood War Films, 1937–1945* (Jefferson, NC: McFarland, 1996).

7. *The Thrifty Pig*, a Canadian war bond promotion short produced by Walt

Disney in 1941, specifically labels the wolf as a Nazi. *Blitz Wolf* (MGM, 1942) parodies *The Three Little Pigs* and pits the porcine trio against "Adolf Wolf."

8. A comic peace conference had also been central to the plot of the feature film *Diplomaniacs* (RKO, 1933).

9. *Lib Cong* MP 5793, and Leonard Maltin, *Of Mice and Magic: A History of American Animated Cartoons* (New York: McGraw-Hill, 1980): 211.

10. Porky's name in this cartoon is a spoof of "Parkyakarkus," a comedian who appeared on Eddie Cantor's radio show and made some film appearances.

11. This cartoon, released in December 1937, also contains a pejorative reference to Japan. When a three-headed monster (a caricature of the Three Stooges) is petrified by the Gorgon into a "see no evil, hear no evil, speak no evil" pose, the description on the pedestal beneath the "statue" reads "Monkeys of Japan."

12. It is not clear if the audience member is frowning at Hitler or because the image on the screen is so distorted. Newsreel parodies were quite popular in animated cartoons of the 1930s and 1940s.

13. Disney's Mickey Mouse, although considered politically benign in the United States, was a figure of some international controversy during the 1930s. At various times, his cartoons were banned in Yugoslavia (for antimonarchical tendencies), in Nazi Germany (for insulting the army), and the Soviet Union (because Mickey allegedly represented the diffidence of the masses under capitalism). However, the cartoon mouse was also recognized as an international symbol of good will by the League of Nations in 1935. See Herbert Russell, "L'Affaire Mickey Mouse," *The New York Times Encyclopedia of Film* 3: 26 December 1937 (NY: Times Books, 1983).

Chapter 4. Meet John Doughboy: 1939–1941

1. Shull and Wilt, *Hollywood War Films*, 84.
2. Shull and Wilt, 85.

Chapter 5. All Out for V: 1942

1. Shull and Wilt, *Hollywood War Films*: 84. The total of 170 reflects 20 additional films discovered since the publication of this book.

2. These include *The Thrifty Pig, The Seven Wise Dwarfs* (1941), *Donald's Decision* (1942), and *All Together* (1942) which includes virtually the entire Disney repertoire. See Richard Shale, *Donald Duck Joins Up: The Walt Disney Studio During World War II* (Ann Arbor: UMI Research Press, 1982).

3. We have not coded cartoons which contain *only* this end-credits bonds message, since it was not part of the individual work but rather a standard message. One of the earliest examples found with the printed message is *The Hungry Wolf* (MGM), released in February 1942.

4. Although most Asian stereotypes in cartoons featured Chinese characters, *The Wily Jap* was an animated segment in Pathé News No. 26 (1915). See *MPW* 17 April 1915: 470. *Japanicky* (1928) was a Felix the Cat entry in which the feline met the "Mikado" and tried to cure the emperor's kneeling subjects of "Japanknees." *Lib Cong* LP25139.

5. Based on viewing about a dozen wartime Japanese cartoons (in the Library of Congress collection), a few observations on *Japanese* stereotyping of *Americans* can be made. In these cartoons, Americans are often overweight, rum-swilling, cowardly, and even at times depicted as one-horned *oni* (demons). *Momotaro no Umiwashi* (Momotaro and the Eagles of the Ocean, 1943) is a 40-minute-long cartoon which recreates the attack on Pearl Harbor, carried out by the three animal retainers of the mythical Peach Boy character. In this film, the hysterically drunken, horned officer of a U.S. battleship resembles Popeye's nemesis Bluto! See Peter B. High, *The Imperial Screen* (Madison: University of Wisconsin Press, 2003).

6. Shull and Wilt, *Hollywood War Films*: 291.

Chapter 6. Seein' Red, White 'n' Blue: 1943

1. See Eugene Franklin Wong, *On Visual Media Racism: Asians in the American Motion Pictures* (New York: Arno, 1978).

2. Sugar rationing had been introduced in May 1942, but the full point-rationing system was not instituted until the end of that year.

3. See Dower, *War Without Mercy*: 121–122, 138.

4. "A Report on the Disney War Effort, " *The Film Daily Yearbook of Motion Pictures 1943*: 201–203.

5. Shale, *Donald Duck Joins Up*: 91.

6. "Schicklegruber" was a frequently used pejorative name for Hitler during the war years. It alludes to the illegitimacy of Hitler's father, whose unmarried mother's last name was Schicklegruber. See Allan Bullock, *Hitler: A Study in Tyranny* (New York: Harper and Row, 1962): 24.

7. A significant percentage of Lantz's work in 1943 was government-sponsored cartoons like *Camouflage*, *Lend Lease* and *Take Heed, Mr. Tojo*. The latter (discussed in the Filmography) was made for the U.S. Navy to promote bond purchases by sailors. *Variety* 6 October 1943: 7, and *MPH* 18 December 1943: 39. Also *Lib Cong* MU 15014.

Chapter 7. Slow Fade on the Home Front: 1944–1945

1. Eshbaugh also produced the non-commercial animated short *Sammy Salvage*, made for the War Production Board-War Activities Committee. It was copyrighted in 1943.

Chapter 8. The Adventures of Private Snafu, or, How to Laugh at the Military While Learning What *Not* to Do

1. Eric Smoodin, *Animating Culture: Hollywood Cartoons from the Sound Era* (New Brunswick, NJ: Rutgers University Press, 1993) 82.

Bibliography

Documents

Catalogue of Copyright Entries, Cumulative Series Motion Pictures, 1912–1939. Washington, D.C.: Library of Congress, 1951.
Library of Congress Copyright Deposit files.
Office of War Information Files, Shorts: 1942–1943 (5 boxes). Washington, D.C.: Library of Congress, Motion Picture and Recorded Sound Division.
OWI (Office of War Information) files, series 208. National Archives and Records Administration, Suitland, MD.

Films

The cartoons themselves are the ultimate source. Cartoon sources included: studio packages owned by local (Washington, D.C., and Baltimore, MD) television stations, cable channels WTBS and WGN (first edition), and The Cartoon Network (second edition), the Library of Congress Motion Picture, Broadcasting and Recorded Sound Division, the Museum of Cartoon Art (Port Chester, NY), rentals (Kit Parker Films), and commercially available videos and DVDs.

Periodicals

Film Comment, January-February 1975.
The Film Daily, January 1939 through September 1945.
Funnyworld, 1969–1980.
Mindrot no. 15.
Motion Picture Herald, January 1917 through January 1920.
Motography, 1917–1918.
The Moving Picture World, August 1914 through January 1920.

Books

CARTOONS AND FILM

Adamson, Joe. *Bugs Bunny: 50 Years and Only One Grey Hare.* New York: Holt, 1990.
_____. *Tex Avery: King of the Cartoons.* New York: Popular Library, 1975.
Alicoate, Jack, ed. *The Film Daily Year Book of Motion Pictures: 1943.* New York: Film Daily, 1944.
_____. *The Film Daily Year Book of Motion Pictures: 1945.* New York: Film Daily, 1946.
Barrier, Mike. *Hollywood Cartoons: American Animation in its Golden Age.* New York: Oxford University Press, 1999.
Beck, Jerry. *The 50 Greatest Cartoons.* Atlanta: Turner Publishing, 1994.
_____, and Will Friedwald. *Looney Tunes and Merrie Melodies: A Complete Illustrated Guide to the Warner Bros. Cartoons.* New York: Holt, 1989.
Cabarga, Leslie. *The Fleischer Story.* New York: Nostalgia, 1976.
Campbell, Craig. *Reel America and World War I: A Comprehensive Filmography and History of Motion Pictures in the United States, 1914–1920.* Jefferson, NC: McFarland, 1985.
Cohen, Karl F. *Forbidden Animation : Censored Cartoons and Blacklisted Animators in America.* Jefferson, NC: McFarland, 1997.
Crafton, Donald. *Before Mickey: The Animated Film 1898–1928.* Cambridge: MIT Press, 1982.
Dick, Bernard F. *The Star Spangled Screen: The American World War II Film.* Rev. ed. Lexington: University Press of Kentucky, 1996.
Floquet, Pierre. *Tex Avery's Comic Language.* London: John Libbey & Co., 1999.
Hoffer, Thomas W. *Animation: A Reference Guide.* Westport, CT: Greenwood, 1981.
Isenberg, Michael T. *War on Film: The American Cinema and World War I, 1914–1941.* East Brunswick, NJ: Associated University Presses, 1981.
Kanfer, Stefan. *Serious Business : The Art and Commerce of Animation in America from Betty Boop to Toy Story.* New York: Scribner, 1997.
Klein, Norman M. *Seven Minutes: The Life and Death of the American Animated Cartoon.* London: Verso, 1993.
Leebron, Elizabeth, and Lynn Gartley. *Walt Disney: A Guide to References and Resources.* Boston: G.K. Hall, 1979.
Lenburg, Jeff. *The Encyclopedia of Animated Cartoons.* New York: Facts on File, 1990.
Maltin, Leonard. *Of Mice and Magic: A History of American Animated Cartoons.* New York: McGraw-Hill, 1980.
Martin, Andre. *Family Tree of the Origin and Golden Age of the American Cartoon Film, 1906–1941.* Montreal: La Cinémathèque Canadienne, 1967.
McCall, Douglas. *Film Cartoons: A Guide to 20th Century American Animated Features and Shorts.* Jefferson, NC: McFarland, 1998.
Morgan Hickman, Gail. *The Films of George Pal.* South Brunswick, NJ: A.S. Barnes, 1977.
Peary, Gerald, and Danny Peary, eds. *The American Animated Cartoon.* New York: Dutton, 1980.
Prendergast, Roy M. *A Neglected Art: A Critical Study of Music in Films.* New York: New York University Press, 1977.

Bibliography   229

Sampson, Henry T. *That's Enough, Folks: Black Images in Animated Cartoons, 1900–1960.* Lanham, MD: Scarecrow Press, 1998.

Schneider, Steve. *That's All Folks! The Art of Warner Bros. Animation.* New York: Henry Holt & Co., 1988.

Shain, Russell. *An Analysis of Motion Pictures About War Released by the American Film Industry, 1930–1970.* New York: Arno, 1976.

Shale, Richard. *Donald Duck Joins Up: The Walt Disney Studio During World War II.* Ann Arbor: UMI Research Press, 1982.

Shull, Michael. *Radicalism in American Silent Films, 1909–1929.* Jefferson, NC: McFarland, 2000.

_____, and David Wilt. *Hollywood War Films, 1937–1945.* Jefferson, NC: McFarland, 1996.

Smoodin, Eric. *Animating Culture: Hollywood Cartoons from the Sound Era.* New Brunswick, NJ: Rutgers University Press, 1993.

War Activities Committee of the Motion Picture Industry. *Movies at War.* Vol. 1 (1942), Vol. 2 (1943), Vol. 3 (1944), Vol. 4 (1945). NY: War Activities Committee of the Motion Pictures Industry, [n.d.].

Watts, Steven. *The Magic Kingdom: Walt Disney and the American Way of Life.* New York: Houghton Miflin, 1997.

Wells, Paul. *Animation and America.* New Brunswick, NJ: Rutgers University Press, 2002.

Wong, Eugene Franklin. *On Visual Media Racism: Asians in the American Motion Pictures.* New York: Arno, 1978.

GENERAL

Bentley, Amy. *Eating for Victory: Food Rationing and the Politics of Domesticity.* Urbana: University of Illinois Press, 1998.

Blum, John Morton. *V Was for Victory: Politics and American Culture During World War II.* New York: Harcourt Brace Jovanovich, 1976.

ten Broek, Jacobus, Edward N. Barnhart and Floyd W. Matson. *Prejudice, War, and the Constitution.* Los Angeles: University of California Press, 1968.

Dower, John W. *War Without Mercy: Race and Power in the Pacific War.* New York: Pantheon, 1986.

Ellul, Jacques. *Propaganda: The Formation of Men's Attitudes.* New York: Vintage, 1965.

Goodman, Jack, ed. *While You Were Gone: A Report on Wartime Life in the United States.* New York: Simon and Schuster, 1946.

High, Peter B. *The Imperial Screen: Japanese Film Culture in the Fifteen Years' War, 1931–1945.* Madison: University of Wisconsin Press, 2003.

Husted, H.H. *Thumb-nail History of World War II.* Boston: Humphries, 1949.

Kennedy, David M. *Over Here: The First World War and American Society.* New York: Oxford University Press, 1980.

Kennett, Lee. *GI: The American Soldier in World War II.* New York: Scribner's, 1987.

Lingeman, Richard R. *Don't You Know There's a War Going On? The American Home Front, 1941–1945.* New York: Putnam's, 1970.

Manning, Thomas G. *The Office of Price Administration: A World War II Agency of Control.* New York: Henry Holt, 1960.

Perrett, Geoffrey. *Days of Sadness, Years of Triumph: The American People, 1939–1945.* New York: Coward, McCann and Geoghegan, 1973.
Rogers, Donald. *Since You Went Away: From Rosie the Riveter to Bond Drives; World War II at Home.* New Rochelle, NY: Arlington House, 1973.
Tuttle, William M., Jr. *"Daddy's Gone to War": The Second World War in the Lives of America's Children.* New York: Oxford University Press, 1993.
Wright, Bradford W. *Comic Book Nation.* Baltimore: Johns Hopkins University Press, 2001.

Articles

"Bugs Bunny, Carrot Crunching Comic." *The New York Times Encyclopedia of Film* 4 (22 July 1945). NY: Times Books, 1983.
Churchill, Edward. "Walt Disney's Animated War." *Flying* 36 (March 1945): 50–51, 134, 136, 138.
Crowther, Bosley. "Cartoons on the Screen: a Momentary Consideration of Who Makes Them, How Many and Why." *The New York Times Encyclopedia of Film* 3 (13 February 1938). New York: Times Books, 1983.
_____. "McBoing Boing Magoo, and Bosustow." *The New York Times Encyclopedia of Film* 6 (21 December 1952). New York: Times Books, 1983.
Dalton, Susan Elizabeth. "Bugs and Daffy Go to War: Some Warners Cartoons of World War II." *The Velvet Light Trap* 4: 44–45.
"D. Duck Joins Up." *The New York Times Magazine* (22 February 1942): 20–21.
Delehanty, Thornton. "The Disney Studio at War." *Theatre Arts* 27 (January 1943): 31–39.
Holliday, Kate. "Donald Duck Goes to War." *Coronet* (September 1942): 20–21.
"Hollywood Censors Its Animated Cartoons." *Look* (17 January 1939): 17–20.
Jacobs, Lewis. "World War II and the American Film." *Cinema Journal* 7 (Winter 67-68): 1–21.
"*The New Spirit*—Disney's Tax Film." *Life* (16 March 1942): 48–50.
Platt, David. "*Victory Through Air Power* Misses the Bus." *The Daily Worker* (21 July 1943).
Russell, Herbert. "L'Affaire Mickey Mouse." *The New York Times Encyclopedia of Film* 3 (26 December 1937). New York: Times Books, 1983.
Strauss, Theodore. "Mr. Terry and the Animal Kingdom." *The New York Times Encyclopedia of Film* 3 (7 July 1940). NY: Times Books, 1983.
"Walt Disney Goes to War." *Life* (31 August 1942): 61–69.

Documentaries

Cartoons Go to War (Teleduction Assoc.—A&E, 1995). Director: Sharon K. Baker.
Ducktators (Netherlands, 1997). Directors: Wolter Braamhorst and Gus Van Wareren.

Text Index

References are to page numbers

36, 43, 45, 46, 51, 56, 60, 62, 63, 65, 66, 69, 71, 72, 77
Holiday for Shoestrings (1946) 78
Hollywood Canine Canteen (1946) 78
Home Defense (1943) 57
The Home Front (1943) 82, 83
Hoover, President Herbert 29
Hopkins, Willie 24
How Charlie Captured the Kaiser (1918) 22, 24
How War Came (1941) 38
Hubley, John 63
Humorous Phases of Funny Faces (1906) 17
Hunting for U-Boats 25
Hurd, Earl 20

I Like Mountain Music (1933) 30, 31, 34
The Invasion of Norway (1940) 4
Ising, Rudolph (Rudy) 5, 8, 82
An Itch in Time (1943) 61
It's Murder She Says (1945) 87
I've Got to Sing a Torch Song (1933) 30

The Japoteurs (1942) 48, 50
Jerry Saves the Navy (1917) 20
Jones, Charles (Chuck) 5, 61, 71, 82
Jungle Drums (1943) 64

The Kaiser, Beast of Berlin (1918) 23, 24
The Kaiser's New Dentist (1918) 25
Katz, Ray 8
Knocking the "H" Out of Heinie (1919) 20

LaCava, Gregory 20, 22
Laemmle, Carl 23
Lantz, Walter 4, 5, 7, 8, 10, 51, 63
The Last Round-Up (1943) 45, 57, 66
Laundry Blues (1930) 31
Leaf, Munro 35
A Lecture on Camouflage (1944) 84
Liberty Bonds (1918) 22
Little Orphan Airedale (1947) 79
Lloyd George, David 26
The Long Arm of Law and Order (1916) 18

MacArthur, General Douglas 13, 69
Magazine Rack see I Like Mountain Music
The Marx Brothers 29
Mayer, Hy 25
McCay, Winsor 17, 22
McCollum, Hugh 62
Meatless Tuesday (1943) 57, 63
Meet John Doughboy (1941) 38
The Mighty NaVy (1941) 38

Mintz, Charles 7, 8
Miranda, Carmen 46
Mr. Bug Goes to Town (1941) 5
Mopping Up (1943) 45, 57
Mother Goose Nightmare (1945) 78
Music Land (1935) 32
Mussolini, Benito 29, 30, 31, 33, 34, 45, 46, 51, 66
My Boy Johnny (1944) 74, 77

Nasty Quacks (1945) 78
The Negro Soldier (1944) 39
Neighbors (1935) 32
The New Recruit (1917) 20
The New Spirit (1942) 41, 42
No Buddy Atoll (1945) 88
Nursery Crimes (1943) 62

Of Fox and Hounds (1940) 38
Of Thee I Sting (1946) 78
Old Blackout Joe (1942) 51, 72
Old Glory (1939) 37
One Man Navy (1941) 38
Operation SNAFU (1945) 88
Opper, F. Burr 20
Our Four Days in Germany (1918) 26
Out of the Frying Pan, Into the Firing Line (1942) 41, 80
The Outpost (1942) 49
The Outpost (1944) 82, 88
Outposts (1916) 18

Pa McGinnis Gets the Boys Out of the Trenches (1915) 18
Pal, George 6, 7
Palmer, Harry 19
Pass the Biscuits Mirandy! (1943) 57, 63
Payday (1944) 83
Peace Conference (1935) 32
Peace on Earth (1939) 33, 34, 37
Pershing, General John J. 18
Petty, George 83
Pigeon Patrol (1942) 51
Pigs in a Polka (1943) 61
Plane Daffy (1944) 70
Plane Dippy (1936) 32
Plenty Below Zero (1943) 62
Pluto and the Armadillo (1943) 60
Poor Little Butterfly (1938) 34
Porky the Gob (1938) 34
Porky's Hero Agency (1937) 33
Porky's Pooch (1941) 79
Porky's Poultry Plant (1936) 32
Post-War Inventions (1945) 77

Filmography Index

References are to entry numbers

Bold numbers refer to main entries for titles. Titles in *italics* are films only referenced in Filmography. Main Filmography titles are in **bold**. Variant names in film credits are listed in brackets after the most frequently-credited version of the name.